STUDIES IN JEWISH LAW, CUSTOM AND FOLKLORE

STUDIES IN JEWISH LAW, CUSTOM AND FOLKLORE

By

JACOB Z. LAUTERBACH

Selected, with an Introduction by
BERNARD J. BAMBERGER

KTAV PUBLISHING HOUSE, INC.

ACKNOWLEDGMENTS

Special thanks are due the Hebrew Union College-Jewish Institute of Religion, publishers of the *Hebrew Union College Annual* and the Central Conference of American Rabbis, publishers of the *Central Conference of American Rabbis Year Book*, for permission to reprint the articles included in this volume.

SBN 87068-013-7

296.3
Lra 55

Manufactured in the United States of America
Library of Congress Catalog Card Number 71-78601

TABLE OF CONTENTS

INTRODUCTION

In 1951, nine years after the death of Jacob Zallel Lauterbach, a collection of his writings entitled *Rabbinic Essays*
was published by the Alumni Association of the Hebrew
Union College—Jewish Institute of Religion. This project
was not only an expression of reverence and affection for
a vastly learned and singularly lovable man, but it was also
a distinct service to the scholarly world. Most of Lauterbach's publications were relatively brief essays; they are
scattered in various periodicals, annuals, and *Festschriften*
which, with the passing of years, become increasingly
difficult of access.

The volume of *Rabbinic Essays* was edited by Dr. Lou
H. Silberman, one of Lauterbach's devoted students, with
the advice and counsel of his senior disciple, Dr. Solomon
B. Freehof. It contained six of the major published writings,
with supplementary notes from the author's own copies; in
addition, two unfinished papers were edited from manuscript. A full bibliography of Lauterbach's work was provided by Dr. Walter E. Rothman. The volume is of great
and enduring value for Jewish and Christian students of
Jewish lore.

Although it is a substantial tome, only a part of those
essays of Lauterbach that are of continuing interest and
value could be included. It was therefore with great delight that I accepted the invitation to edit another selection

of this rich material. I, too, am proud to have been a pupil of this great scholar; and I make no pretence to objectivity about Lauterbach the man. Elsewhere I have attempted to evoke his engaging and colorful personality ("Jacob Z. Lauterbach: An Informal Memoir," *Central Conference of American Rabbis Journal,* June 1963). Here, my purpose is to clarify his aims and methods and to furnish some supplementary details about individual essays.

Lauterbach, born in 1873 in a small Galician town, received a traditional Talmudic education, but was also introduced to secular knowledge. Then he attended the University of Berlin and the Hildesheimer Rabbinerseminar. Despite the strictly Orthodox atmosphere of the Rabbinerseminar, his studies awakened in his mind serious questions concerning the theoretical basis of Orthodoxy. He awakened the ire of some of his fellow students by referring to the Second Isaiah; and ultimately he went to Göttingen to study under the famous Bible critics, Julius Wellhausen and Rudolf Smend. Incidentally, it was Wellhausen who suggested to him that he apply the critical method to the rabbinic literature over which he had such a great mastery. This was some years after David Hoffmann, the rector of the Rabbinerseminar, had published his first attempt at refuting the Wellhausen hypotheses. Yet after Lauterbach had completed his doctoral studies (his dissertation, a critical edition of part of Saadia's translation of and commentary on Psalms, was his only publication prior to his arrival in the United States), he returned to Berlin and received the rabbinical diploma from Hoffmann.

This seemingly contradictory series of events could occur because the young man was still then, and for many years thereafter, observant of Orthodox practice. But plainly his outlook on Judaism had changed. His contact with Bible criticism apparently did not precipitate a spiritual crisis, but helped him resolve prior difficulties. He said to Wellhausen (so he told me in later years) that he had been troubled by the old doctrine of revelation, which seemed to mean that God had arbitrarily chosen Israel to receive the Torah. This difficulty was resolved by the view that the people of Israel had actively participated in a continuing process of revelation.

In 1903 Lauterbach came to New York and worked as an office editor of the Jewish Encyclopedia, to which he contributed no less than 260 articles, some of them quite extensive. Later he was to write articles also for J. D. Eisenstein's Hebrew encyclopedia, *Ozar Yisrael*. These largely routine assignments (a few of the articles in *JE* required more originality, such as the article on "Theology" from the traditional standpoint), were completed competently and responsibly; but he had no desire to continue that kind of work.

Obviously, scholarship has two main aspects. On the one hand it demands patient and tedious effort in assembling materials, correcting texts, verifying facts and dates, summarizing information previously gathered by others, and so on. Such tasks require diligence and accuracy; they are indispensable, though often dull. On the other hand scholarship also has its creative side: the discovery of new facts and new relationships, the framing and testing of hypotheses. Here imagination and ingenuity come into play. Such creative scholarship is both fascinating and risky, and this was the aspect that Lauterbach enjoyed.

He did indeed commit himself to a vast amount of tedious detail work when he undertook to edit the *Mekilta of Rabbi Ishmael,* with an English translation, for the Schiff Jewish Classics Series (Jewish Publication Society, 3 vols., 1933). Ever since its appearance this work has been recognized as a model of meticulous and critical text-scholarship. Otherwise, Lauterbach limited himself to the writing of essays, only two of which extend over more than a hundred pages. Several of these were by-products of the *Mekilta* edition, dealing with the name, divisions, and arrangement of the work, and its relation to the *Mekilta of R. Simeon,* and with the detailed interpretation of certain passages. Perhaps his most important contributions dealt with the inner history of Jewish life in the later centuries of the Second Commonwealth; to this category belong "Midrash and Mishnah" and the great series on the Pharisees (all included in *Rabbinic Essays*). He also edited several small Aggadic texts. In his later years, he concentrated his interest especially on the elucidation of Jewish customs and their folkloristic background. To this task he brought not only enormous erudition, but a special quality of understanding, based on his own childhood memories; for, as he put it, he had the privilege of being born in the sixteenth century.

We have noted Lauterbach's predilection for the new and ingenious. He was, however, too conscientious to be lured by his own cleverness into dubious and unfounded conjectures. He subjected the theories of other scholars to searching, though generally courteous, examination; and he was no less critical in scrutinizing his own theories. Not infrequently, he warns the reader that a suggestion of his should be regarded as no more than an educated guess. And he was not ashamed to admit that some of his earlier opinions required correction in the light of more mature study. In his 1920 article, "The Name of the Mekilta," he explicitly discards the views he had expressed on the subject in his article in *JE*.

His manner of presentation was meticulous. It was his intention that the body of an essay should be comprehensible to any intelligent reader, even if he did not have command of the original sources. So everything was clearly and logically organized; incidental and subsidiary questions were treated in footnotes or excursuses. The language is compact and precise. His articles for the *Jewish Encyclopedia* were written in German and translated by one of the staff, as a matter of efficiency. Thereafter he wrote almost exclusively in English. And the English is excellent, rarely marred by a mistake in word order or sequence of tenses. His Hebrew style was exemplary.

The present volume consists of essays that deal with matters of belief, ethics, ceremony, and custom which in one way or another are relevant to present-day Jewish life. This principle of selection was proposed by Dr. I. Edward Kiev, whose assistance and advice I gratefully acknowledge. The materials brought together here should be of interest and value to many rabbis and Jewish laymen, as well as to Christian students of Judaism. Many important writings have been passed over because they are of value chiefly to the specialist in rabbinic studies or ancient history, who will make the effort to find them in the original publications.

A number of the items in this volume are in the form of responsa presented to the Central Conference of American Rabbis. This fact calls for comment on two points: Lauterbach's attitude to Reform Judaism, and the place of the halakhah in Reform.

As we have seen, Lauterbach acquired an evolutionary view of Judaism during his university days, although he continued to follow traditional practice. After completing his work on the *Encyclopedia,* he served as rabbi of an Orthodox congregation in Peoria. Then he went to another traditional congregation in Rochester, where, however, he found a more liberal element, to whom he was especially close; later, these people were to found a Conservative synagogue.

During his stay in Rochester, Lauterbach delivered a series of lectures on the history of Judaism. He traced the changes and developments that occurred in different lands and ages; and in the concluding lecture he argued that Judaism must adapt itself to the new conditions of American life if it is to survive here with vigor. In this connection, he distinguished between the enduring essentials of Judaism and the changing forms by which the basic values are given outward expression. The tone of the lectures is restrained and conciliatory, but their implications are unmistakable. No doubt it was his progressive outlook that led to his departure from Rochester and his acceptance of a call from the Reform congregation of Huntsville, Alabama. (Lauterbach gave the manuscript of these lectures to Rabbi Louis I. Egelson, who years later handed them on to me. As they represent a relatively early stage in the author's thought, there seemed to be no reason to publish them. I gave them to Dr. Lou H. Silberman, who deposited them in the Hebrew Union College Library.)

By his own testimony, Lauterbach was completely happy in Huntsville, where he had ample leisure to pursue his researches. It was during these years that he allowed himself to discard a good many—not all—traditional observances. Thus, when he was invited in 1911 to become Professor of Talmud at the Hebrew Union College, he was already committed to Reform Judaism in theory and practice. He, however, did not smoke or write on the Sabbath. On occasion, he was severely critical of Reform Jewish institutions and their leadership, but his criticism was that of an insider. He found fault not with the principles of the movement, but with those who professed the principles and did not practice them adequately. At the same time, he looked back with respect and affection to the Orthodoxy of his younger days; and he demanded similar respect from others. When someone in his presence belittled Orthodoxy as "kitchen religion," he retorted, "I prefer a kitchen religion to a parlor irreligion!"

Reform Judaism was never monolithic. It always included moderates, who stressed their links with the Jewish past, as well as radicals, who emphasized their break with tradition. (See the writer's "Continuity and Discontinuity in Reform Judaism," *Central Conference of American Rabbis Journal,* January, 1966.) The tension between these poles was relieved by a common interest in Jewish scholarship. The Reform movement, though it denied the absolute authority of the halakhah, did not reject halakhah altogether, An interesting illustration of this is provided by the following history.

In 1906, Rabbi George Solomon of Savannah (an adherent of so-called "classic Reform") submitted a resolution to the Central Conference of American Rabbis, calling for a committee on responsa. This committee was to answer questions about Jewish custom and tradition, and the answers were to be published in the Year Books of the Conference. The original intent, apparently, was to obtain information rather than guidance. Jews had come to the United States bringing with them a variety of observances from their former homes. These customs in some instances were imperfectly remembered; some may have been peculiar to a single locality or even family. But they could become the subject of discussion, debate, and even conflict. Such circumstances must have perplexed and troubled many rabbis, especially those born and trained in this country.

The Year Books are not entirely clear as to just when and how this resolution was implemented. But within a year or two after the request was made, a Committee on Responsa was in existence, with President Kaufmann Kohler of the Hebrew Union College as its chairman. For a time, inquiries were infrequent and apparently not important, and replies were made directly to the inquirer. In 1913 the Committee made its first extended report, dealing with such questions as the manner of reading the Torah, Bar Mizvah, Kaddish and mourning customs, wedding rites, the blowing of the Shofar on Sabbath—matters which Dr. Kohler deemed important, even though questions had not been submitted on all of them. At this time, also, the Conference agreed that reports of the Responsa Committee were to be regarded as the wise counsel of learned men, not as decisions binding on the Conference members.

As years passed, the questions asked became more numerous and were often of great interest. The responsa were written by Dr. Kohler, Professor Gotthard Deutsch, and several other members of the body. In 1922, Dr. Kohler—then in his eightieth year—became Honorary Chairman of the Committee, and Dr. Lauterbach was made the active Chairman.

In ensuing years, the number and variety of published responsa increased; most of them are by Dr. Lauterbach. Those included in this volume deal not only with ritual questions, but also with issues of ethical and social significance. In the tradition of many great respondents, Dr. Lauterbach did not confine himself to giving practical conclusions, but examined the background of each question and its treatment in earlier sources. Sometimes a simple inquiry led to the writing of an elaborate study, such as the papers on the naming of children, and the covering of the head in worship.

To provide this scholarly apparatus was, in Lauterbach's opinion, an essential part of his function. He was convinced that the rabbinic sources contain much material that is relevant to current problems, and that halakhic literature may provide guidance for Reform Jews. These sources were to be used with freedom; in Dr. Freehof's phrase, they are "for guidance, not for governance." Lauterbach sometimes drew conclusions that admittedly were not explicit in the Talmud and codes. Sometimes, moreover, after consulting tradition, Reform Jews have a right and even the duty to depart from it. But such departures, he held, should be undertaken on the basis of thorough knowledge.

This book had already been planned when I learned that Dr. Lauterbach had left specific instructions concerning the republication of his works. He himself chose the writings included in *Rabbinic Essays*. He further directed that Dr. Freehof and Dr. Silberman were to select the material to be included in any further collections. They have given full approval to the contents of the present volume; they lent me the author's copies containing a few additional notes, and they made a number of helpful comments on and corrections of the introduction and supplementary notes, virtually all of which have been gratefully incorporated. I want to express my warmest thanks to these two colleagues and good friends.

Bernard J. Bamberger

SUPPLEMENTARY NOTES

"The Ceremony of Breaking a Glass at Weddings pp. 1-30.

P. 9, n.12. The author added: comp. R. Briffault, *The Mothers,* III, p. 55, "the bride is strewn with rice and corn . . ." and he connects it with the primitive notion of connecting fecundity of women with fecundity of the earth.

"The Origin and Development of Two Sabbath Ceremonies", pp. 75-132.

This essay, one of the last Lauterbach himself published, is remarkably fresh and engaging. It has a special importance, moreover, in that it deals with some phases of the relationship between Halakhah and Kabbala. Lauterbach had touched on this matter in the essay on breaking a glass (p. 23ff.) and elsewhere; but here the treatment is fuller. This subject is explored by G. G. Scholem, *Major Trends in Jewish Mysticism,* 3rd ed., pp.28ff. and, more recently, in the essay "Tradition and New Creation in the Ritual of the Kabbalists" (*On the Kabbalah and Its Symbolism,* 1965, pp.118ff.) About the authorship of *Hemdath Yamim,* discussed by Lauterbach, p. 114 and n.64, see Scholem, *Major Trends,* p.285 and n.131.

Concerning the magical properties and uses of the myrtle, additional references, including some to classical antiquity, are provided by A. Marmorstein, *The Doctrine of Merits in Old Rabbinical Literature,* (new ed., Ktav, 1968) p.18, n.61.

"Should One Cover the Head When Participating in Divine Worship?" pp. 225-239.

When this responsum appeared in 1928, it received wide publicity, especially in a shortened form, entitled "Hats On or Hats Off?" which was published in the *American Hebrew.* Understandably, it called forth some sharp retorts from spokesmen of the traditional standpoint. The latter generally misunderstood the author's intent. Lauterbach was not defending the practice of praying with uncovered head, but arguing that the issue of "hat or no hat" was unimportant, and should not be the occasion of controversy and bitterness.

In *HUCA* Vol. XIX (1945-1946) Samuel Krauss published an article entitled "The Jewish Rite of Covering the Head," in which he refers to our responsum with high praise and quotes it repeatedly. (Krauss had previously treated the subject in *Talmudische Archäologie*.) He is in full accord with Lauterbach's historical analysis and practical conclusions, and the body of his article is devoted to aspects not treated by Lauterbach.

Krauss takes issue with his predecessor on two matters of detail. He holds that Lauterbach read too much into the Mishnaic expression *sh'hore ha-rosh* (p. 227, Krauss p.143 f.) While the covering of the head was not required in Palestine during the Talmudic period, it is going too far—according to Krauss—to say that "the Mishnah takes it for granted that men go bareheaded." He also denies that the Aramaic phrase *b'resh gale* means "with uncovered head." It means, he says, "publicly, boldly." This is undoubtedly an idiomatic secondary meaning of the phrase; but that does not mean that its original force had completely disappeared. Cf. *Nedarim* 30b, "Men sometimes cover their heads and sometimes bare (*m'gallo*) their heads."

The same year that Krauss' article was published, another contribution to the subject appeared in the *Louis Ginzberg Jubilee Volume*. It is a responsum of Leo da Modena, edited from ms. with notes and introduction by Isaac Rivkind (Hebrew section, pp. 401ff.) In his introduction Rivkind criticizes Lauterbach severely. He too insists that *b'resh gale* means "boldly" (p. 401f., n.1 par. 3). He asserts vehemently that in I Cor. 11.4ff., Paul deliberately urged the rejection of an established Jewish custom; but he does not offer any proof, nor does he refute Lauterbach's argument (p. 228), which Krauss (op.cit. p. 135ff.) fully endorses.

Rivkind correctly notes that Orthodox halakhists became much more rigid on this issue after it was raised by the Reformers. Prior to the rise of Reform, they were more ready to acknowledge that the covering of the head was only a matter of custom. Thus Leo da Modena justified some laxity about bareheadedness because of prevailing Gentile custom, though he did not go so far as to permit the recitation of prayers with uncovered head.

Though Rivkind took Lauterbach to task for writing from the Reform viewpoint, his own approach is hardly objective and detached. As we have noted, Lauterbach wrote not to defend what Rivkind calls "the Reform *mitzvah*" of the uncovered head, but to point out the slight importance of the controversy, and to call for forbearance on both sides.

Rivkind, moreover, refers to decisions made by some Reform congregations in the nineteenth century requiring all men to remove their hats, but does not mention that those rules have long since been discarded, and that in virtually all present-day Reform congregations a worshipper may cover his head without interference or comment. In a few congregations affiliated with the Reform movement, the regular custom is to wear hats.

"Should Women Be Ordained as Rabbis?" pp. 240-246.

This responsum was requested in 1932 by the Board of Governors of the Hebrew Union College. A woman student was scheduled to graduate about two years later, and the faculty had recommended that she be ordained on completion of the requirements. But the Board of Governors, apparently still uncertain about the matter, submitted it to the Central Conference of American Rabbis.

This paper differs from the other responsa in this volume in that it treats the limited traditional material on the subject summarily, as an introduction to the statement of Dr. Lauterbach's admittedly personal opinion. When presented before the Central Conference, it touched off a lengthy discussion, which is recorded in the *Year Book,* vol.

XXXII. Most of the speakers, including several women guests who were invited to express opinions, argued against the responsum. The principle of equality for women, they held, has long been upheld by the Reform movement, and should not be compromised; and they doubted whether the practical difficulties were as great as Lauterbach supposed.

Following the debate a committee was appointed to draw up a policy statement. Rabbi Henry Cohen of Galveston was chairman, and Dr. Lauterbach served as one of the members. The statement produced by the committee and approved by the convention concluded with the words, "We declare that woman cannot justly be denied the privilege of ordination."

This language is hardly enthusiastic, and practical results have been slight. The student whose approaching graduation evoked the discussion dropped out of the College without completing the course. A number of women have studied for longer of shorter periods at various liberal seminaries (Henrietta Szold had been such a student at the Jewish Theological Seminary in the early 1900's), but none has been ordained.

Though the first woman rabbi is yet to appear, it should be noted that the election of women to congregational offices has become a matter of course, and women have served as presidents of several large Reform congregations.

"Burial Practices"

Part I (p. 252) This subject has now been examined more fully and systematically in a responsum, "The Alignment of Graves," in *Current Reform Responsa* by Solomon B. Freehof (1969),pp.132 ff. Dr. Freehof's findings fully support the view given here that no fixed rule governs this question.

Part II (p. 253) The author added: comp. J. G. Frazer, *Folklore in the OT,* 1 vol. ed., p. 230. Perhaps the *"gepelich"* are relics of a ladder put in, by which the ghost ascends to heaven . . . p. 14.

ERRATA

Page	For	Read
12, n.22, 1.10	phylacreries	phylacteries
42, 1.22	Tanhoma	Tanhuma
47, 1.4	Nidah	Niddah
48, 1.31	Gitin	Gittin
60, 1.13	Ketuboh	Ketubot
1.22	p. 3z-4a	p. 3d-4a
65, 1.5	Moel	Mohel
70, n.33, 1.7	שם הגרולים	שם הגדולים
71, n.46, 1.1	קוראבנו	קורא בנו
1.2	הנקראברית	הנקרא ברית
74, n.77, 1.14	עלפלוני	על פלוני
n.81, 1.4	אות	אותו
102, n.40, 1.6	Scheftclowitz	Scheftelowitz
114, 1.20	comes	come
133, 1.26	seems	seem
186, 1.15	תוב	טוב
197, n.6, 1.5	בדטות	בדמות
1.22	בן	בו
1.22	כטוך	כמוך
198, n.11, 1.5	שעטדו	שעמדו
199, n.14, 1.1	לביו	לבין
231, 1.26	הגרייא	הגר"א
235, 1.13	coverinng	covering
242, 1.14	שקיחא	שכיחא
243, 1.24	Barzelona	Barcelona
244, 1.2	Yalkut, Shimeoni	Yalkut Shimeoni
1.2	74i	741
1.7	Jad.	Yad,
249, 1.8	*silencio*	*silentio*

ESSAYS

ESSAYS

ESSAYS

ESSAYS

THE CEREMONY OF BREAKING A GLASS AT WEDDINGS[1]

JEWISH CEREMONIES HAVE BEEN unduly neglected in modern times, both in study and in practice. The effects of this double neglect are reciprocally cumulative. With the decline in the practical observance of the ceremonies, the scholarly interest in them is also waning, so that very few students devote themselves to the study of the origins, and the development of the religious ceremonies. On the other hand, the failure on the part of scholars to choose religious ceremonies as subjects for scholarly research ultimately results in a general ignorance of the actual meaning and significance of the ceremonies. This ignorance of the meaning of the ceremonies naturally causes more neglect of the practical observance of them. For ceremonies are merely a means to an end. They are vessels used to carry ethical ideas, to convey religious lessons. Without a knowledge of the ideas they contain and the lessons which they are to teach they appear empty vessels, meaningless forms, which do not appeal to the people and consequently are ignored and neglected by them.

Yet it cannot be denied that the religious life, as well as the science of religion and folklore lose very much by this double neglect of the religious ceremonies.

[1] It is not my intention in this essay to give a study in comparative folklore. I merely wish to treat the development of a Jewish ceremony. For this reason I consider only Jewish practices and quote only references from Jewish sources as to the ideas underlying these practices, though numerous parallels to these ideas and practices could be cited from the customs and folklore of other people. Only in a few cases where non-Jewish influence is likely to be assumed or where direct borrowing may have taken place, reference to the non-Jewish origin or parallel custom will be given.

Reprinted from *Hebrew Union College Annual*, Vol. II, 1925.

The religious life is deprived of a most powerful auxiliary, for ceremonies are not only a great aid in religious instruction by providing the best means of elucidating the lessons and impressing upon the minds of the people the truths of religion, but they are also of great help in training the people in the habit of putting theories into practice and translating beliefs into actions and thus live their religion.

The science of religion and folklore are deprived of a very valuable source of information about the development of religious ideas and popular beliefs, furnished by the religious ceremonies. For religious ceremonies change in their aspects and in their meaning with the change of beliefs and with the broadening of ideas experienced by those who observe them. The interpretation given to the significance of a ceremony does not merely preserve and reflect the beliefs of those who first introduced or instituted it, but it represents also the ideas of the people who retain the ceremony and who have reinterpreted it so as to meet their own religious standards or advanced theological views.

Such a reinterpretation of the meaning of religious ceremonies has been taking place in Judaism throughout its entire history. Its ceremonies have been constantly developed, more or less changed and modified and reinterpreted from generation to generation and from age to age so as to meet the religious requirements of that age and adequately express, or at least be compatible with, the theological views of that generation. True, it was not always possible to preserve all ceremonies even by means of this process of reinterpretation and continuous adaptation. It happened occasionally that all efforts at reinterpretation of a certain ceremony failed, so that the ceremony could no longer be made to convey any religious idea or be brought into harmony with the prevailing beliefs of the people, and consequently had to be entirely abandoned. But even the record of a discarded ceremony has an interesting story to tell. For it gives us valuable information about the spiritual forces that opposed and combatted it and the strength of the advanced ideas that finally brought about its elimination from Jewish religious practice.

This process of constant reinterpretation and adaptation of the Jewish religious ceremonies with the occasional abolishing or discarding of some ceremonies entirely, has been greatly stimulated and furthered by the continuous struggle which has always been going on in Judaism between the teachers and the masses of the people. The higher ethical principles and pure religious beliefs as formulated and taught by the teachers of Judaism were in constant conflict with some of the popular beliefs and superstitious ideas which lingered on in the mind of the people at large, who besides being disposed to preserve and retain older superstitions of their own, were always easily subject to the influence of environment and prone to borrow superstitions from their non-Jewish neighbours.

The Rabbis have always, directly or indirectly, opposed heathen practices and superstitions but did not always succeed in uprooting them.

The process of the development of a ceremony with its interpretations and modifications frequently takes the following course. The people will sometimes accept and retain a ceremony even if its origin be in an older heathen practice or in a foreign superstition, simply because the masses of the people are not always above these superstitions. The Rabbis will oppose such a ceremony and seek to prohibit its observance. In some cases, they succeed in their efforts and the ceremony is discarded. Sometimes, however, especially in the case of a generally accepted practice, its observance is so widespread that all the objections and protests of the Rabbis can not prevail against it. The people simply persist in observing it, and the Rabbis have to tolerate it. And if the ceremony does not violate an ethical principle and does not interfere with another religious duty, the Rabbis gradually relax their opposition. They acquiesce in its practice, considering it a popular custom, a *minhag*, which has its recognized place in Jewish religious life. All that the Rabbis then try to do is to effect slight changes in the ceremony, to modify it a little so as to remove from it some of its most objectionable features or the elements of crude superstition.

When this is impossible the Rabbis do the next best thing, that is, they ignore the superstitious element altogether. They retain the ceremony as such without giving its meaning or explaining its significance. They never call attention to its origin and do not refer to the superstitious belief on which it is based. The real meaning of the ceremony, being thus suppressed, is gradually forgotten by the people. The next generation, receiving the ceremony without any explanation no longer realizes its original meaning. The teachers of this generation, believing it to be a Jewish ceremony since they received it from their fathers together with other Jewish practices, seek to read into it a meaning which would make it expressive of some Jewish religious idea or at least prove it to be compatible with Jewish teachings. They usually succeed in finding in the ceremony some suggestion of an idea to which they could subscribe and they imagine that this actually was the idea underlying the ceremony. They offer this as a possible interpretation of the meaning of the ceremony. They merely guess at it but the following generation accepts this guess as a certainty and believes that this was the actual significance of the ceremony and the original meaning is almost entirely forgotten. In this manner an ancient superstitious practice may in the course of time be transformed into a Jewish ceremony which is reinterpreted from generation to generation so that even the Rabbis, entirely unaware of its heathen source and oblivious of its original superstitious significance, are likely to acknowledge it as a Jewish custom or even to recommend it as a ceremony with some Jewish religious significance.

The evolution of quite a number of Jewish ceremonies could be cited in illustration of this process. In this essay I shall deal with the ceremony of breaking a glass at weddings. I select this particular ceremony because in the history of its development, with the many changes effected in its details, in the veiled objections raised against it by Rabbis at different times and in the many reinterpretations which it received in the course of time by the teachers of various generations, the process above outlined can be well illustrated and its various stages clearly traced. This ceremony goes back to very ancient times and has its origin in a heathen superstition. It belongs to a group of wedding ceremonies which are based upon a common superstitious belief and have the same significance and purpose. For this reason, while limiting myself to a study of this one ceremony in particular it will occasionally be necessary in the course of the discussion, to refer also to other ceremonies of the group.

The idea underlying this group of wedding ceremonies is an ancient heathen superstition, survivals of which are still found, in one form or another, in Jewish life and practice. It is the belief that the evil spirits or demons are jealous of human happiness and therefore seek to spoil it or to harm the happy individual. The bride and the groom about to be married are, accordingly, the objects of the envy of the demons and liable to be harmed by them. It was believed that the bridegroom was especially exposed to such danger. For the evil spirits, like the arch demons or the fallen angels of old, notice the beautiful daughters of men and desire them.[2] Accordingly, they would seek to kill the bridegroom or otherwise hurt him and prevent him from joining his bride, in order that they might keep the bride for themselves. The story in the book of Tobit about the demon who killed the husbands of Sarah is the classic expression of this belief among the Jewish people in ancient times, and the saying of the Talmud that the bride and groom are among those who need to be carefully watched over and guarded, is generally understood to mean that they need to be guarded and protected from attacks of the jealous demons.[3] During the week of the wedding the bridegroom would, therefore, not dare to go out alone. Friends were especially appointed to guard the groom carefully.[4] Usually the face of the bride would be covered so that the demon should not see her. Sometimes the faces of both the bride and the groom were covered in order to be hidden

---

[2] See my article on Shamḥazai in *Jewish Encyclopedia* XI. p. 228–229.

[3] The saying in the Talmud (b. Berakot 54b) reads: שלשה צריכין שימור חולה חתן וכלה, to which Rashi remarks: שימור מן המזיקין, and he goes on to explain that the bride and the groom need to be guarded against the demons because the latter out of envy and jealousy seek to harm them.

[4] Pirke d. R. Eliezer XVI; TAShBeZ by R. Simon b. Zadok (died 1312), 465 (Warsaw, 1875) p. 80. Among East-European Jews the custom is still observed that the bridegroom does not leave the house to go out alone during, the week of the wedding.

from the demons. The custom for brides to wear a veil and the
ceremony of "Bedecken" that is covering the head of the bride
or, as it was done in some countries, covering the heads of both
the bride and the groom with a black and white cloth[5] or with
a Talith,[6] as well as the custom of having the wedding ceremony
performed under a canopy, though later reinterpreted to
have a certain symbolic significance, were originally simple
devices for hiding the bride and the groom and thus protecting
them from harm by the demons. But this method of guarding
the bride and the groom against the demons merely by having
them hide and trying to escape their notice was not completely
satisfactory. It did not, in itself, offer perfect security. Since
the demons themselves are not visible, the people were never
certain whether by these methods of hiding they succeeded in
making the bride and the groom unnoticeable and invisible
to the demons. The people, therefore, sought other means of
protection from harm by the demons. There were, according
to the belief of the people, three ways of avoiding the danger
of the demons and of effectively warding off any attack by them.

The first was to fight the demons and drive them away.
The second was to bribe them by gifts and conciliate them. The
third was to deceive them by making them believe that the
person whom they envy and seek to harm is not to be envied
at all since he is not as happy as they imagine him to be but is
rather worried and burdened with grief.

Each one of these methods found its expression in special
ceremonies. And the various Jewish wedding ceremonies clearly
show that all three methods were used by the people to obtain
protection from harm by the demons. The method of fighting
the demon was employed by Tobias who upon the advice of
Rafael smoked out the demon and drove him away by the smell
of the heart and the liver of the fish (Tobit VI, 7.VIII, 2–3).
But not all the people have the advice of a Rafael who would
give them special means wherewith to drive away the demons.

[5] *Orḥot Ḥayyim* by R. Aaron ha-Kohen, II, (Berlin 1902) P. 67; *Kolbo*
Hilkot Ishut (Venice 1547) p. 87a.

[6] R. Eleazar of Worms, (died 1238) in his *Rokeaḥ* 353 (Cremona 1557)
p. 64a.

They would, therefore, use other means which in their belief would have the power to drive away the demons. Noises, torches, salt and iron were believed to be effective weapons against the demons.[7] And the custom to make noise and loud music, to carry or throw about torches and light numerous candles at weddings even when they take place in the daytime[8] as well

[7] I shall quote here a few references to Jewish sources where the belief that these means offer protection from the demons or drive them away, is either expressly stated or presupposed. As to noise and shouting see the story in Leviticus r. XXIV, 3 (also in Midrash Tehillim XX, 7 and Tanḥuma, Kedoshim 8 and Tanḥuma Buber ibidem p. 39a) where it is assumed that the noise and the shouting helped in driving away the wicked demon. As to torches and lights see b. Berakot 43b where it is said, where there are two persons the demon might show himself but would not dare hurt them. Where there are three persons the demon would not even dare show himself. And אבוקה כשנים if one person carries a torch with him he is as safe as if he had two other people besides himself, in which case the demon would not even dare show himself. As to salt see Midrash quoted in Tosafot Berakot 40a s. v. הבא מלח and Isserles in Sh. Ar. Oraḥ Ḥayyim 167, 5 and especially Kizzur Shelah (Warsaw 1879) דיני האכילה p. 36 where it is said that salt is put on the table in order to drive away the evil spirits מלח יתן על השלחן לגרש הקליפות. The salt used in the crowns of the bride and the groom (Tosefta Sotah XV, 8, b. Sotah 49b, and p. Sotah IX 34b) also served the same purpose. As to iron see Tosefta Sabbat VI, 13 where the practice of putting iron under one's head (evidently as a protection from the demons) is condemned as a heathen superstition דרכי אמורי. The saying in b. Pesaḥim 112a that when food is put under the bed the evil spirits have access to it even if it be covered with iron vessels, also presupposes that ordinarily iron vessels would protect the food from the evil spirits. In the story in Leviticus r. referred to above, it is also assumed that "beating with iron" מקשין בפרזלא was used to drive away the demon. In a manuscript work by R. Eleazar of Worms, חידושים באותיות חסרות, there is also found the statement להגן מן השדים מקיפין בברזל וכו', quoted by M. Güdemann, Geschichte des Erziehungswesens und der Cultur der Juden I, (Wien 1880) p. 204. In Maharil (Warsaw 1874), p. 6, it is recommended to put a piece of iron into the water, kept in the house during the vernal equinox תקופה so that the demon should have no access to it לתת ברזל אל המים כל זמן התקופה ואו אין רשות למזיק. Comp. also Sabbathai Cohen in his commentary to Yore Deah 115, 6. As to similar beliefs among other people see E. Samter, Geburt Hochzeit und Tod (Berlin 1911) pp. 51, 58, 60, 72, and 151.

[8] R. Eliezer b. Nathan (RABaN) of Mayence (12th century) in his work Eben ha-Ezer (Prague 1610) p. 128c; Orḥot Ḥayyim l. c.; Tashbez l. c.; and Matteh Mosheh (Warsaw 1876) p. 213. RABaN and Orḥot Ḥayyim say that the candles were used for the purpose of increasing the joy משום שמחה,

JACOB Z. LAUTERBACH

as the custom to throw salt[9] over the heads of the bride and the
groom or to have the groom carry in his pocket a piece of iron
during the ceremony;[10] all these were originally intended to
serve the purpose of fighting the demons and driving them
away from the bride and the groom.

The method of propitiating the demons by offering them
gifts also found expression in certain Jewish wedding ceremonies.
The pouring out of wine and oil and the scattering of parched
grain and nuts as well as dried fish and meat before the bride
and the groom[11] were originally intended as offerings to the

Tashbez and Matteh Moshe on the other hand, explain it to be for the purpose
of reminding us of the giving of the Law on Sinai. Both these explanations
are but later reinterpretations by the Rabbis who no longer knew or did not
like the real original meaning of the ceremony.

[9] Rokeaḥ l. c.; also in הלכות ארוסין ונשואין contained in the Manuscript
Siddur of Orleans, see *Zeitschrift f. hebräische Bibliographie* XIII (1909) p.
17. The explanation given by Rokeaḥ that it is to suggest that the marriage
covenant between the bride and the groom be permanent and lasting through
their entire life, is but a later reinterpretation.

[10] Reported by A. Berliner, *Aus dem Leben der deutschen Juden* (Berlin
1900) p. 100.

[11] Tosefta Sabbat VII, 16 ממשיכין יין ושמן בציגורות לפני חתנים וכלות ולא טדרכי
האמורי comp. b. Berakot 50b and in Tractate Semaḥot VII, it is stated more
fully: מבזבזים לפני חתנים ולפני הכלות מחרוזות של דגים וחתיכות של בשר ביכות החמה אבל
לא בימות הגשמים... ממשיכין לפני חתנים ולפני הכלות ציגורות של יין וציגורות של שמן ואין חוששין
משום דרכי האמורי. The very fact that it was necessary to add the statement
that one need not hesitate to perform these ceremonies on the ground that
they are like heathen practices דרכי אמורי proves, to my mind, that these practices were based upon the heathen superstition of offering gifts to the demons. It
is also evident that there were some objections to these practices, raised at least
by some of the Rabbis. For the Rabbis knew very well of the popular superstition and of the practice of some people to offer food and drink to the demons,
for they forbade such practices. The saying in b. Sanhedrin 92a כל המשייר
פתיתים על שולחנו כאלו עובד עבודה זרה שנאמר העורכים לגד שולחן ולמני ממסך is a
protest against the practice of leaving food on the table for the demons
or friendly spirits (see Rashi ad loc. and Sh. Ar. Yoreh Deah 178, 3). The
Rabbis also forbade the practice of saying: "drink but leave something"
as a heathen practice דרכי אמורי (Tosefta Sabbat VII, 7) because it meant,
leave something as a portion for the demons, see below note 35. The Rabbis
had still another good reason to object to these practices and this was on the
ground that they involved the wasting of valuable food. Why then did the
Rabbis tolerate these practices and even declared that one need not object to

demons to bribe them not to harm the bride or the groom. The later forms of this custom which consisted in throwing wheat[12], or wheat and coins,[13] was to serve the same purpose of offering a bribe to the demons, though it has, of course, been reinterpreted and understood in another sense by the rabbinical authorities.

The third method, i. e. the one of fooling the demons by making them believe that the people are sad and mourning and therefore not to be envied, is represented in the ceremonies of putting ashes upon the head of the bridegroom[14] or a piece of

them as being one of the דרכי אמורי? Simply, because these practices were too widespread among the people and the Rabbis were unable to make the people give up these cherished practices. The Rabbis tried at least to modify these practices and limit them to such food as would not become spoiled and wasted by being thrown upon the ground and they prohibited the scattering of food which would get spoiled כל שהוא דבר האבד אין מבזבזין לפניהם (Semaḥot 1. c.; comp. Rashi to b. Berakot 50b s. v. ממשיבין). By these restrictions and modifications they made it less apparent that these foods were intended as gifts to the demons and they could interpret these practices as having another significance either as symbolic acts suggesting plentifulness or as modes of honoring the bride and the groom. Compare also A. Büchler, *Das Ausgiessen von Wein und Öl als Ehrung bei den Juden: Monatsschrift für Geschichte und Wissenschaft des Judentums*, 1905, p. 12–40.

The custom of carrying a hen and a rooster before the bride and the groom at the wedding ceremony, mentioned in b. Gittin 57a, or, as it was done in the middle ages, to let a hen and a rooster fly away over the heads of the bride and the groom (Güdemann op. cit. III, Wien 1888, p. 123) was also intended as a gift to the demons or as a sort of a substitute offering כפרות. See I Scheftelowitz, *Das stellvertretende Huhnopfer* (Giessen 1914) p. 10–11.

[12] RABaN 128c; Vitry p. 589; Tosafot to Berakot 50b s. v. ולא ביטות הגשמים Rokeaḥ l. c.; R. Moses Minz (15th century) in his Responsa No. 109 (Lemberg 1851) p. 100; Maharil p. 64. The explanation given by all these authorities that the practice was merely to be a symbolic suggestion that the couple may increase and multiply, as well as the other interpretation given by Rokeaḥ that it was to be a symbol of prosperity are but later reinterpretations. The mere fact that different interpretations are given shows that those who offered these interpretations were merely guessing and no longer knew the real significance of the ceremony, see above note 8.

[13] Berliner op. cit. p. 47; comp. also Judah Elset מחיי העם in the Hebrew Weekly העברי, edited by Meyer Berlin, New York, XI, No. 2, p. 8–9.

[14] Talmud b. B. B. 60b; Vitry 1. c.; *Kolbo*, Hilkot Ishut p. 86d; *Tur*, Eben ha-Ezer 65; Maharil 1. c.; Moses Minz op. cit. p. 99d; *Matteh Mosheh l. c.*

black cloth upon the heads of both the bride and the groom,
thus making them appear to be mourners.[15] The custom to
cry and wail at weddings indicated already in the Talmud[16]
but especially prevalent among Jews in Eastern Europe[17] also
originated in the belief that the demons might thereby be de-
ceived into believing that the people were grieved and unhappy
and desist from harming them. Possibly the custom for the
bride and the groom to fast on their wedding day[18] was originally
meant to serve the same purpose.

It depended, of course, on the temper of the various groups
of people and their personal preferences as to which one of the

[15] *Kolbo*, Hilkot Tisha be-Ab p. 67c.

[16] Berakot 31a see below note 23.

[17] Compare *Taame ha-Minhagim* by איש שׂוֹרְב I (Lemberg 1911) p. 111
No. 955.

[18] Rokeaḥ l. c. and Tashbez l. c. mention only that it is customary for
the bridegroom alone to fast and they offer different reasons for his doing this.
Rokeaḥ says that he found in an agadic Midrash that the reason why the
bridegroom fasts on the wedding day till after the ceremony is to show his
appreciation of the religious duty which he is about to perform, just as the
pious men of former times used to fast before the performance of every religious duty which they especially liked מה שמתענין החתנים עד לאחר הברכה מצאתי
באגדה מפני שמצוה חביבה עליהם כדרך שעושין חסידים הראשונים שהיו מתענין על
מצוה החביבה כגון לולב ושאר דברים. Tashbez gives the reason that the
wedding day is like the day of the giving of the Torah on Sinai, when
Israel was, so to speak, wedded to God. And just as the Israelites fasted on
that day so should the bridegroom fast on the wedding day. According to
this interpretation, the bride should rather fast, since Israel was the bride.
Matteh Mosheh, p. 213, gives two other reasons for this custom. According
to the one the custom was simply a drastic measure to keep the bridegroom
from feasting and drinking. For in case he should get drunk and enter the
marriage covenant while in a state of drunkenness, the marriage would be il-
legal. The other reason is that the wedding day is for the bridegroom like
a day of Atonement since his sins are forgiven on that day (comp. p. Kilayim
III, 3, 65cd). But one may ask if the marriage itself atones for his sins why
does he need the fasting as another means of obtaining forgiveness. The
same two reasons are also given by Moses Minz l. c. though he says that the
custom is that the groom as well as the bride fast, and for the bride's fasting
there is no reason offered. Isserles Sh. Ar. Eben ha-Ezer 61, I. also says that
both the bride and the groom fast. When so many conflicting explanations
are given for one and the same custom, one is certainly justified in assuming
that they are all merely guesses.

three methods they would employ. Some people chose to fight, others prefered to ingratiate themselves with the demons and still others would seek to deceive them. It may be that these various ceremonies originated at different times and among different groups of the people, and it was only in the course of time that they came to be observed by most of the people. For the people who observe the ceremonies are not always consistent. They often employ ceremonies expressing contradictory tendencies, or are prompted by different and even conflicting motives in the performance of one and the same ceremony, believing it to work in different directions and to serve different purposes. In the ceremony of breaking a glass with which we are here concerned, we find all the three methods expressed. That is to say, in the manner in which it was performed at different times and in some of its details, we can see that the people, possibly at different times or in different countries, understood the significance of this ceremony differently, so that whatever method of dealing with the demons they preferred, they could use this ceremony. In other words all the three methods are represented in the details and various features of this ceremony.

We shall now trace the development of this ceremony and see how all these methods are expressed in it. We shall find that either by slight changes in one of its features or by special emphasis laid upon one of its details, by the meaning ascribed to it by the people or even by the different interpretations given to it by some rabbinic authorities at one time or another, the ceremony could be, and actually was, employed to serve all the three purposes, of fighting, bribing and fooling the demons.

The first mention of this ceremony is found in the Talmud where the following stories are told: "Mar son of Rabina made the wedding feast for his son. When he noticed that the Rabbis were very gay, he brought a precious cup worth four hundred Zuz, and broke it before them and they immediately became sad. R. Ashi made the wedding feast for his son. When he noticed that the Rabbis were very gay, he brought a cup of white glass and broke it before them and immediately they became sad".[19] Significant enough, no express comment is made

in the Talmud about this strange performance on the part of
these two Rabbis, and no direct explanation of its significance
is given.   Judging, however, from what precedes and from what
follows these stories in the Talmud it is evident that the Talmud
understood that the purpose of this performance was to avoid
the danger of provoking the envy of the demons by deceiving
them and making them believe that the people were sad and
grieved.   For, immediately preceding these stories, we are told
the following story: "R. Jeremiah was sitting before R. Zera.
When R. Zera noticed that R. Jeremiah was too gay and hilarious he reminded him of the saying in Proverbs (XIV, 23) which
he took to mean that there is advantage in sadness.   R. Jeremiah,
however, answers saying 'I have the phylacteries on' "[20]   The
meaning of this conversation between R. Zera and R. Jeremiah,
I believe, is this; R. Zera was afraid that the hilarity of R. Jeremiah might provoke the envy of the demons who are not too
friendly to the students and are usually jealous of them.[21]   He,
therefore, advises R. Jeremiah that it would be to his own advantage to appear sad.   R. Jeremiah, however, answers that
he is not afraid of the demons, since he has on the phylacteries
which will protect him.[22]

בת ארבע מאה זוזי ורבר קמייהו ואעציבו. רב אשי עבד הלולא לבריה חזנהו לרבנן דהוו קבדחי טובא
ואעציבו קטייהו ורבר חיורהא דזוניתא כסא אייהי (Berakot 30b–31a).

רב ירמיה הוה יתיב קמיה דר' זירא חזייה דהוה קא בדח טובא אמר ליה בכל עצב יהיה [20]
.מותר כתיב אמר ליה אנא תפילין מנח:א

[21] Comp. b. Berakot 54b and Rashi ad loc.

[22] The popular belief that the Tephillin will protect one from harm by
the demons is expressly stated in the Targum to the Song of Songs VIII, 3
where it is said: אמרת כנשתא דישראל אנא בחרתא מכל עממיא די קטרא תפילין ביד שמאלי
ברישי וקביעא מזחתא בסטר ימינא דדשי תולתא לקבל תיקי דלית רשו למזיקא לחבלא בי .
And in Midrash Thillim XCI, 4 the same idea is expressed in a somewhat
modified form.   Comp. also b. Menaḥot 43b where the additional proof,
added to the saying of R. Eliezer b. Jacob, ואומר חונה מלאך ד' סביב ליריאו
ויחלצם also suggests this idea.   In p. Sabbath VI 8b it is declared prohibited
to put the phylacteries upon a child that is frightened (by demons?) so that it
may sleep.   That the phylacreries will drive away the demons is expressely
stated in p. Berakot V, i (8a) where R. Simeon b. Joḥai says that all people,
even the spirits and demons, will be afraid of thee when they will see the
name of God (meaning the תפלין upon the head, see b. Berakot 6a) upon
thee.   Compare especially b. Berakot 23ab where it is told of R. Joḥanan

Again immediately following the story of R. Ashi's breaking the glass, it is related there in the Talmud that when at the wedding of Mar the son of Rabina, the Rabbis asked Hamnuna Zutte to sing for them he began instead, to lament, crying, "Woe unto us for we must die".[23]   This clearly shows the tendency to deceive the demons by making them believe that the people were not gay and happy but rather worried about their impending death.   It is, therefore, evident from the context that the ceremony of breaking the glass or the precious cup was understood by the later Rabbis of the Talmud, to serve the same purpose of deceiving the demons, by subduing the hilarity of the people and making them appear sad for the moment.

Whether it was also intended as a sort of an offering to the envious evil powers, like "the ring of Polycrates" (Herodotus III, 40ff), as Max Grünbaum, *Gesammelte Aufsätze* (Berlin 1901) p. 111, assumes, or whether it was also believed that the demons can be frightened and driven away by the noise made by the breaking of the glass, is not in any way indicated in the Talmudic report.   It certainly was not so understood by the Rabbis who performed this strange ceremony for they would not have done the act with such a heathen motive.   It may, however, be safely assumed that the original meaning of the ceremony, at least in the popular belief, was to conciliate the envious evil spirits.   For, evidently, this was an old established custom which in the course of time had been reinterpreted by the Rabbis and explained as merely serving the purpose of sobering up the people and causing them to be sad for a moment.   Had this not been an old established popular practice at weddings, R.

that when entering the toilet-roon where danger from demons was commonly assumed he would carry with him his Tephillim, saying הואיל ושרונהו רבנן נטרן since the Rabbis permitted to carry the Tephillim even when entering this place, I might as well carry them with me so that they protect me.   And Rashi there explains נטרן ישמרוני אבנים עמי וישטרוני מן המזיקין Rashi's explanation here that R. Jeremiah meant to say, that the Tephillin prove that he had accepted upon himself the Kingdom of God, is not quite satisfactory, for this would not justify his being hilarious while having the Tephillin on.

[23] אמרו ליה רבנן לרב המנונא זוטי בהלולא דמר בריה דרבינא לישרי לן מר אמר להו ווי לן דמיתנן ווי לן דטיתנן.

Ashi and Mar bar Rabina would not have resorted to such an expensive and wasteful method of subduing the excessive hilarity of their guests. The more so since this practice actually constitutes a flagrant violation of the religious law prohibiting waste בל תשחית.[24]

We are, therefore, justified in assuming that we have here a case of the reinterpretation of the meaning of an older ceremony by the Rabbis who could not succeed in abolishing it altogether. In the popular mind the meaning of this ceremony was to offer a gift to the demons.

This of course was objectionable to the Rabbis, as it meant worshipping other beings besides God. However, being forced by the widespread popular usage to retain the ceremony, they tried to suppress the original idea about its significance by giving it another less objectionable meaning. This theory is further supported by the persistent silence which the Geonim and all the rabbinic authorities up to the twelfth century maintain in regard to this ceremony, for we do not find this ceremony mentioned in Rabbinic Literature before the twelfth century. This silence can only be explained on the theory that the Rabbis did not like this ceremony, they merely tolerated it, hence they did not care to discuss it or comment upon it and they even avoided the mere mention of it. But, much as the Rabbis objected to it, the people persisted in observing it and in a manner which preserved its original significance and refuted the interpretation given by the Rabbis. This is evident from the remarks of R. Eliezer b. Nathan of Mayence, RABaN (first half of the twelfth century) who discusses this ceremony in his work *Eben ha-Ezer* (Prague 1610) § 177, p. 44d. Commenting upon the stories in the Talmud (Berakot 30b–31a), RABaN recognizes the identity of the acts of R. Ashi and Mar b. Rabina with the ceremony of breaking a glass at weddings prevalent in his time.[25]

[24] The Rabbis understood the prohibition לא תשחית (Deut. XX, 19 to apply to all wasteful destruction of food or property, see Midrash Agadah edition Buber (Wien 1894) II, p. 199a and comp. b. B. K. 91b and Maimonides Yad, Melakim VI, 10.

[25] Vitry l. c. and Tosafot Berakot 31a s. v. אייתי כסא and Rokeaḥ l. c. also acknowledge the identity of the later ceremony with the practice recorded in the Talmud.

But he questions very much whether the reason clearly implied in the Talmud for the acts of R. Ashi and Mar b. Rabina would justify the later ceremony.   He also expresses some doubts as to the character of the ceremony itself.   His remarks are, as follows: ותימא לי אם על דבר זה הנהיגו הראשונים לשבר בנשואין כלי זכוכית כי מה עצבון יש בזה שאינו שוה אלא פרוטה ועוד יש לי תימה שנהגו להבזות כוס של ברכה ולשופכו הכל לאיבוד "I wonder whether it was really for this reason, that is, to make the people sad, that the former teachers instituted the custom of breaking a glass at weddings, for what sadness is there in this breaking of a glass which is not worth more than a penny.   Furthermore I am surprised that they instituted such a custom of desecrating the cup over which the benedictions had been recited and pouring out its contents all to waste."

We learn from these remarks a few interesting things.   In the first place, we may conclude from RABaN's words that the ceremony had been observed as an established custom from the time of R. Ashi up to the time of RABaN, so that the latter could well believe it to have been a Jewish custom instituted by the earlier rabbinic authorities.   Secondly, it is apparent that the real significance of the ceremony, having been ignored and suppressed by the earlier teachers, was not known to the later teachers, for RABaN cannot find any other meaning of the ceremony but the one suggested by the context of the Talmudic reports.   And although he finds it unsatisfactory he nevertheless accepts it as the only explanation for the ceremony and cannot think of any other interpretation of its significance. This illustrates the theory stated above regarding the effects which the reinterpretations of a ceremony have upon the course of its development.   When the Rabbis object to a ceremony and are nevertheless compelled to retain it they give it an interpretation which would at least make it less objectionable. This interpretation is then accepted by subsequent authorities who no longer know the original significance of the ceremony. It is also evident that RABaN does not quite approve of the ceremony.   He certainly does not recommend it.   When he describes the ritual of the wedding with all the ceremonies to be observed at it (p. 128abc) he does not mention this ceremony.

It is only in connection with his discussion of the passage in the Talmud that he refers to it here, and from his questioning both the correctness of the interpretation and the propriety of the ceremony it is evident that he does not favor it.[26] Finally we learn from RABaN's remarks another important feature of the ceremony, as it was observed by the people. It did not consist of the mere breaking of a glass, it consisted of the breaking of the glass containing the wine over which the benedictions had been recited, so that with the breaking of the glass went also the spilling of the wine. The spilling of the wine in this ceremony must have had the same significance as the ceremony of pouring out wine and oil and the strewing of wheat, mentioned in the Tosefta quoted above, which was to serve the purpose of bribing the demons. It is evident, therefore, that in the popular belief the purpose of our ceremony was, not to make the people appear sad, but to offer a gift to the demons. If the glass was cheap its contents added to its value as an appropriate offering. No wonder RABaN could not see in the motive implied in the Talmud, that is, to make the people sad, a justification for this ceremony, for in the form in which it was performed in his time the ceremony failed to achieve this purpose. And to the pouring out of the wine RABaN rightly objects. Since he would not countenance the idea of its being an offering to the demons he could regard it only as an unlawful waste and a desecration of the cup over which the benedictions had been recited.

This indirect disapproval of the ceremony by RABaN, which other rabbinical authorities no doubt shared, did not have any effect on the popularity of the ceremony. It continued to be observed by the people and was even endorsed by some of the Rabbis of the time. But such objections as were voiced by RABaN had some effect on the development of the ceremony. For the slight changes and modifications made in it, as we shall note, the emphasis laid on one new feature in it, as well as the altogether new interpretation given to it by later rabbinical

---

[26] R. Joseph Saul Nathanson also understood that RABaN objects to the ceremony, for in his notes שי למורה to Sh. Ar. Eben ha-Ezer 65, he remarks וראב״ן מפקפק על זה.

authorities were in all likelihood due to a desire to meet these
objections and thus render the ceremony less objectionable.

This is clearly shown by the other early reference to this
ceremony which is found in *Maḥzor Vitry* (pp.. 589 and 593)
where the ceremony, with a very significant additional feature,
is prescribed in the following words: וימזוג בו עוד ויברך עליו
שבע ברכות וישתה וישקה וישפוך ומטיח הכוס של זכוכית בכותל ושוברו
"He should refill the glass with wine, recite over it the seven
benedictions, drink from it and give the bride and the groom
to drink and pour out (the rest) and then hurl the glass against
the wall and break it".[27]   We notice here that the objection
to the ceremony had been overcome by some of the rabbinic
authorities at least, for the ceremony is recommended and even
prescribed. Secondly, we notice an altogether new feature
which introduces a new element into the ceremony, or at least
suggests a new motive for its performance. Here it is expressly
prescribed that the wine be poured out. This, no doubt,
was a relic of the older practice of offering wine and food to the
demons. Then after the wine has thus been spilled, the other
part of the ceremony takes place. The empty glass is thrown
against the wall and broken. Formerly, it would seem, the
glass with the wine were both intended as an offering and the
breaking of the glass may have been considered as merely incidental. The main purpose was the offering of the glass and
the wine. This could be achieved only by throwing the glass
with its contents, the wine, at the demons, which act incidentally
resulted in the glass being broken. In the form as prescribed
in Vitry the ceremony is divided into two. The offering, which
is done by pouring out the wine, is separate from the throwing
and breaking of the glass. There must have been a special
reason for this dividing of the original ceremony. I believe that
this new feature of throwing the empty glass was prompted by
a motive entirely different from the one which produced the
original form of the ceremony. It represents the third method
of dealing with the demons, viz. by fighting them or frightening

---

[27] In an addition, תוספות, on p. 593, it is expressly stated that the bridegroom should throw the glass against the wall and break it.

them away. This change in the ceremony may have been made to meet the objections raised against it by the Rabbis. And it was due to this modification that the ceremony could be retained after objections, such as those voiced by RABaN, had been made to it. For, this new feature helped the people to overcome the hesitancy and the scruples which they must have felt in performing the ceremony in its original form when both the wine and the glass were offered to the demons. For offering a gift to the demons is almost like worshipping them to which the religious conscience objected. But fighting the demons is theologically less objectionable. The inconsistency presented by the spilling of the wine which is a form of making an offering and the throwing of the glass which is a form of fighting was probably not realized by the people. The mere fact that the wine was poured out on the ground and not thrown together with the glass in the direction of the demons was sufficient to make it appear that the wine was not intended as an offering to the demons.[28] That the smashing of the empty glass was intended as a method of fighting the demons is further evident from the fact that it was flung at the wall. This plainly indicates that the missile was aimed at the demons. For the demons were believed to lurk under the spouts of the roof close to the wall. (comp. Ḥulin 105b). Of course, Vitry ignores this implied significance. He explains the meaning of the ceremony by merely referring to the Talmudic interpretation of the saying in Proverbs XIV, 23 that there is an advantage in appearing sad.[28] But this interpretation can hardly explain why the wine

---

[28] It may also be that the pouring out of the wine was considered by some of the people to be, not an offering to the demons, but a means of driving them away. Just as the Christians in those days believed that the blessed water had the power of driving away the demons, the Jews could also believe that the wine of the כוס של ברכה would have the same effect. This would explain the special feature of this practice, mentioned in Tashbez l. c. namely to scatter the wine, when pouring it out, over the entire house על פני כל הבית. Tashbez himself, however, explains this feature to have merely a symbolic significance, suggesting that God will bless the house with plenty of good things, comp. b. Erubin 65a.

[29] The same interpretation is also given by Rokeaḥ l. c.

should be poured out and why the empty glass must be broken in this particular manner.

That this throwing the glass in a specific direction was intended to fight or frighten away the demons is also clearly shown by the description of the ceremony as observed by R. Jacob Moellin (died 1427), reported in *Sefer Maharil* (Warsaw 1874) p. 64b–65a, in the following words: כשגמר הברכה נתן לחתן לשתות ואחר כך להכלה והרב החזיק הכוס בידו ואחר כך נתן את הכוס ביד החתן והפך החתן את פניו לאחוריו ועמד נגד צפון זרק את הכוס אל הכותל לישבר ומיד ממהרין עם החתן דרך שמחה להכניסו לבית חתונה קודם הכלה "After he (R. Jacob Moellin) had finished the benediction he gave to the bridegroom to drink and afterwards to the bride, still holding the cup in his hand. Then he gave the cup into the hand of the bridegroom. The latter then turned around and facing the northside threw the cup against the wall so that it got broke. Immediately thereupon they hasten to run away with the bridegroom, in a joyous manner, in order to bring him into the wedding chamber before the bride gets there." The express requirement that the bridegroom turn around and throw the glass against the northern wall is significant. It certainly was done with a definite purpose. And we can readily understand what that purpose was when we remember that it was believed that the demons came from the northside and hence were to be found in their usual haunt along the wall of the northside. This belief that the demons come from the north originated with the ancient Persians[30] but found its way also into Jewish Literature. It is frequently mentioned in many of the younger Midrashim[31] and thus may have become a popular Jewish belief. It is for this reason that the bridegroom, when ready to fight the demons, had to turn northward in the direction where the

[30] Comp. I. Scheftelowitz, *Die altpersische Religion und das Judentum* (Giessen 1920) p. 59.

[31] Pirke d. R. Eliezer III: ושם ׳וברוח צפון) מדור למזיקין ולזועות ולרוחות ולשדים לברקים ולרעמים ומשם רעה יוצאת (ילקוט איוב רמז תתקי׳ז: ומשם יוצאין) שנאמר מצפון תפתח הרעה. comp. also Pesikta Rabbati (Friedmann p. 188) and Midrash Numbers r. II, 10 and III, 12; and Midrash Konen in Jellinek's *Beth ha-Midrash* II, p. 30 where it is said ושם כת סטא׳׳ל; and מדרש אבכיר by A. Marmorstein in דביר I. (Berlin 1923) p. 121.

demons were believed to be, to throw the glass at them, thus
either hurting them with the broken pieces of glass or frightening
them by the noise which the shattering of the glass makes.
The significance of the other feature, mentioned in Maharil,
namely, that immediately after the throwing of the glass they
hurry away with the bridegroom, also becomes clear to us.
Maharil's explanation of this running away of the bridegroom,
as being a joyous manner דרך שמחה is hardly correct, for one fails
to see what special joy there can be in thus running away. In
the popular belief this running away was for the simple purpose
of escaping danger. Before the demons have time to recover
from their fright and rush upon the bridegroom to attack him
the people hasten to get away with him. They were especially
anxious to get him into the wedding chamber before the bride
is there for the demons might endeavour to prevent him from
joining his bride.

It further appears from the description in Maharil that at
that time, that is at the beginning of the 15th century and in
Germany at least, the ceremony was again performed in its
original form, namely, that the glass with its contents, the wine,
were thrown at the demons and not in the form in which it is
described in Vitry, namely, that the wine was first poured out
and then the empty glass thrown against the wall.[32] Thus we
see how in the various features of this one ceremony all three
methods of dealing with the demons found expression. The
people who observed this ceremony believed that by one or the
other of its features it can serve the purpose of effectively warding off the danger of the demons. Whether they preferred to
deceive the demons by appearing sad and unhappy or to bribe
them by offering them the wine as a gift or to fight them by
throwing the glass at them and hurting them, they could well
use this ceremony to achieve their aim.

Of course all these ideas about the efficacy of this ceremony
were entertained only in popular belief. The Rabbis, with
the exception of the few among them who were strongly inclined
to mysticism, did not share in these crude superstitions of fight-

[32] See below reference of R. Pinehas Horowitz to the form in which the
ceremony was observed as late as the 18th century

ing the demons and certainly not in the theologically objectionable idea of offering them gifts, which is a form of worship.   For
this reason Vitry gives only the one explanation of the meaning
of the ceremony that it is to remind us not to be too gay.   And
from the fact that Maharil, though describing the ceremony
in detail, does not give any explanation of its meaning and even
seeks to explain the feature of running away, which clearly
points to the superstition of fighting the demons, as being merely
a "form of joyousness" it is also evident that he did not share
in the popular superstitions and sought to ignore them.   This
illustrates our theory, stated above, about the attitude of the
Rabbis towards popular superstitious practices.   When unable
to abolish an objectionable ceremony simply because the people
in their superstition cling to it, they at least try to ignore the
real meaning of the ceremony and seek to suppress or explain
away the crude superstition on which the ceremony is based.
We may safely assume that the majority of the Rabbis did not
care much for this ceremony, considering that but very few
authorities mention it.   Possibly the ceremony would have
been more strongly opposed and eventually even entirely
abolished by the Rabbis had it not been for an altogether new
interpretation given to it, an interpretation which freed it entirely from all the objectionable superstitious beliefs with which
it had been intimately connected.

This new interpretation is found in *Kolbo* הלכות תשעה באב
(Venice 1547) p. 67, where speaking of the various reminders
of the duty to mourn for the destruction of Jerusalem, the author
also mentions our ceremony in the following words: ועל
זה פשט המנהג לשבור הכוס אחר שבע ברכות "For this reason also the
custom became prevalent to break the cup after the recitation
of the seven benedictions at weddings".   This is an altogether
new interpretation and is probably original with the author of
the Kolbo (14th century).[33]   For, as we have seen, RABaN

[33] Though R. Moses Minz l. c. quotes this interpretation in the name of
the "Zuricher", meaning R. Moses of Zurich, the author of the "Zuricher
Semak".   See about him Dr. Ch. Lauer in *Jahrbuch der Jüdisch-Literarischen
Gesellschaft* XII (Frankfurt am Main 1918) p. 1–36.
Güdemann, op. cit. III (Wien 1888) 122 cites another opinion about

could not think of any other meaning of the ceremony than the one suggested in the Talmud. And Vitry also knows only of one reason for the ceremony, namely the advantage and safety that may come to one from appearing sad, and that even in joy one should tremble. But it did not occur to RABaN or Vitry to connect this ceremony with the duty of mourning for Jerusalem. Evidently, the author of the Kolbo, or whoever first gave this interpretation, objected to the superstition underlying the meaning of the ceremony as suggested in the Talmud, namely that the demons seek to harm the happy people and that by appearing sad the wedding guests may deceive the demons and ward off their attacks. He, therefore, accepted only part of the suggestion of the Talmud, namely, that the ceremony was intended to cause the people to be sad, but he interpreted the purpose of being sad differently from that suggested by the context in the Talmud. He took it not as a means of deceiving the demons, but as a reminder of the destruction of Jerusalem and of our duty to mourn for it on all joyous occasions when we are likely to forget it. It was this interpretation that saved the ceremony and made it acceptable to the majority of the Rabbis. For this interpretation removed from the ceremony the element of crude superstition, so that even enlightened pious people could well observe it.

It took some time before this altogether new interpretation was accepted by the majority of the teachers, but it gradually came to be recognized as the most acceptable interpretation of the ceremony. It is significant that the leading rabbinical authorities of the 16th century who mention this ceremony as Joseph Caro in Bet *Joseph Orah Hayyim* 560, Moses Isserles in *Darke Moshe* and *Shulhan Aruk Orah Hayyim* 560, 2 and *Eben ha-Ezer* 65, 3, and Mordecai Jaffe in *Lebush*, Hilkot Tisha be-Ab 560, 2[34] do not give any details as to how the cere-

the significance of this ceremony, namely, that it was merely a symbolic act, declaring the marriage as legally contracted and valid. This opinion, whose author Güdemann does not mention by name, hardly deserves any consideration.

[34] In Lebush, however, there is still preserved a trace of the original significance of the ceremony, namely, to drive away the demons,. He says:

mony is to be performed, such as are given by Vitry, Maharil and Moses Muenz. They do not even quote these authorities and they also ignore the connection between the ceremony and the story in Talmud Berakot. They only mention the ceremony with the interpretation given to it by *Kolbo*, viz. that it is to serve as זכר להורבן a reminder of the destruction of Jerusalem. Evidently this was the only interpretation of the ceremony acceptable to them and they did not care to point out the details of the ceremony which clearly indicate that the ceremony originally served another purpose. This other purpose, or the original significance, of the ceremony, however, was not entirely forgotten by the people even though the majority of the teachers accepted only the new interpretation. The people, and some of the teachers more inclined to mysticism, continued to take the ceremony in its original meaning and to perform it for the purpose of warding off the danger of the demons. For, as it frequently happens, no matter what the advanced teachings of the enlightened authorities may be the people retain their cherished superstitions and some of the less advanced teachers will encourage them in their superstitious beliefs. Thus we find R. Isaiah Horowitz in his *Shne Luḥot ha-Brit* (Fuerth 1764), section שופטים, p. 378a, quoting Recanate, gives the following explanation of the significance of the ceremony: ועל כן תקנו לשבור את הכוס בשעת חופה פירוש כדי לתת למדת הדין חלקו ועל ידי כן ועולתה תקפץ פיה "Therefore have they instituted the custom of breaking the glass at the wedding, in order to give to the accuser his due portion whereby iniquity will close her mouth." Here it is expressly stated that the purpose of the ceremony is to offer a bribe to Satan or the demons, for THE ACCUSER and INIQUITY are but circumlocutions for Satan and the demons.

וטעם זה נוהגין לשבור הכוס תחת החופה להבהיל ולמעט השמחה. The word להבהיל "to terrify" or "dismay" can only mean to terrify the demons and frighten them away, for whom else would they wish, or believe, to frighten at the wedding. Possibly, the words ולמעט השמחה may have the same significance which is implied in the Talmud and in Vitry and Rokeaḥ, namely not to appear too happy. The author of the Lebush may have repeated this interpretation from another source in which the ceremony was understood in its original significance, though Lebush himself, no doubt, understood the ceremony as being a זכר לחורבן for he mentions it in Hilkot Tisha be-Ab.

This plain statement about the purpose of the ceremony
made by Recanate in the fourteenth century and endorsed
by R. Isaiah Horowitz in the beginning of the seveteenth century, is very interesting. It shows that in the fourteenth
century, at about the same time when Kolbo gave his new interpretation to the ceremony, the people and some authorities
still held on to the older meaning of the ceremony as being a
means of warding off the danger of the demons. It also shows
that in the sixteenth or the beginning of the seventeenth century after all the leading rabbinic authorities had accepted
Kolbo's interpretation, there were still some great teachers,
like Horowitz, who, because strongly inclined to mysticism, accepted and endorsed the older explanation of the significance
of the ceremony.[35] This clearly proves the correctness of the
statement made above that even after the official authorities
reinterpret a ceremony to harmonize with their theological
views the original meaning of the ceremony with its underlying
superstititions does not entirely disappear from the mind of
the people and even of some of the teachers. This observation
will also help us to understand some of the changes and modifications subsequently made in our ceremony.

The new interpretation of the ceremony as serving the
purpose of reminding us of the destruction of Jerusalem, though
accepted by the majority of the rabbinical authorities, did not
preclude further developments of the ceremony. On the
contrary, quite a few significant changes and modifications were
made in the performance of this ceremony after the new interpretation had been accepted by the majority of the Rabbis.
In the first place we notice that in the 16th century the ceremony
was observed not only at weddings but also at engagement
parties. This extension of its observaece was compatible with

_____

[35] According to Shelah, the ceremony was performed in the older form,
i. e. to smash the glass with the wine in it, thus spilling the wine as an offering
to the demons. For the breaking of an empty glass could not be considered
as offering to the demons their due portion. The idea of bribing the demons
by giving them their due portion is clearly stated in *Matteh Mosheh*, 306 and
504, where the pouring out of part of the wine at the Habdalah ceremony is
explained to be such an offering to the demons.

the new interpretation. For, if the purpose of the ceremony was to remind us on all joyous occasions of the destruction of Jerusalem, then it should by right be observed also on the joyous occasion when we celebrate the engagement. And so the custom of breaking pots and dishes at engagement parties came into use.[36]

Another significant change made in the ceremony was that instead of breaking the cup over which the seven benedictions, or ברכות נשואין had been recited, as prescribed by Vitry and Maharil, they would break the cup over which the benediction over the bretrothal, or ברכות אירוסין had been recited. What caused this change was a superstitious fear of another danger that might threaten the bride and the groom besides the danger from the jealousy of the demons. Superstition is not consistent. Superstition which originally considered the ceremony of breaking the glass as a sort of protective measure, believing it to have the effect of warding off the danger of harm by the jealous demons, now sees in this very ceremony a new danger. It considers the breaking of the cup over which the marriage benedictions had been recited a bad omen since it might augur a possible breaking of the marriage bond, suggesting a dissolution of the

[36] The earliest direct reference to this custom that I could find, is R. Yomtob Lippmann Heller (died 1654) in his *Malbushe Yomtob*, quoted by R. Elias Spira in *Elijahu Rabbah*. Commenting on the passage in Shulḥan Aruk Oraḥ Ḥayyim (or Lebush?) 560, 7, R. Elias Spira quotes from Heller's work the following remark: ונראה לי שזהו הטעם שמשברין הקדירה בכתיבת התנאים "It seems to me that this (i. e. to remind us of the destruction of Jerusalem) is also the reason why they break pots at the time of the writing of the engagement pact." He does not explain, however, why just pots be broken at the engagement party and not a glass as at weddings. The fact is that this interpretation of the custom of breaking earthen vessels at engagement parties is not correct. Its real purpose was to drive away the demons for which broken pottery was considered more effective. Just as the Germans would break pots on the evening before the wedding, Polterabend, in order to drive away the demons that threaten the bride and the groom, see Samter, *op. cit.* p. 60. That this was also the purpose of the Jewish custom is evident from the fact that just at the moment when the pots are broken the people present make noise and shout כזל טוב "good luck". For, certainly there would be no reason for making noise and shouting Mazel Tob at the moment when one is to be reminded of the destruction of Jerusalem and of the duty to mourn for it.

marriage just now contracted. That this was the reason for substituting the cup of the ברכת אירוסין for the cup of the ברכות נשואין is plainly stated by R. Moses Muenz (*Responsa* No. 109, Lemberg 1851 p. 100a) when he says וראיתי רבותי נהגו ליקח הכוס הראשון לזרוק ולשבר ולא זכיתי לשאל מהן טעמא מאי למה דוקא כוס ראשון ונראה קצת טעמא כיון דיש עתה שני כוסות טוב ליקח ולשבר כוס של אירוסין כי כוס של נישואין אתי לגמר הזיווג ומברכין והתקין לו ממנו בנין עדי עד לכן אין סברא לשבר כוס של נישואין שמורה חס ושלום על שבירת העניין כי אמרינן סימנא מילתא And Isserles (*Darke Moshe Oraḥ Ḥayyim 560* and *Sh. Ar. Eben ha-Ezer 65, 3*) likewise says that the custom in his city was that the bridegroom would break the cup over which the ברכת אירוסין had been recited. Isserles also tells us of another change in the ceremony as it was observed in the city of Cracow where he lived, and this was to recite the ברכת אירוסין over an earthen cup, and this was done because of the fact that they would break this cup and not the cup of the ברכות נשואין. He says: ובעירנו נוהגין שהחתן שהחתן משבר הכוס שמברכין עליו ברכת אירוסין ולכן נהגו לברך ברכת אירוסין על כוס של חרס, He does not explain how the use of an earthen cup for the ברכת אירוסין was the necessary consequence of the custom of breaking this cup instead of the one over which the marriage benedictions had been recited. He must have had in mind the custom of breaking pottery at the engagement ceremony. Since the betrothal אירוסין is more of an engagement than a wedding hence when the ceremony of breaking the cup is performed at that part of the wedding ceremony which represents the betrothal the cup to be broken should be of the same kind as the vessels broken at engagement parties.[37] This custom of using an earthen cup for the ברכת אירוסין seems to have been merely a local custom in Cracow and was not accepted in other places. From all the references to this ceremony that I could find it appears that the distinction between breaking dishes at engagement parties and breaking the cup at weddings was strictly maintained. For the former they required earthen pots or dishes while for the latter they insisted upon a glass. Various explanations are offered for this dis-

---

[37] Compare R. Joseph Teomim (1727–1793) in his משבצות זהב to Oraḥ Ḥayyim 560,4 who gives a fuller discussion of Isserles' statement.

tinction and reasons given why specifically pottery should be broken at engagements and a cup of glass should be broken at the wedding.[38]

The custom, however, of breaking the cup of the ברכת אירוסין instead of the one of the ברכות נשואין was almost universally accepted.   And to my knowledge there is but one reference to the custom in some place of breaking both the cup of the ברכת אירוסין as well as the one of the ברכות נשואין.[39] Besides the reason given by R. Moses Muenz as quoted above there are other explanations offered by some authorities why the cup of the ברכות נשואין should not be broken. These other explanations give the entire ceremony an additional symbolic aspect suggesting the relation between God and Israel. Thus R. Joseph Trani, the younger (1573–1644) in his *Zofnat Paaneaḥ* to section Matot (Venice 1653 or 1648), p. 196c, states that the custom is to break the cup of the ברכת אירוסין and that it must be of glass. And the reason why it must be of glass only is because then the ceremony not only reminds us of the destruction of Jerusalem but at the same time also suggests the hope that the breach in the relation between God and Israel caused by

[38] R. Joseph Teomim l. c. makes the following remark: ויראה לשבור תחת החופה כוס שלם ואין משום בל תשחית כיון שעושים לרמו מוסר למען יתנו לב מה שאין כן בתנאים שעושין להבהיל ולמעט השמחה ראוי ליקח קדירה שבורה חרס מחרסי האדמה לשבור והבן זאת. He does not say whom the broken pottery is to terrify, להבהיל, and by adding the words, והבן, he apparently hints at something which he does not care to express. He must have had in mind the popular belief about the purpose of this ceremony. See above note 36 and comp. Elset in Haibri X, No. 39, p. 10–11. For another suggestion why glass should be broken at weddings, see R. Samuel Edels in his Novellae to Berakot 31a. R. Elija Gaon of Wilna is reported to have said that the reason why just pottery must be broken at engagements is in order to suggest that just as the broken earthen vessels cannot be repaired so engagements should never be broken: אמר בשם הגאון זצ"ל שמזה הטעם שוברין בעת התנאים כלים של חרס שכיון שנשברו אין להם תקנה כן אסור לבטל התנאים ובחופה שוברין כלי זכוכית שיש לו תקנה להדבק כן יש תקנה להפרד בנט (quoted in סדר שערי רחמים p. 10 also in ספר תוספת מעשה רב Jerusalem 1896 in שאלתות p. 19 No. 134. The same interpretation is ascribed by others to R. Israel Baal Shem (Besht), see *Taame ha-Minhagim* I. p. 113a.

[39] See R. Ḥayyim b. Israel Benveniste (1603–1673) in his כנסת הגדולה to Eben ha-Ezer 65.

the destruction of Jerusalem will yet be repaired just as a broken vessel of glass can be repaired (comp. b. Ḥagigah 15a). This hope, he goes on to say, is further emphasized by taking another cup, a whole one, and reciting over it the marriage-benedictions, suggesting thereby that God will again be glad to do good to His people and betroth them unto Him in faithfulness forever.[40]

While Trani explains the practice to keep the cup of the marriage-benedictions unbroken as a symbolic sign that in future the relation or the bond between God and Israel will be everlasting, there is no doubt that in the popular belief the keeping of the cup of the marriage-benedictions intact was to suggest a good omen that the marriage bond of the couple whose wedding had just been celebrated will remain unbroken. Compare also R. Joseph Teomim (1727–1793) in his משבצות זהב to Oraḥ Ḥayyim 560, 4.

While these Rabbinical authorities thus explained the ceremony as reminding of the destruction of Jerusalem and as suggesting the hope of a renewal of God's relation with Israel as of old, the people, in some countries at least, continued to perform the ceremony in its original form and for the original purpose of giving the demons a bribe. This is evident from a statement of R. Pinehas Horowitz (died 1805) in the קונטרס אחרון of his ספר המקנה (Offenbach 1786) p. 256. Horowitz like R. Joseph Teomim (op. cit.) explains away the objection that might be raised to the ceremony of breaking the glass on the ground that it involves a violation of the law of בל תשחית. But he strongly objects to the manner in which the ceremony was performed in his time in Germany, that is, the breaking of the cup while it is full of wine מה שנהגו באשכנז לשבור הכוס מלא יין. This he thinks is wrong since the spilling of the wine is an act of ביזוי אוכלין a slighting of food and thus despising God's gifts. We see from this that even as late as the second half of the 18th century the custom in Germany, or at least in certain parts of Germany, was to throw the cup of wine to the ground, thus smashing the glass and spilling the wine. Evidently then

it was intended as a gift to the demons.[41]   This is clearly stated
by a contemporary of Horowitz, R. Uri Feivel b. Aaron in His
אור החכמה. Part II (Laszczow 1815) p. 6b.   He describes this
throwing of the glass with the wine as the portion due to the
"Other Side" which is always desirous of bringing about destruction and separation והוא חלק לסטרא אחרא שרוצה תמיד בחרבן ופירוד
The "Other Side" is a designation for Satan and the evil spirits.
They are desirous of doing harm and bringing about separation,
hence we give them a bribe to desist from harming the marrying
couple or trying to separate them.   Thus we see that all the interpretations of the Rabbis and their efforts to make this ceremony
merely of a symbolic character were not sufficient to uproot from
the mind of the people the old superstition that the ceremony is
intended as a bribe for the demons to make them more friendly
to the marrying couple.   It was left to another superstition
to defeat this old supersition, and remove it from the mind of
the people at least in connection with this ceremony.

It seems that the people began to be afraid of breaking even
the cup over which the benedictions of the betrothal were recited.   Since both the ברכת אירוסין and ברכות נשואין are at present
parts of the ritual by which the marriage is solemnized, the people
entertained the fear that the breaking of the cup over which
either one of these benedictions had been recited might augur
a breach in the marriage bond.   The custom was, therefore,
introduced of breaking another glass altogether, i. e., one which
has not been used in connection with the performance of the
marriage ceremony at all.   They usually have in readiness
another glass especially for the purpose of being broken.   This
is now the general practice as far as I know and the earliest
reference that I can find is one by R. Joseph Teomim in his משבצות
זהב l. c. where he says: "But I have seen the custom that
they take a glass cup for the benedictions of the betrothal.
It seems however that they do not break this cup after the marriage benedictions but it is another glass that they break after
the recital of the seven benedictions." אבל ראיתי המנהג שלוקחין
כוס זכוכית לאירוסין ומכל מקום נראה שאין שוברין אותו אחר נישואין כי
אם כוס אחר שוברין אחר שבע ברכות

[41] See above notes 32 and 35.

This latest form of the ceremony has also revived and developed some other superstitions. The idea of fighting the demons seems to have been revived and the successful smashing of the glass by the bridegroom is taken as a good omen, auguring that he will subdue and smash all his enemies.[42] If however the bridegroom should fail to crush the glass with the first stamping of his foot, as would happen if the glass slips away from under his foot, then it augurs ill for him. It might suggest that his enemies will escape from him or that he will fail to defeat them. To avoid the occurrence of such a bad omen it is customary to wrap the glass in a handkerchief so that it will not slip away when he steps on it and thus he will be sure to crush it with the first stamping of his foot.

[42] There is a suggestion of this popular belief in the mystic saying ולאחר החופה שוברין כוס שהוא בסוד הפח נשבר שהוא שבירת הקליפות quoted in Taame ha-Minhagim I. p. 111 No. 955. The Palestinian Jews also wrap the glass in a handkerchief and while it is being broken the assembled guests recite also the verse from Ps. 124, 7: "The snare is broken and we are escaped". The wrapping of the glass in a handkerchief also serves the purpose of preventing any of the broken pieces from getting lost. It is a popular belief among the Palestinians Jews that if one familiar with witchcraft got hold of the broken pieces he could by means of it bewitch the groom, making him sick and preventing him from joining the bride. Hence they are very careful to gather up all the pieces of the broken glass and bury them. See A. M. Luncz, *Jerusalem* I (Wien 1882) Hebrew section p. 7–8.

THE NAMING OF CHILDREN IN JEWISH FOLKLORE, RITUAL AND PRACTICE

THE NAMING OF CHILDREN IN JEWISH FOLKLORE, RITUAL AND PRACTICE

Names of persons, among the Jews as among other peoples of antiquity, were considered of great importance, and regarded as possessing special significance. They were not merely designations whereby a person might be distinguished from other persons in the group. They were believed to serve other purposes besides those of identification and recognition. To the question: "What is in a name?" the ancient Jews—and to a certain extent, their later descendants—would answer: "There is a whole lot in it." Hence, great importance has been attached among the Jews of all times to the selection of a proper and fitting name for the newly-born child.

The Bible does not expressly tell us by what considerations one should be guided in the selection of a name, nor does it clearly formulate any definite theories about the significance of names. But, from the numerous casual remarks about individual names, scattered through the Bible, we may gather what ideas and beliefs prevailed among the people of Bible times, in connection with personal names and their significance.

Without entering into a lengthy discussion of the Biblical names, their meaning and significance,[1] we may safely state that the following ideas as to the purpose, function and significance of personal names were current among the people of Bible times.[2]

(1) The purpose of a name is to describe adequately the personality of its bearer, to identify him and make him recognizable as a distinct individual not only by his fellow human beings but also in the world of the spirits by angels or demons, who might have something to do with him as a distinct individual. This purpose of adequately describing the person and marking him as a distinct individual is accomplished by choosing a name which

Reprinted from *Central Conference of American Rabbis Year Book,* Vol. XLII, 1932.

would point to some characteristic, or indicate some peculiarity in the person himself, or allude to his origin, the station or social position into which he was born, the circumstances surrounding his birth, or the conditions prevailing at the time of his birth in the world in general or in his family or group.

(2) The name has still another purpose in that it may be prophetic of the fortunes and the experiences of the person to whom it is given. It has, accordingly, the function of suggesting what the person is to be. It predicts his future and determines his fate.[3] It presages his history and experiences in life, pointing to the great things he will accomplish, as in the case of Noah (Gen. 5, 29), or to the conditions that will prevail or the events which will happen during his lifetime, as in the case of Peleg (Gen. 10, 25) and of Solomon (I Chr. 22, 9). In other words: Nomina sunt omina.

(3) Even more, the belief in the power of the uttered word, namely, that by merely saying something we might actually bring it about—a belief current among Jews in Bible times as among other ancient people—caused another notion to be cherished in connection with proper names. This was that, by giving the child a certain name, we produce in him the qualities indicated by that name. The name given to a person, so it was believed, may influence his character and actually make him what the name would suggest him to be. Thus Jacob's conduct towards his brother Esau was suggested and, as it were, predetermined by his very name (Gen. 27, 36). A man's character, so it was believed, is what his name pronounces it to be. "For, as his name is, so is he" (I Sam. 25, 25).

(4) As a corollary of the belief in the absolute identity of the name with the personality, there was another belief current in Bible times, namely, that when the two no longer coincide they must be made to coincide. When a change takes places in the person there must go with it a corresponding change in the name.[4] In other words, when a person's name, for one reason or another, no longer adequately describes his personality or expresses his character and fortunes, or when a change in the character and fortunes or position is wished for, the name must accordingly be changed. The practice of changing the name of a person is re-

corded in many instances in the Bible. The names of Abram and Sarai are changed to Abraham and Sarah (Gen. 17, 5 and 15) to suggest and, in a manner, make possible the change in their position and fortunes. Jacob's name is changed to Israel to indicate a change in his character and to point to his achievements which gave him a new position (Gen. 32, 29; 35, 10). Jacob changes the name of his second child from Rachel whom the mother had called "Ben Oni, the son of my sorrow" to "Benjamin, the son of my right hand" (Gen. 35, 19), probably to suggest better luck for the child. Likewise, Moses changes the name of Hoshea the son of Nun to Joshua (Num. 13, 16), probably also to suggest success and good luck on his trip with the spies.[5] And Naomi expressly says, "Call me not Naomi, that is Pleasant; call me Marah, that is Bitter, for the Almighty hath dealt very bitterly with me" (Ruth 1, 20).

(5) Still another belief intimately connected with, or resulting from, the belief in the mystical identity of the personality with the name, was that one cannot exist without the other. Just as a man's name lives with him as long as he is alive, so also he lives with his name as long as the latter is kept alive. It was believed, then, that if, and as long as, a person's name is kept alive and remembered, the person himself continues to live. Complete obliteration of a man's name meant his utter destruction. He is "cut off from the land of the living and his name is no more remembered" (Jer. 11, 19). "To make their memory (i.e., of people) cease from among men" meant to "make an end of them" (Deut. 32, 26).

Hence, great importance was attached to the preservation of the name of a person, which meant the securing of a sort of immortality for that person. Preservation of the name merely meant remembering the name. This remembering of the name, however, was, in Bible times at least, not to be achieved by calling other persons, children or descendants, by the same name. It was to be insured by leaving someone or something, children or property, which, having belonged to that person, would always be identified with his name, so that subsequent generations, in referring to his descendants or his property, would mention the name of the person who was the ancestor of those descendants or the original owner or builder of that property.   In this manner would his name be recalled and remembered.   That this—and not the naming of descendants by the same name—was the manner in which the memory of a name was to be insured, is evident from a few instances in the Bible.   Thus the daughters of Zelophehad could see no other way of preventing their dead father's name from being "done away from among his family" than by obtaining a possession among the brethren of their father (Num. 2, 4), for this possession which was due their father would be known as their inheritance from their father Zelophehad, and thus his name would be remembered.   If the name of the father could have been kept alive and remembered merely by naming their children after their father, they would have had no valid reason for their claim to a possession among the brethren of their father.

Again, Absalom, who had no son to keep his name in remembrance, reared up for himself a pillar which was called "Absalom's monument" and thus caused his name to be remembered (II Sam. 18, 18).   Likewise, to prevent the name of the brother who died childless from being blotted out of Israel, the firstborn that his widow bears to his brother, her second husband, must "succeed in the name of the brother that is dead" (Deut. 25, 5–6).   This means not that he should be named like the dead brother but that he should be known as and called the dead brother's son, thus keeping the dead brother's name in remembrance.   It did not mean that he should be called by the same name as the dead brother.[6] This is evident from the fact that the son that Ruth bore to Boaz was called Obed and not Mahlon, like Ruth's first husband (Ruth 4, 17).   But he must have been called Obed the son of Mahlon, so that the women in calling him by this name could well say: "There is a son born to Naomi."   For Naomi's son Mahlon was in a manner reborn, because his name would from then on be kept alive and remembered.

Likewise, when Jacob in blessing Joseph and his children said, "And let my name and the names of my fathers Abraham and Isaac be called on them" (Gen. 48, 16), he only meant that by people calling or referring to Ephraim and Manasseh as the descendants of Abraham, Isaac and Jacob, the latter names would

thus be recalled and remembered. He certainly did not mean that
Ephraim and Manasseh or any of their children should be named
after their grandfathers and be given the name of Abraham or
Isaac or Jacob.[7] For, as far as the Biblical records show, no child
was ever named after Abraham, Isaac or Jacob. In fact with but
one possible exception we do not find in the Bible any instances
of, or reference to, the custom in pre-exilic times[8] of naming
children like parents or grandparents, deceased or alive. This
absolute and persistent silence about such a custom strongly suggests that not only was such a custom not in vogue but that there
were positive objections to, and a determined avoidance of, such
a practice. These objections to, or avoidance of, this practice
seem to have been based upon the very belief in the mystical
identity of the name with the personality.

This belief in the absolute identity of the person with the name
precluded, at least in the popular mind, the possibility of two
persons in the same family, or the same group, having the same
name. For it would mean having one and the same individuality,
designated by and identical with that name, exist as two, which
of course is impossible. There could be two persons having the
same first name given to them in order to predict success or
describe similar circumstances which prevailed at the time of the
birth of both (or of each one) of them, or to express the same ambi-
tions cherished for each by its parents. In such a case each one, being further described as "the son of so-and-so," or "of the tribe or
family of so-and so," would thus be marked off as a separate and
distinct individuality, different from the one with the similar name
belonging to a different group or family. But in one and the same
family no two persons could conceivably have one and the same
name.

The individuality and character expressed by, and absolutely
identical with, a certain name could belong to only one person in
the same group or family. To give the name of one person to
another of the same group or family would, according to popular
conception, mean to transfer the very being, the individuality of
the one person, so identical with the name, to the other person
in the family, with the result that the one from whom the name—

with the personality identical with it—is taken must cease to
exist. The same consideration would keep people from naming
children after deceased relatives or ancestors. To give the child
the name of a departed ancestor would, according to the popular
conception in Bible times, not have the effect of keeping the
memory of the name of the deceased alive. It would have just
the opposite effect. It would destroy and wipe out the remembrance of the departed. For all that goes with his name, his
very being, his memory, and the mystical associations connected
with it, would have been transferred to another person to whom
the name had been given and would now be identical with that
other individuality. At the mention or recall of the name, subsequent generations would have in mind and keep alive the memory
of the second bearer of the name and not the original bearer of
the name from whom it had been taken away.

It may, therefore, be stated with absolute certainty, that in pre-
exilic times the selection of a name for a child was determined
solely by consideration for the child itself. The name was to
serve the purpose of adequately describing and identifying the
person by pointing to his origin and history, suggesting his character or predicting his future. The consideration for the memory
of another person, parent or grandparent, never entered into the
selection of a name for a child. For the name *per se* given to any
person was not to serve as a reminder of any other person who
previously may have had the same name. We do not find in the
Bible any indication of the custom, in pre-exilic times, of naming
children after their ancestors. We have no record in the Bible
of a person in pre-exilic times being named after his grandfather,
with but one exception. Nahor the brother of Abraham had the
same name as his grandfather. For Terah's father's name was
likewise Nahor (Gen. 11, 25–26).[9] But even in this one exceptional case we have no indication that the reason for Terah's
naming his son Nahor was to keep alive the memory of his father.
Most likely the same circumstances or conditions that determined
the selection of the name for the grandfather prevailed also in the
case, or at the time of the birth, of the grandson and these, not
the consideration for the memory of the grandfather, determined

the selection of the name. In the genealogical list of the kings of the house of David no two persons appear with the same name.[10] Likewise in the list of the high priests of the first Temple, as given in Ezra 7, 1–5 and I Chr. 6, 35–38, no name is repeated.[11]

In post-exilic times, however, and especially beginning with the Hellenistic period, we notice a remarkable change in the practice of selecting names for children. In the list of the names of the high priest of the second Temple and of the Maccabean rulers, and later on in the family of Hillel, as well as of later talmudic teachers, we find many instances of a grandson having the same name as the grandfather. This clearly points to the prevalent practice of naming children after their grandparents. Now, among the Greeks it was the general custom to give the children the name of their grandparent. It would, however, be a mistake to assume with L. Löw[12] that the Palestinian Jews of the period of the second Temple borrowed this custom from the Greeks. For we find instances of a grandson having the same name as his grandfather among the Palestinian Jews of post-exilic times, even before they came in contact with the Greeks.[13] Then again we find that among the Elephantine Jews, children were named like their grand-parents.[14] As the custom of naming children after ancestors was prevalent among the Egyptians, the Elephantine Jews no doubt borrowed this custom from their Egyptian neighbors. And it is reasonable to assume that from the Elephantine Jews the custom came to the Palestinian Jews, if indeed they did not get it from the Egyptians directly. But, no doubt, changed conditions or beliefs among the Palestinian Jews must have helped to make this foreign custom generally accepted. Certainly the innovation of a practice unknown in pre-exilic times could not have been introduced without corresponding changes of ideas, or at least certain modifications of those ideas, prevailing in pre-exilic times, which precluded or prevented the practice represented by the innovation.

That this new custom of naming children after ancestors represented a departure from the custom prevailing in pre-exilic times and was recognized by the people as such, is expressly stated by two Rabbis of the second century, who also advance theories of their own as to the reasons for this innovation. The statements

of these two teachers, R. Jose b. Halafta and R. Simon b. Gamaliel, are found in the Midrash Gen. r. 37, 10, and read, as follows:

רבי יוסי אומר הראשונים על ידי שהיו מכירים יחסיהם
היו מוציאין לשם המאורע אבל אנו שאין אנו יודעין את
יחסינו אנו מוציאין לשם אבותינו. רבן שמעון בן גמליאל
אומר הראשונים על ידי שהיו משתמשין ברוח הקודש היו
מוציאין לשם המאורע אבל אנו שאין אנו משתמשין ברוח
הקודש אנו מוציאין לשם אבותינו

"R. Jose says: The ancients, or former generations, who well knew
their genealogical descent would name their children according to
special occasions or with reference to some event. We, who do
not so well know our genealogical descent, give our children the
names of our ancestors. R. Simon b. Gamaliel says: The ancients,
because they could make use of the holy spirit, would name their
children according to special occasions or with reference to some
event. We, who cannot make use of the holy spirit, give our
children the names of our ancestors." [15]

It should be stated first that both these teachers agree as to
the time or the period in which the new practice came into vogue.
They differ only as to the reason for, or the cause of, the innovation. For under "the ancients" or "former generations" הראשונים
they both understood the people of pre-exilic times or the generations up to Ezra, as contrasted with the generations after Ezra,
or the people during the time of the second Temple and after its
destruction.

According to talmudic tradition, there were especially two features which distinguished the period of the second Temple from
that of the first Temple, marking off the former as inferior in
comparison with the latter. The one characteristic of the period
of the second Temple was the absence of the revelation of the
holy spirit or the cessation of prophecy. For "with the death of
the last of the prophets, Haggai, Zachariah and Malachi (i.e., at
the very beginning of the period of the second Temple), prophecy
ceased in Israel and the holy spirit no longer revealed itself"

(Tosefta Sotah XIII, 2, and B. Yoma 9b). The other feature was the presence, to a considerable proportion, of foreign elements in the population. Among the people who returned with Ezra and formed the new community—not to mention those who had remained in the land and later formed a part of the new community—there were many people of non-Jewish descent or at least such as, unable to trace their genealogies, could not prove their Jewish descent (M. Kiddushin IV, 1).[16]

It was the one or the other of these conditions prevailing during the time of the second Temple and distinguishing it from the period preceding it, that, according to the respective opinions of R. Jose or R. Simon b. Gamaliel, was responsible for the innovation of naming children after ancestors. According to R. Jose, it was the composite character of the population, the fact that not all the people could accurately trace their genealogy and prove with certainty their purely Jewish descent, that prompted many people to call their children by the names of their fathers, thus pointing to their Jewish origin and indicating by their very names that they were descended from Jewish ancestors. This theory of R. Jose, however, is insufficient to explain the change in practice. For, on the one hand, we find, as far as our records show, that the practice of naming children after their grandparents was first introduced among the families of the high priests, about whose pure Jewish descent there was not the least doubt and who, therefore, did not need to indicate by the names which they gave their children that the latter were descended from good Jewish families. On the other hand, we find that proselytes were called by such names as Judah and Benjamin.[17] Hence, even names of great Jewish forefathers would not necessarily prove the pure Jewish descent of their bearers. These two facts are sufficient to disprove the theory of R. Jose.

According to R. Simon b. Gamaliel, it was the absence of the Holy Spirit, the fact that they could no longer make use of divine inspiration in order to suggest or determine by the very name which they gave their children what the latters' fate and destiny should be, that caused the people to name their children after their ancestors. This theory is not satisfactory either. In the first place, even in pre-exilic times, in the age of prophecy, the Holy Spirit was not poured out over all flesh, and not all the people were favored with divine inspiration; and yet all the people gave their children's names לשם המאורע, according to the occasion or alluding to certain conditions or events. And in post-exilic times, notwithstanding the fact that prophecy had ceased, the Holy Spirit was not altogether absent and there were, according to talmudic reports, instances of manifestations of the Holy Spirit even during the times of the second Temple.[18]

Accordingly, the difference between the pre-exilic and post-exilic times as regards the manifestation of the Holy Spirit was merely one of degree. Furthermore, the people in general during the period of the second Temple and even after its destruction, without claiming any prophetic powers, nevertheless believed, as we shall see, in the suggestive, if not the absolutely determinative, influence of the name upon the fortunes and character of its bearer. Hence, the cessation of prophecy or the infrequency of the manifestation of the Holy Spirit could have been no reason why the people should not continue as in former times to give their children such names as would express their hopes and aspirations for their children's future, or suggest their children's fortunes. At any rate, such names as are not of a prophetic nature and do not seek to express any hopes for the future, but merely point to a characteristic of the child or refer to the circumstances at the time of its birth, as e.g., Isaac, Perez, and Zerah could certainly have continued to be given by people who not only disclaimed any prophetic powers but even disbelieved in the suggestive powers of any uttered name.

Accordingly, neither R. Jose nor R. Simon b. Gamaliel with their respective theories satisfactorily explain why the older practice of pre-exilic times should not have continued in post-exilic times. In fact upon a closer scrutiny of their statements, we find that these two Rabbis do not even say that the older practice was discarded. For they do not say: אין אנו מוציאין לשם המאורע "We no longer give our children names referring to an occasion or event." All they say is: "We give our children names like the names of our ancestors." This by no means implies an abolition of the older practice. Indeed, the older custom was never abolished or discarded. It has continued, though not so universally as before, throughout the talmudic period and up to the present day.[19] Hence, what is historically accurate in the statements of these two teachers is that the innovation of naming children after ancestors came into use not to the exclusion, but alongside, of the older practice. Their theories as to the cause of, or reason for, the innovation we have found to be insufficient. But if the older practice was never abolished and the innovation merely represented an additional practice which gradually became more and more universally accepted, it is perhaps a mistake to ascribe it to one cause or to seek to account for it by one reason only. Undoubtedly, the custom of naming children after their ancestors so prevalent in talmudic times and ever since was the result of a long and gradual process whereby a foreign custom, finding its way into the life of the people, was helped and furthered by, and in turn effected, changes and modifications in some popular beliefs which were opposed to such a practice.

We must, therefore, seek to ascertain what ideas were current among the people in talmudic times in regard to the function, purpose and possible effects of proper names, and examine to what degree they represent developments and modifications of ideas of Bible times. This will explain how a custom unknown in pre-exilic times came to be so prevalent in post-exilic times, and also help us to understand all the practices that obtained in talmudic times in connection with naming children.

There is especially one popular belief current in talmudic times which will help us understand the ideas which the people entertained in regard to the selection of names. This is the belief in the power of the uttered word, that is, that by merely saying that a thing will or shall happen we can bring it about that it actually come to pass. This belief was also current in Bible times. But in talmudic times it is more pronounced and developed, and almost universally accepted. From many indications in the Talmud we can learn how such a belief in the miraculous power of the word originated among the people and what its basis was. It seems that the basis of this belief in the power of the uttered word—or at any rate intimately connected with it—was the notion that the agents of the heavenly administration, both good and bad angels, or angels and demons, were, like human agents, liable to misunderstanding and mistakes. When these heavenly agents or floating spirits hear the word uttered by any human being, they are not always quick to recognize that it is a human voice speaking. They sometimes mistake it for the voice of a spirit or of a heavenly authority, giving them an order which they must carry out.[20] If the uttered word pronounces something good, the good angels, eager to do good, hasten to fulfill it in the belief that they are carrying out a command from on high. On the other hand, if the word uttered is of an evil nature, the floating bad angels or demons, always eager to do harm, seize upon it quickly and hasten to bring about the evil,[21] believing that in doing so they act under authority of a higher command. These two beliefs, the one in the power of the uttered word and the other in the fallibility of the spirits, largely determined the attitude of the people in the selection of names for their children.

Because of the power attached to the uttered word, it was believed that the name given to a person actually influences his character and determines his destiny and his future. This belief is clearly expressed in the following statement of the Talmud (B. Berakot 7b): מנא לן דשמא גרים? אמר רבי אלעזר דאמר קרא לכו חזו מפעלות ד' אשר שם שמות בארץ אל תקרי שמות אלא שמות

How do we know that the name is a determining factor in the character and destiny of a person? said R. Eleazar. Scripture says: "Come, behold the workings of the Lord who hath accomplished *shmot* (שמות) in the earth" (Ps. 46, 9). Do not read "*Shamot*," which is rendered "desolations," but read "*Shemot*," meaning "names." In this verse, then, R. Eleazar finds expressed the idea that in dealing with human beings the Lord through His agents carries out what their names suggest or, as Rabbi Samuel Eidels in his comment on this passage explains it, שפעולות השם נמשכים אחרי השם של אדם שהוא גורם the divine workings are controlled by or follow the suggestions contained in

the name of the person. This simply means that the heavenly
agents take a person at his name's value. Believing that the
name of a person had been decreed or pronounced upon him by
a higher authority, they proceed to carry out all that the name
implies and endow that person with goodness or wickedness, or
bestow upon him happiness or misery according to the meaning
of the name. R. Meier, a famous teacher of the 2nd century,
seems to have been very much addicted to this belief, and he
always paid special attention to names. From the very name of
a man he would draw conclusions about his character. Thus, in
the well-known story told in Yoma 83b, he concluded from the
very name of the innkeeper that the latter was a wicked man,
and he proved to be right. Here the Biblical idea that a man is
what his name pronounces him to be again comes to the fore. The
name given to a person cannot remain ineffective. It is bound to
make his character coincide with it. Hence, in a later Midrash
it is strongly recommended that one should be careful in examining
the meaning of names, so as to call his son by a name which would
destine him to become a righteous man, for indeed often [22]
the very name causes goodness or badness of character לעולם
יבדוק אדם בשמות לקרוא לבנו הראוי להיות צדיק כי
לפעמים השם גורם טוב או גורם רע (Midrash Tanḥoma
Haazinu 7).

The idea which we found current in Bible times, that the identity
of the name with the person demands that they both coincide and
that a change in the one of necessity requires or automatically
produces a corresponding change in the other, was also current
in talmudic times. In talmudic times, however, one aspect of it,
namely, that a change in the name effects a change in the status
or destiny of the person, is more developed and more emphasized.
The other aspect of this idea, namely that a change in status or
position requires a corresponding change of the name, is not so much
emphasized, though from many indications we may conclude that
it also obtained in talmudic times. Thus, e.g., R. Meier whose
original name was Measha is said to have been given the name
Meier, which means "enlightener," after he had become a great

scholar, one who enlightened the eyes of the wise in the study of the Law (Erubin 13b; see Dikduke Soferim ad loc.).

The belief that a change in the name effects a change in the status was strongly developed and almost generally accepted in talmudic times, because of its connection with, or the support it derived from, the other notion so generally accepted in talmudic times, namely, the fallibility of the spirits. It was believed that if a person is called by another name, the spirits, angels or demons, who look for him under his old name cannot find him. For under the new name they imagine him to be another person, a person about whom they have no order or against whom they have no charge or grudge. Thus to escape danger from demons, it was considered an effective protection for husband and wife to exchange their names, he calling himself by her name and she by his. The demons who might seek to harm the gentleman would find a person who, judging by the name, was a lady, whom they would refrain from harming. Likewise, the demons who might pursue the lady would give up their evil designs if they should find instead of the lady a person who, as the new name indicates, was a gentleman—not at all desirable. The Talmud (Sabbath 67b) describes this practice of exchanging names as heathen superstition, *darke ha-Emori* דרכי האמורי,[23] and is inclined to object to it. Yet the Talmud considers it perfectly good Jewish belief, that by a change of name one might escape the punishment decreed against him by the heavenly court. There are four procedures by which a person may cause the evil decree, issued against him, to be torn and destroyed, says a Baraita (R. H. 16b). One of these is changing the person's name. Some people say that a change of place or residence may also have the same effect.[24]

It is possible, though rather doubtful, that the old idea that a man's character is what his name declares it to be and that by changing the name an actual change in the character is effected also underlies this belief that a change of name nullifies the verdict against the person, as indeed some medieval authorities would explain it.[25] The person whose name has been changed, so these authorities rationalize, has by repentance actually become another, better person no longer capable of persisting in the sins committed

by the person with the other name and the wicked character.
Hence, he is not to suffer punishments for them. But the real
reason for the favorable effects of the change of name, at least
to the popular mind, was that the change of name, like the change
of residence, furnishes the person an escape from the danger of
the evil decreed against him. The decree against him simply cannot be executed. The agent charged with carrying out the decree
simply cannot locate or is unable to identify him.[26] The angels
go only by name and address. And if they come to the given
address and, looking there for a person with a certain name, do
not find such a person there, either because he has moved away
or because the occupant goes by a name different from the one
they are looking for, they report back that they could not find
him or that no such man can be found in the designated residence.
The verdict is then destroyed as useless.

That the angels can and do make such mistakes in persons,
mistakes which might even result in a miscarriage of justice by
the heavenly administration, is evident from the following story
told in the Talmud (Hagigah 3b–4a): The angel of death was
ordered to put to death Mary the hairdresser,[27] but by mistake
he put to death an innocent little school teacher by the name of
Mary, whom because of the similarity of names he mistook for
the woman sentenced to death.[28] And while his heavenly superiors
pointed out to the angel of death the mistake he had made, and
perhaps reprimanded him, the life of young Mary the school
teacher was not restored. She remained in the other world whither
she had been transferred by the mistake of the angel.[29]

When giving their children names like those of their ancestors,
people were influenced to a great extent by these beliefs in the
suggestiveness of the name and in the fallibility of the angels and
demons. They would select the name of an ancestor whom they
believed to have been a good man and a successful man. The
benefits of such a name for the child were twofold: In the first
place, since גרים שמא the name is a determining factor in
the destiny of the person, this name which manifestly had been
so successful in the case of its former bearer, the ancestor, would
presumably have the same good effects upon the destiny and char-

acter of its new bearer, the child.[30]   Secondly, in case the angel should make a mistake in the person by the similarity of names, it would be in favor of the child. The child might be mistaken by the spirits for the ancestor whose name he bears and treated with the consideration due to the ancestor, or credited with the achievements recorded in heaven to the account of the ancestor.

They would avoid naming a child like an ancestor or relative who was wicked (Yoma 38b),[31] for fear of the twofold danger involved in such a procedure. In the first place, the name may actually make the child's character and destiny be like the wicked relative's. Secondly, the child might be mistaken by the spirits for the older wicked person by that name. All the evil decrees against that former bearer of the name, all the accusations recorded against him might be charged to the child who might thus be made to suffer all the punishments for them.[32]

The primary consideration in choosing a name for the child was still the welfare, future and destiny of the child itself—how it might be affected by the name. It seems, however, that during talmudic times there was combined with this chief consideration a secondary consideration, namely, the effect upon the person after whom the child was to be named, whether the memory of that person should be kept alive or let rot and fall into oblivion. Due to the gradual spread of the custom of naming children after ancestors there developed a modification of the belief in the absolute identity of the name with the person, which had made it impossible in Bible times for two persons belonging to the same family or group to have the same name. It is true, the persistent avoidance of giving children such names as Abraham,[33] Moses,[34] Aaron[35] or David,[36] which is so pronounced throughout the talmudic period, would suggest that at least in regard to certain great names the ancient biblical belief was still strong.[37]   In general, however, it seems that the fear that by naming a child after an ancestor the memory of the latter would be forgotten, because all that had been associated with his name was transferred to the new bearer of the name, was apparently no longer entertained. It seems that somehow the people came to believe that it was possible for two individualities to be referred to or designated by the same name,

and that by giving a child the name of an ancestor the memory of
the latter is thereby preserved and kept alive.   Whenever the
child would be called or referred to by the name, so it was believed,
people would also be reminded of the former or original bearer
of that name.   Hence, as already stated, to the considerations for
the welfare of the child in choosing the name of an ancestor there
was added, in the popular mind, the secondary consideration of
preserving the memory of the name of the ancestor who was believed to have been a righteous man.   And to the reason for avoiding
the giving of the name of a wicked person to a child because of the
danger of the child there was now added another motive, namely, the
desire to cause the name of the wicked to rot, and to avoid preserving his memory by having some one bear his name.

Likewise the fear, that by giving the name of one person to
another the very being, the personality identical with the name,
is transferred to the other person, and the one from whom the name
is taken must therefore cease to exist, a fear which, as we have
seen, was also a result of the belief in the absolute identity of
the name with the person, was also generally abandoned.   Not only
were people not afraid of their lives when children were named like
them, but they were even pleased with it and welcomed it, since it
meant that the preservation of their memory was thus assured
them even in their lifetime.   Thus R. Nathan, a teacher of the
second half of the second century, reports that in his travels he
occasionally was able by his advice to save the lives of newborn
children.   The parents of those children, out of gratitude to him—
and probably also to suggest that their children grow up and become men as good as R. Nathan—named their children Nathan,
after him (Hullin, 47b).   And R. Nathan was rather pleased with
this expression of gratitude.   Hence, we find throughout the entire
talmudic period that not only would people name their children
after departed ancestors but that there was no hesitancy even to
name children after living parents or grandparents, relatives or
friends.[38]   It is true that in many instances reported in the Talmud
of a son's having the same name as his father or grandfather, we
cannot definitely ascertain whether the father or grandfather was
still alive when the child named after him was born.   But in some

instances, at least, there is no doubt that the father or grandfather was still living when the child was named after him. Thus in the case of R. Hananiah the son of Hananiah mentioned in Tosefta Nidah V, 15, there is no doubt that the father was living when the son was named after him. For we are told that when the son was still a minor the father made the vow for him which caused him to become a Nazirite. Likewise in Luke I, 60 it is reported that the child John was originally called Zachariah after the name of his grandfather who was then still living. One may wonder that in spite of the belief that the angel of death was liable to get confused and mistake the one person for another of the same name, the people were nevertheless not afraid lest when the angel of death comes to call for the old grandfather he might by mistake take the child having the same name. But one need not expect superstition to be consistent. The older man may even have hoped that the stupidity of the angel of death might work in his favor. And when the angel of death comes to take his life, the old man might be able to put him off and fool him by declaring that his time has not come yet, for a certain number of years had been allotted to him—as the heavenly record would show on the account of the name of his junior—which he has not yet completed.[39]

Which of the grandfathers, paternal or maternal, was favored in naming the grandchild, we cannot state definitely. There are no regulations about this in the Talmud. In many instances known to us from the Talmud of a grandson's having the same name as his grandfather it is the name of the paternal grandfather that the grandson bears. The custom among the Greeks was to name after the paternal grandfather. And among the Jews in post-talmudic times this was also the rule. It may, therefore, be assumed that in talmudic times, likewise, the general practice was to choose the name of the paternal grandfather for the child. But it was not a fixed rule. There must have been instances where the son was given the name of his maternal grandfather. Thus we read in the Book of Jubilees (XI, 14–15) that Terah's wife's name was Edna and her father's name was Abram. Terah called the son which Edna bore him "Abram by the name of the father of his mother, for the latter had died before his daughter had conceived a son." Although this legend is contradicted by the talmudic tradition, according to which Abraham's mother's name was Amatlai the daughter of Karnebo (B. B. 91a), yet the report in the Book of Jubilees at least reflects the custom in certain Jewish circles of naming the son after the maternal grandfather.

As to Hebrew or non-Hebrew names, there was in talmudic times no real distinction made in practice. It is true that we find some agadic utterances against the practice of changing a Hebrew name into a foreign one. And one of the virtues because of which Israel was redeemed from Egypt is said to have been that they retained their Hebrew names and did not change them to non-Hebrew ones שלא שינו את שמם (Mekilta Pisḥa V and Lev. R. 32, 5). But these utterances seem to have been directed against those who by changing their names or calling their children by foreign names would seek to deny their Jewish identity, and not against the foreign names as such. A good Jew could well have borne a foreign name. And we find even among the Rabbis themselves many whose names were non-Hebrew, like Antigonos, Alexandri, Romanus, and others. In some instances, these non-Jewish names, especially among the Palestinian Jews, may have been accompanied by another, Hebrew, name שם הקודש, as in the case of Judah Aristobolus and others. For the practice of being called by or having more than one name is already found in talmudic times.[40] In some instances again these non-Hebrew names would be substitutes for or merely translations of original Hebrew names. But there are also many instances where the non-Hebrew name was the original and only name unaccompanied by any other.[41]

Throughout the entire talmudic period, then, the people would not hesitate to give their children non-Hebrew names. And of the Jews outside of Palestine it is expressly reported that the majority of them had names like the gentiles (Gitin 11b).

In post-talmudic times no radical change in the attitude towards names took place, and no marked development of the ideas governing the selection of names can be noticed. In the main, the beliefs and popular notions as to the purpose, significance and function of proper names which were current in talmudic times have been retained almost universally throughout the post-talmudic and later rabbinic times. Some slight modification of one idea or the other may have been made, or more or less emphasis may have been laid upon certain notions by one group or another. In some instances, even a reversal to older, more primitive ideas, which had been suppressed or rather ignored in talmudic times, took place. These slight modifications in the popular beliefs and mild changes in the attitude towards proper names, however, brought about some changes in practice and very often put certain restrictions upon the selection of proper names, restrictions unknown in talmudic times. But these changes and new practices are not universal. They differ among different groups of Jewry, and sometimes vary in the various communities of even one and the same group.

One change we notice in post-talmudic times that is almost universally accepted and this is in the attitude of the people towards the names, Abraham, Moses, Aaron, and David. The hesitancy of calling children by these names which we have noticed in talmudic times has been entirely overcome. And ever since Geonic times these names have become very frequent among all groups of Jewry. The belief or fear upon which this hesitancy in talmudic times rested seems to have been entirely abandoned. Only in a modified form, as we shall see, we may find it still effective in later times, at least in some exceptional cases.[42]

As regards the other changes that took place in post-talmudic times, we must distinguish between the Sephardic and the Ashkenazic groups of Jewry. Most of the changes developed among the latter group. Among them the superstitious elements of the ideas of talmudic times became more pronounced and were more emphasized, while the former group in general followed a more rational course in their attitude towards names and adhered more closely to the general practices of talmudic times. Thus we find that among the Sephardic Jews there was no fear or hesitancy in naming a child after a living person. There are many instances of a grandson being given the name of his grandfather even when the latter was still alive. To mention but a few outstanding examples, Judah Halevi had a grandson who was likewise named Judah to whom he seems to have been much attached, for in one of his poems he refers to this grandson with the words: "How can Judah (the grandfather) ever forget Judah" (the grandson)? [43] Likewise R. Isaiah b. Elijah de Trani, an Italian rabbinical authority of the 13th century was named like his maternal grandfather, R. Isaiah b. Mali de Trani. The grandfather lived to see the grandson, named like him, grow up to become a prominent scholar, and he pointed to him with pride and satisfaction as his heir and successor who would take his place in the scholarly world.[44] Likewise when the daughter-in-law of Naḥmanides, who was the daughter of R. Jonah Girondi, gave birth to a boy, Naḥmanides, the paternal grandfather of the child, said: Although, as custom requires, the child should be called by my name (Moses), I forego the privilege and am willing that he be called Jonah, like his maternal grandfather.[45]

We also find among the Sephardic Jews the practice of calling the son by the name of the father, even when the father is still living. This practice, however, is less frequent and some of the Sephardim consider it rather strange. Thus, H. J. D. Azulai in his commentary to Sefer Ḥasidim No. 460, (ed. Lemberg, 1862) p. 44b says: A man does not call his son by his own name.[46] At the same time he mentions an instance of a man by the name of Mordecai whose son was also named Mordecai. Azulai finds this rather strange. But we know from other sources that the practice was not infrequent among the Sephardim. Thus Jacob Saphir in his Eben Saphir I (Lyck, 1866) p. 51 reports that it is the custom among Jews in Yemen to name the child like the father, especially in a family that has previously lost children.[47] It was considered a protection to give the child the name of the father. By this means, so it was believed, the life of the child so named would be safeguarded and it would not share the fate of its brothers or sisters who died young. To a certain extent this practice may have been motivated by the belief in the suggestive power of the name שמא גרים which would make the child grow up and be like his father or grandfather. But this was not the only determining factor in this practice. There seems to have been underlying it another superstitious idea which we found current in talmudic times, viz., the belief in the fallibility of the angels.

For in some circles of the Sephardic Jews, it was also believed that a father might be assured of a long life by naming his son like him.[48] It seems, therefore, that whatever belief in the fallibility of the angel of death was entertained among the Sephardic Jews it not only did not deter them from naming children like living fathers or grandfathers but it even encouraged the practice. For it was hoped that the mistake the angel of death might make by confusing the names would be in favor of the person whom he is after. He will refrain from taking the life of the person sentenced to death by mistaking him for another person by the same name against whom no decree of death was issued.

Among the Ashkenazic Jews, however, such risks were generally avoided. They would not rely on the hope that the angel of death would make a mistake in favor of the living. Hence with but few exceptions the general practice among the Ashkenazic Jews has been not to name a child after a living parent or relative. That this practice is based upon superstition is frankly admitted by the authorities. But believing in safety first, they find no fault with the people who, governed by certain superstitious beliefs, avoid certain practices. Thus in Sefer Ḥasidim (ed. Wistinetzki, Berlin, 1891) No. 377, p. 114, we find the following statement:

כל הניחושים כנגד המקפידים גוים שקורין לבניהם בשם אביהם ואין בכך כלום ויהודים מקפידים על כך. ויש מקומות שאין קורין אותו אחר שמות החיים אלא אחר שכבר מתו

"Superstitions work harm only upon those who heed them. Non-Jews call their sons by the names of their father, and no harm results. But the Jews are careful not to do so. And in some places they do not name after living persons at all, but only after such as have already died." What these superstitious fears were that caused the Jews to avoid naming children after living persons is not stated here. We can learn them, however, from other passages in the Sefer Ḥasidim as well as from utterances in other sources originating among German mystics.

One of these superstitions was that due to the carelessness of the angel of death harm may come to a child named like an older living person. For when the time will come for that older person to die, the angel of death, receiving instructions to take the life of the older person by that name, might instead take the life of the younger person of the same name. This belief in a possible mistake on the part of the angel of death which we have found expressed in the story of the Talmud (Hagigah 3b–4a) cited above, was especially current and strongly believed in among the Ashkenazic Jews. This is evident from the following story told in Sefer Ḥasidim (ib.) No. 375, p. 114: An older teacher and a young student happened to get married in one and the same week. The young student died during the very week of his wedding. In a dream he appeared to his mother and told her that he actually had many years yet to live but his untimely death was brought about by a mistake on the part of the angel of death. The latter received the order to take the life of the bridegroom who got married during that week. Of course, the order referred to the older teacher who also got married during the same week. But the angel of death did not understand the order correctly. And when he met the young student bridegroom alone on the street [49] he thought that the order for the bridegroom of the week was meant for him, and so he killed him. The story goes on to tell that all the years which had been allotted to the young student and which he had not lived out were then—by another mistake of the heavenly clerks—assigned to the old teacher, thus prolonging his life. Finding on their records, that the bridegroom who married during that week—referring to the young student—had yet so many years to live, and finding only one living bridegroom who got married that week, and this was the older teacher, they concluded that all these years allotted to the bridegroom of that week must belong to the old teacher, and they accordingly credited his account with that number of years.

There is no doubt that out of consideration for the safety of the child, and as a precaution against possible danger resulting from mistakes on the part of the angel of death, they avoided naming the child after a living father or grandfather, or—as the custom was in some places—after any living person. And it was not

only fear for the death of the child but also fear for sickness or
any other punishment that might be decreed against the older
person and which the angel charged with the execution of that
decree might by mistake inflict upon the child having the same
name.[50] For the angel of death is not the only one among the
angels that is stupid and careless. The other heavenly officers are
not much smarter and no more careful than he.[51]

There was still another consideration which prevented people
from naming children after living parents or grandparents, and
this was fear for the life of the parent or grandparent. This fear
was based upon the old idea of the absolute identity of the soul
or the very being of a person with his name, according to which
it would be impossible for two persons to have one and the same
name. This old idea was revived and found strong expression
among German mystics. Thus in the *Sefer Ziyyuni* by R. Menahem
b. Meier of Speyer (Cremona, 1560) p. 26, we find the statement
גופו הוא אדם של שמו "A man's name is the very essence
of his being." Ziyyuni then goes on to quote from a ספר החײם
probably by R. Eleazar of Worms,[52] to the effect that "a man's
name is his soul." [53] This in a manner suggested the notion that
by giving the child the name of a living person we cause, as it were,
the soul of that person, identical with his name, to enter the child.
The necessary consequence resulting from this notion was the fear
of naming a child after a living parent or grandparent. For since
the one soul identical with the name cannot at the same time be
in two places or occupy two bodies, its entrance into the body of
the child which is effected by giving the child the name identical
with that soul, would necessitate its withdrawal from the other body
and the latter would have to die. In other words, only one person
in possession of a certain soul identified with a special name can be
living on earth. Giving to children the name of a living parent or
grandparent would cause the death of the latter.[54]

We need not be surprised to find another result of this emphasized belief in the absolute identity of the soul of a person with
his name. If the identity of the soul with the name made it, in
the popular belief, impossible for two persons of one group or
family living on earth to have the same name, because it would mean

that one and the same soul occupies two bodies or is in two places
on earth at the same time, then it should also preclude the possibility of two persons of one family or group having the same name,
even if one of them has already departed this earthly life. For it,
likewise, involves the absurdity of assuming that one soul, identical
with a certain name, occupies two places at the same time; that
is, one in heaven in the assembly of the souls of the righteous, and
one on earth in the body of the person to whom the name identical
with the soul was given. And just as to give a child the name of
a living parent means to remove the soul of that parent from its
abode in the body of that parent and transfer it into the body of
the child, so also to give the child the name of a departed parent
must needs mean to cause the soul of the latter to leave its heavenly
abode, to come back to earth and to reenter the body of the child.
This notion, as we have suggested above, was probably the reason
why in Bible times no child was named after a departed parent or
grandparent. The same notion, while not common in the Middle
Ages, must have been in the mind of some mystics who as a consequence would object to their descendants being named after them.
This seems to me to have been the case with R. Judah b. Samuel
He-Ḥasid. One of the mandates (No. 61) in his Testament (published in the Sefer Ḥasidim, edition Lemberg, 1862, p. 2) was that
none of his descendants should be called by his name Judah nor
by his father's name Samuel לא יקרא איש מזרעו את בנו
יהודה ולא שמואל The reason for this strange request has not
been satisfactorily explained, though various theories about it have
been advanced.[55] One of these theories is that Judah was conscious
of having committed the sin of making use of the Holy Names. And
he had a tradition that the punishment for this sin is inflicted
upon any of the descendants of the offender throughout all generations who are called by his name. Hence, to spare his descendants
the suffering of the punishment for this sin, he commanded them
not to call any of their sons by his name. Not being called by
his name, they will not be held responsible for his sin.[56] The only
interesting point in this theory which is said to have been advanced
by the descendants of Judah he-Ḥasid is the notion which it implies, that a descendant having the same name as the ancestor might

be held responsible for the sins of that ancestor, but is not responsible for these sins if he does not bear the same name as the
offending ancestor. This is but another way of saying that the
heavenly authorities may get mixed up in persons of one family
having the same name, confusing the one with the other and by
mistake inflicting upon one punishments intended for the other.
But as an explanation of the motive of Judah he-Ḥasid's strange
mandate it is unsatisfactory. For at most it would only explain
why he did not want any of his descendants to bear his own name
Judah. But it cannot explain why he forbade his descendants to
call any of their children by the name of his father Samuel. He
could not have been so disrespectful to his father as to imply that
he likewise committed any such grave sin for which all his descendants might have to suffer. The real reason for this strange request
seems to me to have been the desire that he and his sainted father
should not be disturbed in their heavenly bliss and should not be
forced to leave the heavenly abode, to come down to earth again
and to enter the body of one of their descendants who would be
named after them.[57]

This instance of R. Judah he-Ḥasid, however, is an exception to
the rule that prevailed almost universally of preferring to have
descendants named after their ancestors. People in general were
very eager to leave, as it were, a name behind them. Even those
people who believed in the absolute identity of the soul with the
name, and that with the name given to the child the soul formerly
identical with that name is made to come down from heaven and
enter the body of the child, would not hesitate to name their children
after departed ancestors. Superstition is usually overcome by another superstition. And, in this case, the belief that by preserving
the name of the departed ancestor, we preserve his soul, and in a
manner secure for him a sort of immortality, counteracted the
superstitious fear that he might be disturbed in his eternal rest and
be forced to come down to earth again. People, in general, as it
seems, did not consider it such an unpleasant thing to be reborn
again and, as it were, renew their life here on earth.

Of course, some people would consider it a misfortune to be
reborn as a woman. For, what man would like to live the life of

a woman! Certainly, not one who all his life had daily recited the benediction thanking God for not having made him a woman. Hence, as we shall see below, some people objected to giving a girl the name of a male ancestor.[58] For this would mean making the soul of that ancestor enter the body of the girl and thus live the life of a woman. But otherwise it was not considered so bad for the departed to be invited again to a visit on earth. With the gradual spread of the belief in the transmigration of the soul, *gilgul*, it was believed that the souls of the departed, even of the great and righteous men, reenter this world and are reborn.[59] Hence, assuming that the soul of the departed in coming down to earth by the process of *gilgul* would naturally prefer to enter the body of a new-born child of his own family, it was even considered necessary and proper to give the child into whose body it was hoped the soul of the ancestor would enter the name of that ancestor. Thus, according to Isaac Lurya, when the father of an unborn child dies before the birth of the child, his soul enters the body of the child when it is born, and therefore the child should also be given the name of the father.[60]

A contemporary of Lurya, the famous Joseph Caro, even went so far as to say that with the name which a person receives he also receives something of the character of the very first or original bearer of that name. Thus, if one is named Abraham he will be inclined towards kindness.[61] This is but another way of saying that with the name there is associated and intimately connected the soul, or at least a spark of the soul, of the original bearer of that name. For even though the person is named Abraham only after his grandfather by that name and not directly after the biblical Abraham, indirectly he is named after, and has at least part of the soul or character of the biblical Abraham. For the grandfather after whom the child is named was in turn named after his grandfather and the latter again after another, and so forth up to the one first named after the biblical Abraham. All the intermediary bearers of the name Abraham were merely temporary possessors of that name.[62] And each one of them in his turn transmitted it together with the spark of the soul of Abraham associated with it, to all those who in the course of time were called Abraham. Caro,

as is evident from his reference to the saying of the Talmud
(Berakot 7b), has also in mind the idea of שמא גרים, that
the name determines the fate and character of the person. This
belief in the suggestive power of the name has been retained all
through the post-talmudic times and was combined with the practice
of naming children after departed parents or ancestors. With
Caro, however, it seems to have undergone a slight modification.
It meant that when we give the child the name of a certain ancestor
we thereby give the angel in charge of providing the body of the
child with a soul, directions, so to speak, as to which or what kind
of soul he should put into the child, namely, the soul once associated and identical with the name of that ancestor, and thus we
bring it about that the character and the fate of the child be like
that of the former bearer of that name. The angels, who, as we
have seen, according to popular belief in the power of the uttered
word, heed sometimes orders by human voices mistaking them to
come from a higher authority, in this case also heed the directions
contained in the name, believing that the name was given by a
higher authority. Indeed, according to Lurya, when the father gives
a name to his child, it is really not the father but God speaking
through the mouth of the father who gives the name. God puts
the name in the mouth of the father, and causes him to call his
son by that name.[63] Thus even in the age when prophecy had
long ceased in Israel and when people could no longer make use
of the Holy Spirit, names even when given by any ordinary father
were believed to have been determined upon by an act of inspiration, and actually divinely ordained. No wonder then that the
people believed in the power of the names to determine the fate
and reveal the character of the persons to whom they were given.
This belief in the suggestive, if not determinative, power of the
name which with more or less emphasis has been current among
the people throughout all times, accounts for the continuation of
the practice of naming children with reference to some event, hope
or expectation לשם המאורע. This practice has been retained
all through the ages [64] up to modern times. Especially frequent is
the practice of determining the choice of a name for a child by the
date or season of its birth. A child born on a Saturday may be

called Shabbetai. One born on a holiday is named Yomtob, one born on the Day of Atonement is called Raḥamim, one born on the 9th of Ab is called Menahem, and one born on Purim or one whose circumcision takes place on Purim is called Mordecai or if a girl is born on Purim she is called Esther. Sometimes the name is taken from the Scriptural portion read during the week in which the child was born. When the child is born during the week when the *sidra* Noah is read, he is called Noah. When born during the week of the *sidra* Vayera, which contains the account of the birth of Isaac (Gen. 21), he is named Isaac. When born during the week in which the *sidra* Shemot, containing the story of Moses, is read, he is called Moses.[65]   But there are also names referring to special conditions prevailing at the time of the birth. Thus S. D. Luzzato called one of his sons, born at the time when he was lecturing on Isaiah, by the name of Isaiah. Another son, born at the time when he was engaged in his work on the Targum Onkelos, he called Philoxenos, or Oheb Ger. Of course, Luzzato meant these names merely to be commemorative, and was not influenced in his choice of them by a belief in the suggestiveness of names (see Hillel Della Torre in Kerem Hemed IV, No. 19).

But the majority of the people, whether giving their children names after departed relatives or with reference to some occasion or event, have been and consciously or unconsciously still are influenced in the selection of a name by the above discussed beliefs as to the possible influence of the name upon the child or its effect upon the one after whom it is named. As these beliefs or superstitions are not shared by all people in a like degree, there developed among different people certain restrictions upon the selection of names, which may have been accepted and heedèd by some people or even the majority of the people, but ignored and disregarded by others. These restrictions, originating in the popular beliefs, are endorsed or rejected, by the respective authorities according to the degree in which they, the authorities themselves, accept, share in, or tolerate the underlying popular beliefs or superstitions. In the following I mention a number of such restrictions without attempting to be exhaustive:

1) Some authorities object to the practice of giving to a boy

the name of a girl and vice versa. (See Moses Konitz in his ספר המצרף I, No. 86 (Wien 1820, p. 56). But this practice has been widespread. In talmudic times there were certain names common to men and women. Thus, one of the daughters of R. Ḥiyya was named Pazzi (Yebamot 65b). And Pazzi is also found as the name of a man.[66] In medieval and in modern times we find the name Simḥah used as a name for a boy as well as for a girl, though in the latter case it is sometimes translated into German and it becomes *Freude* (see R. Samuel b. David ha-Levi in his נחלת שבעה (Koenigsberg, 1858, p. 122). And it is a common practice to name a grandson after his grandmother, and a granddaughter after her grandfather. In cases where the name of the grandmother is not thought quite suitable for a boy they change it slightly, giving a masculine form to the feminine name, e.g., when the grandmother's name was Dinah they call the grandson Dan. Some people, however, object to calling a granddaughter after her grandfather. The reason for this objection is that it might be unpleasant to the departed grandfather, if his soul, identical with his name, would have to enter the body of a girl, and thus be made to live the life of a woman.[67]

2) Some people would refrain from naming a child after a person who was killed or murdered by non-Jews for fear of bad luck, lest the sad fate of the former bearer of that name also befall the one named like him.[68] The same superstitious fear underlies the hesitancy to name a child after a person who died young. For it is feared that it may have been the name that caused the untimely death of that person.[69] And the child having the same name might suffer the same fate and be as shortlived as the former bearer of that name. In both these cases the fear is based upon the belief that the heavenly agent or angel of death might possibly make a mistake and confuse the one person with another of the same name. If, however, the people wish to preserve the name of the one who was killed or died young by naming some one after him, they usually combine with his name the name of another person who lived to a ripe old age and died a natural death. The child then, since it has two names, is clearly marked as another person, and mistakes on the part of the angel of death will thus be avoided.

3) The same fear prevents some parents from naming their child after another child of theirs that died. Most authorities, however, declare it permissible.[70] Some authorities, however, advise for safety's sake to combine with the name of the child that died another name, and call the new child by two names. It is reported of R. Elijah Wilna that he recommended to a family whose children would die young to call their new child by two names, one after its dead brother or sister and one after another person. This, he is said to have declared, to be a potent means by which to safeguard the life of the new child.[71] Some authorities would even permit two living children in the same family to be called by one and the same name.[72] They cite the case of R. Ḥisda who had two sons who were called by the same name (see Rashi to Ketuboh 89b s.v. מר ינוקא and comp. Tossafot to B. B. 75, s.v. מר ינוקא) It is, however, thought advisable to avoid such practice for fear of the "evil eye."

4) Some authorities would declare it prohibited to give a child the name of any biblical personage prior to Abraham. This, however, is ignored by most authorities, as indeed names like Adam, Mahalalel, Noah, Enoch, and even Jephet have been frequent among Jewish people (see H. J. D. Azulai in his *Shem ha-Gedolim* I (Wien, 1864) p. 3z–4a).

5) There are a few authorities who would object to non-Hebrew or non-Jewish names (Commentary to Sefer Ḥasidim No. 1139 (editio Lemberg, 1862) p. 84a, and R. Moses Schick in his Responsa תשובות מהר"ם שיק part of Yoreh Deah, No. 169 (Munkacs, 1881) p. 52d). But, as we have seen, even in talmudic times non-Jewish names were in vogue among the Jews. And it has continued to be the practice in post-talmudic times all through the Middle Ages and up to the present times to call children by non-Jewish names. Many great rabbinical authorities had non-Jewish names. Rabbinic law recognizes this practice and seeks to regulate the correct spelling of these non-Jewish names for use in legal documents, especially in bills of divorce (see *Shulḥan Aruk*, Eben ha-Ezer 129 and commentaries, and comp. Naḥalat Shib'ah, pp. 110–122).

In most cases, however, these non-Jewish names are accompanied

by a Hebrew name designated as the שֵׁם הַקּוֹדֶשׁ,[73] the latter being
used especially when the person is being called up to the Torah
and in certain prayers recited by or on behalf of the person.
The need for calling a person by a Hebrew name in connection
with any religious performance and especially in the recitation of
prayers is based upon the belief that the heavenly administration
is conducted and all its records kept in Hebrew. The ministering
angels are not believed to be great linguists. At any rate, whether
they have any knowledge of foreign languages or not, they would
ignore any communication addressed in any language other than
Hebrew. They would not even pay attention to petitions expressed
in Aramaic which is cognate to Hebrew (Sabbath 12b).[74] Hence
it is deemed advisable, according to popular belief, that when dealing with the heavenly administration a person should be called and
referred to by his or her Hebrew name.[75]

In this connection another peculiar practice in regard to mentioning a person's name for purposes of accurate identification, in
dealings with the heavenly authorities, should be mentioned. In
certain special prayers recited by or on behalf of a person,[76] it is
customary to add to the name of the person for further identification the name of the person's mother and not that of the person's
father. The person reciting the prayer for himself introduces himself with the phrase: "I, Thy servant so and so, the son of Thy
handmaid so and so." When others pray for him he is described
in the prayer as: "So and so, the son of Mrs. so and so." Certain
popular notions hinted at in the Talmud and enlarged on and
more clearly expressed in the Zohar are the bases for this practice.
In certain incantations occasionally used or recommended by the
Rabbis of the Talmud, the person is referred to as the son of his
mother פלניא בר פלניתא (Sabbath 66b, Pesahim 112a). And
Abaye quotes his nurse who so often gave him information about
popular beliefs and superstitious practices to the effect that in all
magical formulas the person must be identified by giving his
mother's name (Sabbath l.c.). The Talmud seemingly tolerates
this practice in dealings with the demons. The assumption is that
the demons either do not recognize marriage and still follow the
customs of the age of the matriarchate, or that they may have

their doubts as to who a person's father is (comp. Zohar, Shemot (Lublin 1872) p. 17b). The Zohar however goes farther and assumes that even when dealing with the angels or when wishing to get something from the powers above, one should identify himself in no uncertain manner and hence mention the name of his mother and not that of his father (Zohar, Lek Leka, (Lublin 1872) p. 84). This, of course, is contrary to the Jewish rule that children follow the father and should be recorded and identified as belonging to the family of the father (comp. B. B. 109b). Furthermore it is not quite nice, to say the least, and rather disrespectful to the mother if a prayer recited by or on behalf of her son contains the implication that there are some doubts as to who the actual father of her son is. So one could raise serious objections to this practice. But it has persisted and become widespread. [Comp. R. Elijahu Gutmacher (1796–1874) in his work, Sukat Sholom, ch. 5 (Jerusalem 1883) pp. 295–334 who discusses the question very thoroughly. He would compromise and consider the practice proper in such cases where the prayer, even though addressed to God, indirectly aims to have some restraining effect upon the demons, seeking to forestall or counteract any harm they might seek to do.]

As a result of this belief that the heavenly authorities know and can identify a person only on the basis of the description furnished by his full name: "So and so, the son of so and so," there developed in the course of time a whole system of tricks by which to hide a person from the heavenly agents and protect him from the dangers that threaten him from them. We have found that already in talmudic times there was current the belief that a change in the name of a person can have the effect of nullifying the evil decree issued against him. For the heavenly agents are unable to identify and apprehend him, since he now goes by another name.

In post-talmudic times this belief became more pronounced and more generally accepted. Hence the practice of changing a person's name when he is sick became widespread, and a special ritual for performing such a change of name was developed already in Geonic times.[77] The angel of death, so it was—and still is—believed, who comes to that person with a warrant to take his life, fails to identify him. He does not recognize in the person now going by another name the one upon whom the death sentence was decreed. To make this change of name more effective, and make doubly sure that the angel of death would not be able to harm the person with the changed name, it is deemed wise to select as the new name one which in itself suggests long life. They usually select names like Ḥayyim, *Life*, Alter, *Old Man*, Zeide, *Grandfather*.[78] The angel of death will thus find before him not only a person against whom he has no warrant but one whose very name declares that he must continue to live, grow old and become a grandfather; certainly the angel of death will not dare to touch him. But there is still another danger threatening the person even after his name has been changed, and this is that the angel of death might be looking for him merely as the child of his parents. This he is likely to do especially when death has been decreed upon the child because of the sin of the parents,[79] and the death warrant therefore calls for a child of so and so. Or he may simply ignore part of the name which in full reads "so and so, the son of so and so" and seek to identify the person merely as the child of so and so with no regard to its first or proper name. To meet this danger, a very ingenious practice was developed which frustrates all possible efforts of the angel of death to get at the sick child. This practice consists in changing the second part of its name, that part of it which contains the names of the parents, so that the child is no longer called "the son of Mr. and Mrs. A." but "the son of Mr. and Mrs. B." This is done not by giving the parents another name but by giving the child other parents, as it were. The real parents sell their sick child to another couple,[80] to people against whom, judging from the fact that their own children are all alive and healthy, there seems to be no charge in the heavenly records. The sick child is now considered the child of Mr. and Mrs. B., the new parents who acquired him. This transaction absolutely confounds the angel of death. If he looks for the child not under his first personal name but under the name of his former parents, as the child of Mr. and Mrs. A., he cannot find it, for the child is no longer called so. And if his order was to punish the parents by taking their child away from them, he finds that these parents no longer have a child that could be taken away from them. For the parents have sold their child and no longer own it. In either case, the angel of death has to report back to heaven that he could not execute his order.

Still another method of safeguarding the life of a child is not to give it any name at all, or when a name is given to it to keep it secret for a time so that it is not registered in the heavenly records. Of course, when the child has no name or when its name is not recorded the heavenly authorities do not know it. They cannot issue any decree against it and there is no way of finding it. This method is resorted to by families whose children die in infancy. They leave the child unnamed for a certain time, until as they believe, there is no more danger for the child or until it passes the critical period of infancy. Then they give it its name.[81]

As to who should give the child the name, there has never been any inflexible rule or fixed regulation. In biblical times it was usually the father who would give the name to his child. In many instances, however, it was the mother. We also have an instance of the foster mother's naming the child, as was the case with Moses (Exod. 2, 10). Sometimes it was done by neighbors, as was the case with Obed the son of Ruth and Boaz (Ruth 4, 17). In one instance, the prophet in the name of God gave the child a name in addition to the name given by the parents, as was the case with Solomon whom the prophet named Yedidyah (2 Samuel 12, 25).

In talmudic times it seems no change was made in the custom which obtained in biblical times, although we have no definite report in the Talmud on this point. In Midrash Kohelet R. (to Kohelet 7, 1) there is a reference to the name given to a person by his father and mother. And in Pirke de R. Eliezer (ch. 48) it is said that both parents of Moses gave him a name. But this may only mean that both parents agreed upon the name by which he should be called, and not that they both actually pronounced the name upon him. It may be assumed that the practice in talmudic times was the same as in biblical times. When the father was there he would actually name the child. When he was not there the mother would do it. In one instance reported in the Talmud (M. K. 25b) of a child born after the death of his father, it is said that "they"— the people present, neighbors or members of the family—gave the child the name of his father. This practice would correspond to the practice of neighbors naming the child as recorded in Ruth 4, 7. In post-talmudic times and up to modern times the same rule has obtained. It has, however, become customary that another person, the Moel, the Rabbi or cantor, or whoever the father delegates to do so, actually performs the rite of naming the child. The father merely pronounces the name and tells the officiant that that is the name which he wishes to give to his child. But it is still the right of the father to decide upon the name. Popular custom in some countries gives the mother the right to decide upon the name of her firstborn child and to name it after her parents or relatives.[82] But most authorities object to this custom, insisting that it is the indisputable right of the father to decide upon the name of the child.[83] In practice, however, these questions are first settled between the parents. And after they both agree upon the name, the father tells it to the officiant who pronounces it over the child.

With respect to the time when the name should be given to the child there have been some developments in the course of time. In biblical times the child was given its name immediately at its birth (see Löw, op. cit. p. 94 and comp. A. S. Herschberg, Hatekufah XXI, p. 257 for references). In talmudic times, though no express regulation about it can be found, it seems that it was the usual custom to name the male child at the circumcision on the 8th day after its birth (see Luke I, 59 and II, 21; and Pirke de R. Eliezer, ch. 48).[84] This has become the established practice in post-talmudic times up to this day.[85] In case the circumcision is postponed, because of the sickness of the child, the naming of the child is also postponed, till the time of the circumcision. In case a child is to remain uncircumcised, as when it comes from a family whose children die as a result of circumcision ערל שמתו אחיו מחמת מילה, the name is given to the child at the time when his father is called up to the Torah. And there is difference of opinion as to whether it is preferable to do so before the child is eight days old or after.[86] In case of girls there has been no uniformity of practice. Among the Sephardim in the Orient, the naming of a baby girl is a home ceremony. The parents invite guests to a meal at which the name of the newly born daughter is announced. Among the Italian and Ashkenazic Jews it was customary to name the girl in the Synagog on the Sabbath when the mother for the first time after birth of the child could visit the Synagog (Löw, op. cit. p. 104). There is, however, no fixed rule about this. Present day custom among Polish-Ashkenazic Jews varies in different localities. In some places it is still customary to name the girl right after she is born.[87] In others the name is given in the Synagog on the Sabbath or on a Monday or Thursday when the father comes to the Synagog and is called up to the Torah.

The prayer recited at the naming of a boy has become part of the service at a circumcision. The prayer at naming a girl now usually has a very short form. In the prayer "He who blessed" מי שברך recited for the mother, there is inserted the phrase "May He also bless the girl that was born to her and whose name should be called so and so."[88]

SUMMARY

As a result of the above survey of the different attitudes towards names and the various rituals and practices resulting from them, we may state that there have never been any definite laws or uniform fixed regulations on these questions. It was all a matter of custom and usage, which were not uniform. Custom is subject to changes from time to time and from place to place. And the customs in connection with the naming of children are no exception to this rule. Since these customs are governed by certain ideas and beliefs which not all people share in the same degree, it is not strange to find that the customs themselves differ so. Some people are more superstitious, others are more rational. It is well to recall the saying, quoted above, of one who himself was inclined to superstition, the author of the Sefer Ḥasidim: "Superstitions can affect only those who believe in them." Hence, while it is but proper to follow the custom established by the community or the group, it actually makes no difference what names we give to children. For no matter what name a person is given by others, what ultimately counts is only the name which he makes for himself by his actions and his conduct.

NOTES

[1] Comp. on these questions Cheyne-Black, *Encyclopaedia Biblica*, III, pp. 3264–3307.

[2] Comp. Walter Schulze, Der Namensglaube bei den Babyloniern, in *Anthropos* XXVI (1931) pp. 895–928, where the ideas as to the significance of names in Bible times among the Hebrew and the other Semitic peoples are also discussed, and the literature on the subject given.

[3] Comp. Schulze, *op. cit.*, p. 909.

[4] Comp. *ibid.*, p. 906. The change in the names of Joseph (Gen. 41, 45), of Eljakim (II Kings 23, 34), of Mattaniah (*ibid.* 24, 17), and of Daniel, Hananiah, Mishael and Azariah (Dan. 1, 17) were made because of the change that had taken place in their position. Likewise when, as the prophet predicts, God will in the future "call His servants by another name" (Isa. 65, 15) it will be in order to indicate the change in their fortunes or position. See also *ibid.* 62, 2.

[5] So it was understood by the Rabbis of the Talmud (Sotah, 34b). Comp. also Mekilta, Amalek III (Friedmann, 57ab).

[6] The possibility of such an interpretation of the phrase יקום עַל שֵׁם אָחִיו הַמֵּת is rejected by the Rabbis of the Talmud. See Sifre, Deut. 289 (Friedmann, 125b) and Yebamot 24a.

[7] Comp. however Mekilta, Pisha 5 (Friedmann, 5a) where the passage וְאוֹמֵר הַמַּלְאָךְ הַגוֹאֵל וכו' is probably a later interpolation.

[8] It is true that in I Chron. 3, 6–8 in the list of David's children, Eliphelet is mentioned twice and according to Rashi *ad loc.* David had two children by the name of Eliphelet, and the second child was named after that one that had died. But aside from the fact that these lists are not reliable (comp. the list of David's children in II Sam. 5, 14–16 where it is stated that only one child by the name of Eliphelet was born to David), the Book of Chronicles was written at a late period, and it reflects the ideas of its time, not of the time of David.

[9] Perhaps it was thought that, since the father of the grandfather was named Serug so that the grandfather's full name was "Nahor, the son of Serug," he was by his full name sufficiently distinguished from the grandson whose full name was "Nahor, son of Terah" and thus marked as a separate individuality. Hence, since the circumstances at birth or other considerations made it desirable to call the child Nahor, it was deemed proper and safe to call him so. A custom, however, to name after grandparents would involve the repetition of the full name, e.g. if Nahor, the son of Terah, would name his son Terah, there would be two persons by the full name of Terah, son of Nahor, indistinguishable from one another. This was inconceivable.

[10] Comp. L. Löw, *Die Lebensalter in der juedischen Literatur* (Szegedin, 1875) p. 94 and note 49 on p. 385.

[11] The list in I Chr. 5, 30–41 which disagrees with the two lists in Ezra is not to be considered as authentic. Comp. Löw, *op. cit.*, p. 385, note 50.

[12] *Op. cit.*, pp. 94–95.

[13] Against Zunz, Namen der Juden, in *Gesammelte Schriften*, II (Berlin, 1876) p. 19. The name Jadua mentioned in Neh. 12, 11 and 22 is probably the same as Yojada. So Jadua had the same name as his grandfather (or great grandfather?). And he was given this name long before Alexander came to Palestine, that is, before the Jews had any contact with the Greeks.

[14] See G. Buchanan Gray, Children Named After Ancestors in the Aramaic Papyri from Elephantine and Assuan, in *Studien Zur Semitischen Philologie und Religionsgeschichte*, Julius Wellhausen zum Siebzigsten Geburtstag (Giessen 1914) p. 163ff.

[15] I quote according to the reading in the edition of Theodor-Albeck. Comp. commentaries. The reading given in Yalkut to Chronicles 1073: הראשונים

על ידי שלא היו מכירין את יחוסן היו מוציאין לשם המאורע

אבל אנו שאנו מכירין את יחוסינו אנו מוציאין לשם אבותינו

is a gross mistake based upon the misunderstanding of the purport and meaning of R. Jose's saying.

[16] The term שתוקי "a silent one" designates one who could not prove his pure Jewish descent, as the records were silent about him. Hence Abba Saul would designate him as בדוקי "one who is to be investigated." The meaning of these terms was misunderstood, hence the fanciful interpretations in the Gemara Kiddushin 70a and 74a and Yebamot 100b. As to these records or family-registers which were kept in the archives of the Temple, see Lauterbach, *The Three Books Found in the Temple at Jerusalem* (New York, 1918), and comp. also S. Klein in *Ziyyon* (Jerusalem, 1930) vol. IV, who, without having seen my Essay, independently arrived at almost the same conclusion, that the three books kept in the Temple were genealogical records and not Torah copies.

[17] An Amonite proselyte by the name of Judah יהודה גר עמוני is mentioned in the Mishnah (Yaddayim, IV, 4) and an Egyptian proselyte, a disciple of R. Akiba, by the name of Benjamin, is mentioned in the Tosefta Kiddushin V, 4, though some texts have the reading מנימין instead of בנימין, but it is the same name.

[18] Comp. A. Marmorstein, Der heilige Geist in der rabbinischen Legende, in *Archiv für Religionswissenschaft*, XXVIII (1930) pp. 286–303, especially p. 291ff.

[19] Thus Jesus is reported to have been given his name ישוע to suggest or predict that "he will save his people from their sins" (Mat. 1, 21). Whether this actually was the intention of those who gave him his name, or they merely named him so after a relative, is for our purpose irrelevant. It at any rate shows that the writers of the Gospel assumed the prevalence of the custom of naming children לשם המאורע. The names חסדא, טביומי in talmudic times were names לשם המאורע. So also no doubt were the names כידור and לכלוכית. See below Note 64.

[20] This, in my opinion, is the meaning of the phrase הואי כשגגה שיוצאה מלפני השליט which occurs in the Talmud (Ketubot, 62b and *passim*) in explanation of how the evil spoken, even without the intention to wish it, came to happen. I hope to deal with this subject more exhaustively elsewhere.

[21] Hence one should never open his mouth to say something which Satan might hasten to bring about אל יפתח אדם פיו לשטן. (Berakot, 19a and parall.) There is another aspect to this belief which is not connected with the belief in the fallibility of the angel. And this is that Satan may simply cite the statement uttered by the person, as an argument against him, claiming that the person himself admitted his guilt or invited the misfortune.

[22] The expression לפעמים "sometimes" or "often," is merely put in in order not to deny the principle of free will.

[23] הוא בשמה והיא בשמו יש בו משום דרכי האמורי and Rashi comments on this: הוא ואשתו מחליפין שמותיהן זה בזה בלילה משום ניחוש

ד' דברים מקרעין גזר דינו של אדם. אלו הן צדקה צעקה [24]
שינוי השם ושינוי מעשה . . . ויש אומרים אף שינוי מקום

Yet there is no instance of an actual practice of changing the name in case of sickness recorded in the Talmud. Comp. Löw, *op. cit.*, p. 108.

[25] See R. Nissim (Gerondi) in his commentary to Alfasi *ad loc.* who explains:

שינוי השם שמשנה שמו וטעמא דמילתא דשנוי השם גורם לו
לעשות תשובה שיאמר בלבו איני אותו האיש שהייתי קודם לכן
וצריך אני לתקן מעשי

[26] Thus M. Coucy in his סמ"ג *Commandments*, 17 (Venice, 1547), p. 90a, plainly explains: שינוי השם שמשנה שמו כלומר שאני אחר ואיני אותו האיש שעשה המעשים that the one who changes his name as much as declares—to the angel looking for him or to whomsoever it may concern—"I am not the person you are looking for, I am not the one who committed the sins you charge me with." Mohammed also believed that by changing the name of a person the person himself also becomes changed. See J. Wellhausen, *Reste Arabischen Heidentums* (2nd edition, Berlin, 1897) p. 199.

[27] Some authorities would identify this Mary the hairdresser with Mary the mother of Jesus. See Tossafot, *ad. loc.* s.v. הוה שכיח and comp. S. Krauss, *Das Leben Jesu nach juedischen Quellen*, (Berlin, 1902) p. 274f. note.

9. Perhaps, however, מגדלא שער נשיא does not mean "hairdresser" but one who herself had long hair, and there may be here an allusion to the Mary who "anointed the feet of Jesus and wiped his feet with her hair" (John 12.3).

[28] As to the heavenly agents carrying out their orders, sometimes without exact knowledge as to what they are doing, see רשב"ם quoted by Tossafot Yomtob to M. Abot III, 16, who prefers the reading in the Mishnah מדעתן ושלא מדעתן and interprets it as referring to the agents or collectors who exact payment from man. Comp. also saying in Mekilta Pisha XI (Friedmann 11b) which according to the correct text established in my forthcoming edition of the Mekilta reads: משניתנה רשות למלאך לחבל אינו מבחין בין צדיק לרשע

[29] The idea that the ministering angels are liable to make mistakes in the identity of a person if that person is referred to merely by name is in my opinion presupposed in the following statement in the Talmud (Berakot 34a): כל המבקש רחמים על חבירו אין צריך להזכיר שמו שנאמר אל נא רפא נא לה ולא קמדכר שמה דמרים When one prays for mercy for his fellowman it is not correct (אין צריך here does not mean "it is not necessary" but rather "it is not correct" לא נכון, see Jacob Reischer in עיון יעקב, commentary to En Jacob, ad loc.) to refer to him by merely mentioning his name. For when Moses prayed for Miriam it is said: "Heal her now, O God, I beseech Thee" (Num. 12, 13). He pointed to Miriam and did not merely refer to her by name. By pointing to the person for whom one prays mistakes on the part of the angels are less likely to happen.

[30] Thus Abba b. Abba the father of the famous Babylonian Amora of the first generation Samuel, called his son by the name of the prophet Samuel, no doubt, to suggest that his son may become like the prophet. He thereby wished to help bring into fulfillment the promise which R. Judah b. Bathyra

had given him, that he would have a son who would be like the prophet Samuel. See Midrash to Sam. X, 3 (ed. Buber, Krakau, 1893), p. 39a.

[31] The expression דלא מסקינן בשמייהו which literally means "we do not bring (them) up by their name" may have an allusion to the belief that, if you call the name of the ghost it appears. Hence we do not wish to name a child like them, for fear that whenever we will call the child by its name we might, by the mere mentioning of the name, cause the ghost, the original bearer of that name, to come up from the grave and appear before us. Comp. the remark by Schulze (op. cit., p. 924): "Der Namesruf bewirkt die Gegenwart seines Trägers. Man vermeidet deshalb Namen, dessen Träger unheilvoll sind."

[32] Comp. Pithe Teshubah to Yore Deah 116, 6, s.v. לידי סכנה

[33] The name Abraham, it seems, was never given to a child in talmudic times. In the passage of Gen. r. 49, 1 the words אברהם יצחק יעקב are omitted in some editions (see Theodor, ad. loc. and comp. S. Krauss, *Talmudische Archäologie,* II (Leipzig, 1911) p. 13 and note 136 on p. 440). There occurs, however, the name Abram—the original name of Abraham—as the name of an Amora (Gittin 50a). See, however, Krauss, *op. cit.* note 138 on p. 440 and comp. H. J. D. Azulai in שם הגדולים I, s.v. אברהם No. 34 (Wien, 1865) p. 3b. It is likely to assume that since father Abraham was not to be called by his former name Abram there was no hesitancy felt in calling children by the latter name. But they would avoid calling a child Abraham.

[34] The name Moses occurs but once in the Talmud (B.B. 174b) as the name of a man משה בר עצרא who, as it seems, was not a teacher. No teacher of talmudic times, Tanna or Amora, was ever called by the name of Moses (See Azulai op. cit. s.v. משה No. 110 p. 59a, who assumes that there was a mystic reason for avoiding to give the name Moses to any teacher (לא היה שום תנא או אמורא שנקרא משה והוא פלא וסוד. The name מיאשה is not identical with משה as assumed by Graetz (*Gesch.* vol. 4, note 19 (Leipzig, 1908) p. 433). Comp. also Krauss, *op. cit.,* note 140 on p. 441.

[35] Aaron occurs only once (B. K. 109b) as the name of a teacher of the last generation of the Babylonian Amoraim. The saying in *Aboth de Rabbi Nathan,* Version A ch. XII is merely of a homiletical nature. Comp. Krauss, *op. cit.,* p. 441, note 140.

[36] David occurs but once according to some variant reading in Yebamot 115b. See marginal note in Talmud edition Wilna 1908. This reading, however, is doubtful. It is missing in the text of the other editions.

[37] Krauss, *op. cit.,* p. 13, assumes that it was merely reverence for those great ancestors which prevented people from calling a child by their name, just as Christians would not call a child by the name Jesus. But mere reverence would not constitute a mystery which Azulai assumes as the reason. To me it seems that the avoidance of calling children by the names of these ancestors was due to a hesitancy to transfer the very being or soul of any of those ancestors to another person, which would be effected by giving that other person the name of the ancestor. These great souls should not be disturbed and made to come to earth again.

[38] See for references to some instances, Krauss, *op. cit.,* II, p. 440, note 131, and A. S. Herschberg, in *Hatekufah* XXV, p. 396, note 4, to which many other instances could be added. Comp. also Jacob Mann, *Rabbinic Studies in the Gospels,* in Hebrew Union College Annual I. (Cincinnati, 1924) p. 328.

[39] This, as we shall see, was actually the belief among the oriental Jews in later times who would seek to secure for the older man a prolonged life by naming his child or grandchild like him. See below Note 48.

[40] Comp. Herschberg, *Hatekufah* XXV, p. 392ff.

[41] Comp. Zunz, *op. cit.*, p. 15 and Herschberg, *op. cit.*, p. 395f.

[42] As in the case of Judah he-Ḥasid and his father, see below Note 57.

[43] ואיך ישכח יהודה את יהודה Divan, ed. S. D. Luzzatto (Lyck 1864) 3b; comp. Luzzatto's note 9, *ibid.* p. 4a.

[44] See Weiss, *Dor* V (Wilna 1904) p. 94.

[45] אע"פי שצריך⸤לקרותו על שמי אני רוצה שיקרא יונה על שם זקנו אבי אמו משום וזרח השמש ובא השמש עד שלא זרחה (לשוי נקיה תחת שקעה?) שמשו של זה זרחה שמשו של זה ספר הר"שב"ש Quoted by R. Solomon b. Simeon b. Zemah in his responsa No. 291 (Leghorn, 1742) 56d.

[46] Comp. also ספר ולכל המנהגים אין אדם קוראבנו בשם עצמו. שרביט הזהב החדש הנקראברית אבות by R. Schabsza Lipschitz (Muncacs, 1914) ch. VIII, No. 11, p. 59b.

[47] זאת מנהגם לסגולה מי אשר לא יקיימו בניו רחמנא ליצלן יקרא לבנו בחייו כשמו

[48] See Lipschitz, *op. cit.*, ch. VIII, No. 16 (p. 60b) quoting S. A. Wertheimer of Jerusalem: אצל אחינו בני ישראל אנשי ארץ ספרד בירושלים מקובל לסגולה לאריכת ימי האב שיקרא בנו בחייו בשמו

[49] Which according to popular superstition he should not have done. See *Pirke de R. Eliezer* ch. 16 חתן אינו יוצא לבדו לשוק and comp. Berakot 54b.

[50] In this connection, it should be noticed that the warning against a marriage in case the bride has the same name as the mother of the groom or the bride's father has the same name as the groom, expressed in the *Testament of R. Judah he-Ḥasid* צוואת ר"י החסיד (published in *Sefer Ḥasidim* (Lemberg 1862) p. 1b) is also based upon the fear of an error by the heavenly agents, who might not know to distinguish between two persons by the same name in one family or one household, and by mistake inflict upon the one person ills decreed against the other with the same name. This danger is especially great in case the names of the respective parents of the two persons with the same name were also alike, as when e.g. the father of the girl is Isaac the son of Abraham and the groom's name is also Isaac the son of Abraham, or the name of both be Jacob the son of Isaac the son of Abraham (משולשים) (*Sefer Ḥasidim*, 477, Lemberg, 1862, p. 45d, and comp. R. Abraham Danziger in his ספר חכמת אדם 123, 13 (Warsaw, 1914) p. 140). For in such cases the angel will be absolutely at a loss to distinguish the one from the other. Comp. the interesting remark in *Sefer Ḥasidim* (ibid): "Although one should not believe in superstitions, yet it is better to be heedful of them." אע"פי שלא לנחש יש לחוש. This is a sort of apology for advising all these precautions.

[51] See above Note 28 characterization of the heavenly agents according to Rashbam's reading in the Mishnah, Aboth III, 16.

[52] See Benjacob, *Ozar ha-Sefarim,* No. 560. Benjacob's suggestion (*ibid.*, No. 559) that Ziyyuni may have had reference to another ספר החיים ascribed to Ibn Ezra does not seem plausible.

[53] ומצאתי בספר החיים כי שמו של אדם הוא נשמתו

[54] Of course, if the older person whose life is thus endangered by his name being given to the child, does not mind the risk, his name is given to his grandchild. There have been such exceptions even among Ashkenazic Jews. See נוהג כצאן יוסף by Joseph ben Moses Kossman (Hanau 1718) p. 22a.

[55] Comp. Jacob Emden in his בירת מגדול עוז (Jitomir, 1874) p. 12.

[56] Comp. Responsa משבצות זהב by R. Nathan Amram No. 42 (Leghorn, 1851), p. 39, and in the מפתחות there p. 73d where he cites this theory in the following words: שהוא (ר"י החסיד) זצוק"ל להוראת שעה השתמש
כמה פעמים בשמות הקודש ולפי שהיה מתיירא לנפשו הטהורה
לשמא ח"ו יענישוהו על ככה תמיד כל הימים לכך צוה ויעמוד
לבל יקראו בשמו עולמים שכן היה מסורת בידו ז"ל שכל מי
שהשתמש בימיו בשה"ק כל זמן שיהיה נמצא בזרעו השם ההוא
עצמו בהכרח לשיגללו עליו את הכל ולכן לא מצא תרופה לזה
אם לא בהשבית זכרו מיוצאי חלציו זכותו יגן עלינו.

[57] See above Note 42.

[58] See below Note 67.

[59] See Hayyim Vital in ספר הגלגולים Chap. IV (Frankfurt, 1684) pp. 3bff. and 35b–36b.

[60] See Emanuel Riki in משנת חסידים (Amsterdam, 1727) p. 33b ומי
שמת והניח אשתו מעוברת ויולדת בן הוא מתגלגל בו and comp. Lipschitz, *op. cit.* ch. VIII, No. 37, p. 64a.

[61] See מגיד מישרים to section שמות (Amsterdam, 1708) p. 21a רזין
דשמהן . . . דמאן דאיקרי אברהם נוטה לצד עשיית חסד

[62] See עמוד העבודה by R. Baruch b. Abraham (Czernowitz, 1854) p. 41cd.

[63] See Jacob ibn Ḥabib in הכותב to *En Jacob* on Berakot 7b who interprets the saying of R. Eleazar to mean that God put into the mouth of Leah the name which she gave to her son כי השם יתברך שם בפיה קריאת
שם זה
See also Emanuel Riki (*op. cit.* p. 85): והשם שקורא לבן הק"ב"ה
מזמינו בפיו and comp. R. Bezalel b. Solomon Slutzk in his עמודיה
שבעה (Prague, 1674) No. 33, p. 4.

[64] Comp. such names as (יום טוב=) טביומי and חסדא in talmudic times, and חפץ or מצליח in Geonic times. See above Note 19.

[65] See A. J. Glassberg זכרון ברית לראשונים (Berlin, 1892) p. 256; Lipschitz, *op. cit.*, ch. VIII, No. 31, p. 62b and comp. R. Joseph Hahn in יוסף אומץ (Frankfurt, 1928) p. 240.

[66] See Hyman תולדות תנאים ואמוראים s.v. p. 1010. Likewise in the Bible we find that the names: Atalyah, Abiyah, and Noadjah were used as names for men as well as for women. See Ch. D. Ginsburg, The Massorah, vol. III (London 1885) p. 194.

[67] See Lipschitz, *op. cit.*, ch. VIII, No. 37, p. 64.

[68] Id., *op. cit.*, ch. VIII, No. 10, p. 59a, where, however, the remark is added that if one does not mind this fear of bad luck God will protect him from harm ומאן דלא קפיד בזה שומר פתאים ד'.

[69] Comp. *Sefer Ḥasidim*, No. 363–364.

[70] See Responsa אדני פז by Ephraim B. Samuel Hekshir No. 25 (Altona, 1743) p. 38 (and comp. Pithe Teshubah to Yore Deah 116, 6). Responsa בית יצחק by R. Isaac Schmelkes to Yore Deah part II, No. 163 (Przemysl, 1895) p. 129.

[71] See ספר עליות אליהו by Heshil Lewin, (Wilna, 1856) p. 67, note 51.

[72] Responsa אדני פז No. 34, p. 40a.

[73] This שם הקודש is sometimes a retranslation of the foreign name. But in some cases it is an altogether different name. See Zunz, op. cit. p. 26f. In this connection should be mentioned the ceremony of *Hollekreisch* which according to some authorities took place in the case of boys when they gave them their secular name, after the שם הקודש had been given the child at the circumcision. As this ceremony was performed while they placed the child in the cradle, the name given to him at that occasion is designated as שם העריסה. For a description of this ceremony of הוליקרייש or חולקרייש, the etymology of the word and the superstitions suggested in it or connected with the ceremony, see Löw, op. cit. pp. 104–105; J. Perles, Die Berner Handschrift des kleinen Aruch, in *Jubelschrift zum Siebzigsten Geburtstage des Prof. Dr. H. Graetz* (Breslau, 1887) p. 26, and M. Güdemann, *Geschichte des Erziehungswesens,* etc. III (Wien, 1888) p. 104f.

[74] The saying in the Talmud reads: שאין מלאכי השרת מכירין בלשון ארמי and Asheri (quoted in Beth Joseph to Orah Ḥayyim 101) explains it to mean that the angels would not recognize the Aramaic language, it is disdainful to them; hence they would not pay attention to petitions spoken in it לשון זה מגונה בעיניהם להזקק לו. It does not mean that they do not understand it. Comp. also Responsum by Sherira Gaon in Harkavy's תשובות הגאונים (Berlin, 1885) No. 373, p. 188.

[75] In this connection another popular belief with regard to Hebrew names and the angels should be mentioned. As soon as a man has died and been buried, so it was believed, the angel of death comes to his grave and beats him and asks him for his name, for the purpose of identifying him and examining his record. See ילקוט הרועים in מסכת חבוט הקבר (Warsaw, 1885) p. 80 and comp. the commentary חסד לאברהם ad loc. Of course, the person must give his name in Hebrew, otherwise the angel would not pay any attention to his answer and keep on beating him. It is, therefore, necessary for every person to make sure that he will remember his Hebrew name after death. This he can do by reciting every day after his daily prayers a verse from the Bible in Hebrew which contains his name or at least some allusion to or reminder of his name. See תקון חבוט הקבר in קיצור של"ה by R. Jehiel Michael Epstein (Warsaw, 1864) p. 101b–102b.

[76] Especially in a prayer מי שברך for the sick, also in the prayer beginning רבש"ע recited on the Three Festivals at the opening of the Ark before taking out the Torah scrolls.

[77] R. Jeroham b. Meshullam (1st half of the 14th century) in his ספר
תולדות אדם וחוה part I. נתיב כ"ח (Kopys, 1808) p. 182a, refers to,
and in part quotes, a ritual for effecting the change of name, instituted by the
Geonim. שנוי השם שתקנו הגאונים It is to be recited in an assembly of
ten persons by an expert reader who also holds a scroll of the Torah in his
hands. The ritual in full is found in *Maḥzor Bologna* (1540) Sig. 23 leaf
4 and in סדור התפלה עם היוצרות *Ritus Rome* (Mantua, 1557) p. 227b
ff. Comp. also קיצור של"ה by Epstein (Warsaw, 1864)
p. 101b. In this ritual the sick person is given a new name and the heavenly authorities are notified and requested to take cognizance of this change
in name and to consider the person with the new name as not identical
with the person with the old name, so that whatever decrees may have been
issued against the person with the old name should not be executed upon
this person with his new name, ואם נקנסה מיתה, עלפלוני זה לא נקנסה
ואם נגזרה גזרה רעה, על פלוני זה לא נגזרה דאיש אחר הוא
וכבריה חדשה הוא וכקטן שנולד לחיים טובים.
Comp. also H. J. D. Azulai in his עבודת הקודש (Warsaw, 1879) סנסן
ליאר p. 109 where it is assumed that the change has also the effect of
bringing into the person a new and purer and holier soul להמשיך לו נפש
חדשה וקדושה.

[78] There are some who follow another method for selecting the new name.
The scroll of the Torah is opened and the first name of any of the Biblical
heroes they happen to strike upon is selected as the new name for the sick
person. See S. Baer ספר תוצאות חיים (Rödelheim, 1862) p. 19.

[79] See Sabbath 32b.

[80] See *Sefer Ḥasidim* (ed. Wistinetzki) 365 and comp. Azulai's *Commentary
to Sefer Ḥasidim*, (editio Lemberg) No. 245.

[81] See Lipschitz, op. cit. VIII, No. 28, p. 62, and comp. commentary on the
Torah by the בעלי התוספות to Gen. 5, 28 (Warsaw, 1904) p. 5; משותלח
הצדיק נתן לו (וללמך) עצה שלא ימהר לקרוא לו (ולבנו נח) שם
לפי שאנשי הדור מכשפים היו ויהיו מכשפים אות אם ידעו שמו

[82] See Lipschitz, op. cit. VIII, No. 35, p. 63ab.

[83] Ibid. Comp. also Abraham Mejuhas ספר שדה הארץ part III Responsum No. 22 (Leghorn, 1788) p. 41a.

[84] Comp. Krauss, *Archäologie* II, ch. V and note 123, p. 439; also J. Mann,
op. cit., p. 326.

[85] See הגהות to ספר מנהגים by Tyrnan (Warsaw, 1709) p. 67, and
compare Kaufman Cohen in ספר חוקי דעת (Sadilkow, 1835) p. 66b.

[86] See Glassberg, *op. cit.*, p. 248 and Lipschitz, *op. cit.*, VIII, No. 2, p. 58b.

[87] Lipschitz, *ibid.*, No. 3, p. 58b.

[88] As to the original longer forms of this formula, see Glassberg, *op. cit.*,
pp. 256–7.

THE ORIGIN AND DEVELOPMENT OF
TWO SABBATH CEREMONIES

JEWISH religious ceremonies have their histories and their fates. They come into being in different ways and have different origins. They may be enacted by divine law; formally introduced by the leaders of the people and decreed by the religious authorities; imported from foreign lands; or borrowed by the people themselves — from non-Jewish neighbors — and then gradually, even if reluctantly, tolerated and accepted by the religious authorities. They may even be born of mere habits which have become fixed, or grow out of mere customs of convenience which gradually acquire some religious significance and thus, in time, become generally accepted. But, no matter what their origin, after they have been recognized as Jewish ceremonies, they all start a certain course of development and begin their history. They change more or less in form and content, flourish and live on, or decay and die.

When, in the course of time, due to the general progress of civilization, new ideas arise among the people and major or minor changes in their beliefs take place, all ceremonies observed by the people in an earlier period, or in a previous cultural stage, meet with difficulties. They are exposed to the dangers either of neglect or of antagonistic criticism which threaten their very existence. In the one case they no longer appeal to the people who now cherish ideas other than those which gave rise to the ceremonies or different from those expressed by these ceremonies. In the other case they may become objectionable to more advanced ways of thinking and be attacked by the cultural leaders. In either case they experience difficulties in maintaining themselves.[1]

[1] Comp. Lauterbach, "The Ceremony of Breaking a Glass at Weddings" in *HUCA*, II (1925), 352 f.

Reprinted from *Hebrew Union College Annual*, Vol. XV, 1940.

In this struggle against new hostile ideas and unfavorable conditions, not all ceremonies fare alike. Some ceremonies possess a special aptitude for adjusting themselves to changed conditions and have the capacity of making their peace with advanced ideas and new beliefs. They lend themselves to modifications by which they can retain their appeal to the changed popular fancy; and they readily submit to a process of repeated interpretations by which they assume new meaning and fresh significance in keeping with the newer ideas in vogue among the more thoughtful of the people. They are thus enabled to continue performing some function or serving some purpose, even though it may be a function or a purpose altogether different from the one for which they were originally intended or which they served in a previous period.[2] At any rate, they maintain themselves and remain a part of the cultural or spiritual life of the people.

Other ceremonies are not so successful. By attempts at adaptation to changed conditions and new ideas they too seek to prolong their existence, and they may manage to achieve some passing success. Gradually, however, they lose their adaptability and are unable to withstand the attacks by the hostile forces of a different spiritual climate or a changed cultural environment. Sooner or later they are rejected by the leaders of thought and are neglected even by the people, and thus disappear entirely.

In some instances a ceremony meets obstacles which make it difficult or impossible for it to continue functioning in its totality. It then may break up into parts, each of which forms a separate ceremony that can avoid the difficulties encountered by the parent ceremony as a whole. These new ceremonies, less objectionable than the original ceremony as a whole, pursue their own course of development and are capable of continuing to function as independent religious ceremonies.[3] This method of splitting

---

[2] Even after acquiring a new meaning and being given a new purpose, a ceremony may still retain some of the notions originally associated with it and, in the mind of some people at least, continue to serve the old purpose alongside of the new one. See Lauterbach, *Tashlik*, (Cincinnati 1936) pp. 1–3, and pp. 110–111.

[3] Such an instance is the original ceremony out of which developed *Tashlik*, and *Kapparot*. See Lauterbach *op. cit.*, p. 56 ff., p. 71 f., and p. 131.

itself into parts, however, does not always save the ceremony or any of its parts. In some cases the parts are no more successful in maintaining themselves separately than was the whole. The separate ceremony, formed out of a fragment of the broken up older ceremony, may, for a time at least, show greater adaptability to a changed environment. It may develop a certain capacity for associating itself with new ideas whereby it acquires a new significance and a different character which gives it a fresh appeal to a certain class of people. This does not, however, assure its permanent existence or continuous function. Like the older ceremony of which it was merely a part, it, sooner or later, may face criticism and meet with disapproval; sometimes because the objectionable character of the parent ceremony may still be noticeable in the part, notwithstanding the newer significance and different character given to it, or sometimes the new character itself assumed by the part or the fresh significance assigned to it which at first imparted to it a fresh appeal, provokes new antagonism or meets with objections on the part of some other group of the people. The result is that the ceremony, notwithstanding or even because of its new character, is attacked by hostile forces which cause it to be officially discarded or neglected by the people.

In the following I shall describe the course taken by two Jewish ceremonies observed respectively on Friday evening and Saturday night. Both of these ceremonies grew out of a mere custom or habit and originally were similar in character and form. The one, after being recognized as a religious ceremony, experienced in the course of time, (due probably to some objections raised against it) some reinterpretations. With some modifications, it has been preserved to this day. The other seemingly met with greater obstacles. And even though, or just because, it was given some new mystic significance and assumed a new character, it was not generally favored. It encountered strong objections and was discarded by the great majority of the people, so that it finally fell into utter disuse and became almost completely forgotten.

There seems to have been a custom among the Jews in Palestine in ancient times of providing their table on the Sabbath

with fragrant plants or aromatic herbs.[4] The primary and chief
purpose of these plants was to enhance the pleasures of the table
by affording the participants of the meal the additional enjoyment of the aroma or pleasant fragrance. They were simply a
substitute for the incense, or smoke of spices, *mugmar*,[5] which
it was customary to provide at the end of every meal.[6] This

[4] We have no explicit reference in the Talmud to such a custom but some
indications point to it. Thus the description of a table in the house of a wealthy
Jew on a Sabbath mentions that it was laden with all kinds of food and deli-
cacies and aromatic herbs כל מיני מאכל וכל מיני מגדים ובשמים (Sab. 119a), though
the Munich Ms. does not have the word ובשמים. See Rabbinovicz דקדוקי
סופרים *ad loc. Še'eltot* I (Wilna 1861) p. 6; *'Or Zaru'a* II, p. 10; and *Šibbole
Ha-leḳeṭ* 55 (Wilna 1886) p. 43, when quoting this passage omit the word
ובשמים. And *Sefer Ha-'ittim* (Berlin 1902) p. 241 has פירות instead of בשמים.
The Midrash, Lev. Rab. 23.6 speaks of the use of the rose for Sabbaths and
Holidays שושנה מתוקנת לשבתות וימים טובים מטלטלין עצי בשמים. See also Beẓ 33b
להריח בהם, and Men. 43b בשבתא וביומי טבי טרח וממלי להו באיספרמקי which Rashi
s. v. באספרמקי correctly explains as בשמים. Comp. I. Löw, *Aramaeische Pflanzen-
Namen* (Leipzig 1881) p. 152. Likewise Persius Flaccus, a Roman satirist of
the first century, describing the table in a Jewish home on the Sabbath, says :
"The lamps are arranged and adorned with violets" which probably refers
especially to the Friday evening ceremonies. Cf. Buechler, "Graeco-Roman
Criticism of Some Jewish Observances and Beliefs" in *The Jewish Review*, I
(London 1910), 133–134. And last but not least, the story in Sab. 33b to
be discussed below, unmistakably points to such an early custom.

[5] מוגמר from גומרא, glowing coal. See Jastrow, *Dictionary* s. v. p. 738.

[6] The Mishna (Ber. 6.6) prescribes that "the one who recites the Grace
after the meal over a cup of wine, also says the benediction over the *mugmar*"
adding "although they usually serve the *mugmar* only after the meal." והוא
אומר על המוגמר אף על פי שאין מביאין את המוגמר אלא לאחר הסעודה. "After the meal"
לאחר הסעודה, is understood by the commentators to mean after the meal is
over and Grace has been recited. Some commentators add that it only means
that it was the usual custom to serve it after the Grace following the meal
had been recited but that they would some times also serve it after the eating
was finished, before the recitation of the Grace. See *Tosefot Yomṭob ad loc.*
and פירוש בעל ספר חרדים on the Palestinian Talmud to Ber. 6.6 in edition
Wilna 1922, p. 96 and p. 98. Whether the *mugmar* had, in the mind of some
people, the additional purpose of driving away the evil spirits as the smoke
of the incense קטורת was reputed to do (*infra*, note 40), we cannot tell. The
statement in the Mishna Beẓ. 2.7 permitting the preparation of the *mugmar*
on a holiday מניחין את המוגמר ביום טוב indicates that the Rabbis, at least, understood its purpose to be solely for enjoyment or to help the digestion; hence
the work in preparing it like all work for preparing food, אוכל נפש, was permitted on a holiday.

mugmar consisted of some aromatic herbs strewn upon a pan of live coals which thus produced a pleasant aromatic smoke. On week days or even on holidays on which the making and using of fire was allowed, such a pan of live coals could be prepared and, with the aromatic herbs or spices scattered on them, placed upon the table. On the Sabbath, however, when fire could not be made and live coals were neither obtainable nor allowed to be moved or handled, it was impossible to prepare this *mugmar*. Yet the people did not like to do without it on the Sabbath; they did not like to make the Sabbath-day meals less enjoyable than those on the other days of the week. A substitute was, therefore, introduced which did not involve any violation of the Sabbath law. They placed on the table during or at the beginning of the meal[7] fragrant plants, flowers, or perhaps other kinds of aromatic herbs and spices, מיני בשמים which would give out a pleasant fragrance without the necessity of putting them on the fire first. Of course, they recited a separate benediction בא"י אמ"ה בורא עצי בשמים over this substitute, just as they recited the very same benediction over the *mugmar* on week days and just as one had to recite a separate benediction over any kind of extra enjoyment that may have been brought to the table which did not form an integral part of the meal. But the reciting of a benediction over this extra enjoyment did not make the custom of having plants at the table a religious ceremony. Hence, no express reference to such a custom is, to my knowledge, to be found in the *Talmud* or *Midrashim*, nor any discussion of its details. It was just a table custom like the *mugmar*, for which it was substituted, which likewise is nowhere prescribed as a religious ceremony and the details of which are likewise not discussed except in the casual remark in the *Mishnah* (Ber. 6.6), that the one who says the benediction over the wine brought in after the meal also says the benediction over the *mugmar*.

[7] See preceding note. In the case of the *mugmar*, they could not place it on the table at the beginning of the meal for the coals might die out during the time of the meal and the aroma would not last till the time after the meal when they really wanted it. But, in the case of flowers, their fragrance is more lasting and would continue till after the meal, even though placed on the table at the beginning of or even before the meal. *Infra*, note 16, and note 25.

This table custom was not limited to one particular meal of the Sabbath and it was not especially a Friday evening custom, as one might assume from the description by Flaccus.[8] It was a custom for the whole Sabbath, observed at all of its meals, since fire for the preparation of the *mugmar* could not be used.[9]

Before the new system of reckoning the day from evening to evening was introduced, when the Sabbath extended from Saturday morning to Sunday morning,[10] there were only *two*[11] meals partaken of on the Sabbath — as on any other day — one in the morning or forenoon and the other in the evening or late afternoon.[12] And, of course, at *both* of these meals, flowers or plants had to be used as a substitute for the *mugmar*. Since the evening, under that system, belonged to the preceding, not to the following day, Friday evening was not yet part of the Sabbath; hence, the meal on Friday evening was not yet a Sabbath meal: it was simply the second meal of the week day, Friday. Fire, then, could still be used and live coals could be obtained, hence there was no need of using plants as a substitute for the *mugmar* at the Friday evening meal. With the innovation of reckoning the day from sunset to sunset, which made the Sabbath extend from Friday evening to Saturday evening, the character of the Friday evening meal was greatly changed, and the character of the Saturday late afternoon or evening meal was likewise greatly affected. Both of these meals were made

[8] Flaccus mentions the violets as an adornment of the lamps, which can have reference only to Friday evening. *Supra*, note 4. This merely means that, on Friday evening, they arranged the flowers together with the lamps but it does not mean that, on the Sabbath day, they did not have these violets or other flowers on the table, even though no lamps were burning.

[9] They have also occasionally enjoyed the fragrance of these flowers even between meals. See Beẓ. 33b and Men. 43b quoted *supra*, note 4.

[10] This innovation, as I prove elsewhere, was introduced during or near the end of the Greek period. Comp. J. Morgenstern, "The Sources of the Creation Story" in *AJSLL* XXXVI (1919–1920), 176, note 1 to p. 179.

[11] The rule for taking three meals on the Sabbath developed much later. I hope to discuss this (later) development elsewhere. Cf. *infra*, note 19.

[12] There were no fixed hours for all people. Different classes of people had their meals at different hours. But in general it can be said that one meal was taken in the forenoon and the other in the late afternoon or evening. See S. Krauss, *Talmudische Archäologie* III (Leipzig 1910), 28–31.

the occasion of emphasizing the new mode of reckoning the day, by declaring, through solemn ceremonies at the table, that Friday night, now belonging to the following day, was part of the Sabbath; and Saturday night, belonging to the following day, Sunday, was no longer part of the Sabbath. This involved some changes in the arrangement of those two meals by introducing these new ceremonies and fitting them in, or adjusting them to, the older habits.

Now, changes in old habits or established customs are not so easily made. It is in the nature of human beings to cling to accustomed ways. And, in their inertia, people yield but slowly and reluctantly to the need of new customs or of changes in old ones if, indeed, they do not, actively or passively, altogether resist their introduction. Even those persons who recognize the need of changes, and even the authorities who advocate new practices and seek to introduce new ceremonies, are very often anxious to retain along with the new practices as much as possible of the older forms. Of course, not all of the older forms can be retained, as not all are compatible with the principles of the advocated changes and newly introduced practices. It then becomes a question of individual judgment or personal preference as to which part of the old is more valuable and should be retained and which should be abandoned. Some people prefer the one feature of the older custom which they claim should be retained even in the new system of practices; others again, emphasize the importance of another feature or principle which they insist should be retained even under the changed conditions. But all of them seek, as much as possible, to minimize the break with the past, and to introduce the new practices without upsetting the older forms and the established order too much. This was also the case when it was necessary to adjust the changed status of Friday evening and Saturday night to the older customs and to combine the new ceremonies necessitated by that new status with the older forms.

In the case of the Friday evening observances, this adjustment of older habits to the new order was not so difficult. Once the innovation of considering Friday night as part of the Sabbath was accepted — and for this there was a good precedent in the law about the Day of Atonement,[13] which was also called a Sabbath — there was no difficulty in arranging the customs or ceremonies at the meal of that evening to suit its new character as a Sabbath evening. All that was necessary was to make the meal a little more festive and to connect with it the Kiddush service, signifying the beginning of the holy day and consecrating it.[14] The fact that the lights had been kindled before sunset or before the starting of the meal did not in any way affect the order and arrangement of the meal.[15] This was left as it had previously been, except that it was considered a Sabbath meal. And instead of the *mugmar* which now could not be provided, since no fire could be used, the substitute for it, the plants, were provided as for the meals on the Sabbath-day.[16]

---

[13] The law in Lev. 23.32 about the Day of Atonement, a "Sabbath of solemn rest" שבת שבתון, which reads, "From even unto even shall ye keep your Sabbath," was simply taken to apply to all Sabbaths, not only to the Day of Atonement. To be forbidden to work on Friday evening was not a hardship. And this restriction was probably not much noticed by the people, as night work was not common in those ancient times. The only inconvenience to the people resulting from this innovation was the impossibility of making fire or producing light on that evening. This inconvenience, however, was soon remedied. For it was declared that only the labor of producing fire and light was forbidden but, if prepared before the evening, fire and light could be kept in the house. So, all in all, as regards Friday evening, the innovation did not cause an unpleasant break with the former habits of the people and they could well, even by mere inertia, accept the new status given to Friday evening. They probably welcomed the additional joy and the solemnity provided for it by the ceremony of the Kiddush.

[14] There was as yet no other act or rite announcing the arrival of the Sabbath. The תפלת ערבית had not yet been introduced; at any rate, it had not yet been generally accepted. Comp. I. Elbogen, "Eingang und Ausgang des Sabbats" in *Festschrift zu Israel Lewy's 70tem Geburtstag* (Breslau 1911) p. 179 ff.

[15] The הדלקת נר שבת was originally not a positive obligatory ceremony. It was just a permission to have lights on Friday evening, if kindled before dark. It was accordingly merely a preparatory act, performed before the advent of the Sabbath but not one greeting or welcoming the Sabbath. It was only some time later that it came to be regarded as a duty מצוה or even an obligation חובה. Cf. *supra*, note 13.

[16] They could not well prepare the regular *mugmar* before dark, as the aroma might soon dissipate and not last till the end of the meal when they wanted it most. *Supra*, note 7.

Yet no regulation about this is found, nor is it especially mentioned that or when, in the order of the Kiddush service or the meal, the benediction over these plants, the substitute for the *mugmar*, should be recited. It was taken for granted that like the *mugmar* itself, the substitute for it, the plants, properly belonged at the end of the meal and the benediction over them was to be recited following the recitation of the Grace after the meal. Thus, when the arrangement of the Friday evening meal is discussed, only the new feature or the ceremony added to it after and because it became a Sabbath meal, i. e., the Kiddush service, was considered. This was a new ceremony, and differences of opinion as to which part of it should come first could be entertained. The Shammaites and Hillelites, accordingly, merely discussed the order of the benedictions recited in the Kiddush service, at the Friday evening meal, i. e., whether the benediction over the wine should precede the one declaring the consecration of the day or vice versa (Ber. 8.1). But no mention is made of the benediction over the plants, the substitute for the *mugmar*, which followed the meal. Evidently the feature of having plants instead of the *mugmar* at the Friday evening meal had, as yet, no special significance which might have caused the teachers to consider the question of assigning the benediction over them any special place. Hence there was no need of even mentioning it.

It was different in the case of Saturday night which now, under the new system, was no longer part of the Sabbath. Here the adjustment of the older practice to the new status was more difficult. The meal on that evening, even though it may have been partaken of or, at any rate, finished after dark, was still considered, as it had always been in the past, one of the Sabbath meals. In fact, it was the second meal or the evening meal of the Sabbath-*day*[17] which, however, because the people were free from work, may have begun a little earlier in the afternoon.[18] This meal extended through the twilight until nightfall, when it was followed by the Habdalah rite which declared that the

---

[17] See Elbogen *op. cit.*, p. 183.

[18] See Yer. Ber. 8.1 (11d) היה יושב ואוכל בשבת וחשכה מוצאי שבת, and cf. the commentaries to the Mishnah, Ber. 8.5.

Sabbath was over and that the week day in which work may be done was beginning.[19] A concrete demonstration of this distinction was the lighting of the light, an act which could not be performed during the Sabbath. These were the new features introduced in connection with that meal. But the meal in itself still retained the character of a Sabbath meal. Hence, no *mugmar* was used at this meal but plants were substituted as was done at the other Sabbath meals. The question then arose how the new features, i. e., lighting the light and reciting the Habdalah, should be combined with the older established practices of saying Grace after the meal and serving the substitute for the *mugmar*. All agreed that the meal, being the second meal of the Sabbath *day*, had to be finished and Grace recited after it, before the other ceremonies marking the going out of the Sabbath could be started. They also agreed that the recitation of the Habdalah, declaring that the Sabbath was over, had to be the last feature.[20] Differences arose only in regard to the arrangement of the other ceremonies. In keeping with the tendency, described above, of seeking as far as possible not to disturb the established order of older practices by the addition of new ones, there were three lines of arrangements that could be advocated,

[19] In the course of time the connection between the Habdalah ceremony and the last meal of the Sabbath became severed. This last meal of the Sabbath had to be finished before the evening service תפלת ערבית was recited, while the Habdalah ceremony took place after it. This caused great difficulty to some of the commentators who tried to explain talmudic passages, reflecting the older practice, in harmony with the later practice as they knew it. See Tosafot to *Pes.* 102b s. v. מניחו לאחר המזון and 105a s. v. והני מילי. In gaonic times, the distance separating the Habdalah and the last meal of the Sabbath was still further extended, as the time for the latter was set before the afternoon prayer תפלת המנחה. Some Gaonim cite a custom, which they characterize as מנהג אבותינו תורה היא, not to have any meal on the Sabbath between the מנחה prayer and the ערבית prayer. See *Šibbole Ha-leḳeṭ* 127 (p. 50) and cf. Tosafot to Pes. 105a s. v. והני מילי. More of this in the discussion of the development of the custom of having three meals on the Sabbath, referred to *supra*, note 11. Cf. also Elbogen *op. cit.*, pp. 183–184.

[20] Ber. 52a. א"ר יהודה לא נחלקו ב"ש וב"ה על המזון שבתחלה ועל הבדלה שהיא בסוף. Of course המזון here means ברכת המזון, the grace after the meal. In Yer. Ber. 8.1 (12a), the saying of R. Judah reads: לא נחלקו ב"ש וב"ה על ברכת המזון שהיא בתחלה ולא על הבדלה שהיא בסוף: *Infra*, note 24.

and actually were followed, by different groups of people. As already pointed out, all agreed that the new ceremony, i. e., the recitation of the Habdalah benediction should be at the very last, when the Sabbath was actually over. They also agreed that the Habdalah, like the Kiddush, should be recited over a cup of wine. In fact, as R. Johanan puts it, its very origin was in connection with a cup, שעיקרה בכוס, i. e., from the very start it was ordained that the Habdalah declaration be made over a cup of wine.[21] But as to the arrangement of the other acts,

---

[21] There can be no doubt that the practice of reciting the Habdalah over a cup of wine was the original practice and older than the one of mentioning it in the prayer. For it was even older than the whole institution of the evening prayer תפלת ערבית. The very statement אנשי כנסת הגדולה תקנו להם לישראל ברכות ותפלות קדושות והבדלות (Ber. 33a) implies that the recitation of the Habdalah was something separate from and independent of, not merely embodied in, the prayers. But the Palestinian Talmud expressly tells us that this was so. To the question, how could the teachers in the Mishna (Ber. 5.2) disagree about the place of the Habdalah in the Saturday evening prayer if there had been an older traditional practice דבר שהוא נוהג ובא חכמים חולקין עליו?, R. Johanan gives the answer: על ידי שעיקרה בכוס שכחוה בתפלה. Because originally they recited it over a cup of wine, the teachers did not remember — more correctly, did not know — which place it should be assigned in the prayer. And the Gemara, there, adds expressly that this statement of R. Johanan declares that the original institution of the Habdalah was to recite it over a cup מילתיה אמרה שעיקרה בכוס (Yer. Ber. 5.2 (9b)). In the Babylonian Talmud (Ber. 33a), the answer of R. Johanan is reported in a different form which does not make very good sense. There it reads as follows: בתחלה קבעוה בתפלה העשירו קבעוה על הכוס חזרו והענו קבעוה בתפלה והם אמרו המבדיל בתפלה צריך שיבדיל על הכוס. "At first, presumably because people could not afford wine, the teachers instituted it to be recited in the prayer. When the people became rich and could afford wine, they instituted its recitation over a cup of wine. But when they again became poor, they instituted its recitation in the prayer. However, at the same time, they declared that even if one had recited it in the prayer, he must recite it again over a cup of wine." One cannot see how the poor people who could not afford wine were helped by the institution that it should be recited in the prayer if, at the same time, it was insisted that, even after having recited it in the prayer, one must still recite it over a cup of wine. It seems that the Babylonians sought to harmonise the report about the original institution of reciting it over the cup with their later practice — after the תפלת ערבית had been accepted as obligatory — of reciting it in the prayer and repeating its recitation over a cup of wine. It should be noticed that there is no discussion of the question whether, after having recited the sanctification of the day, the Kiddush, in the prayer, one should recite it again

marking the going out of the Sabbath, and in what order the benedictions over these acts were to be recited, there were differences of opinion. Some authorities argued that the older order should not be disturbed at all: that the Sabbath meal, begun late in the afternoon, be completely finished, and Grace after it be recited over a cup of wine and then followed by the *mugmar* substitute, aromatic herbs or some fragrant plants, as had always been and still was the order at the other Sabbath meals. And only after all this was finished, there should follow the new features, marking the end of the Sabbath, i. e., lighting the lights which in a concrete manner marks the end of the Sabbath. and the recitation of the Habdalah which declares the distinc-

over the cup of wine, as there is in the case of the Habdalah recitation (Ber. 33a; Pes. 107a). For even after the תפלת ערבית had been introduced and considered obligatory and the sanctification of the day קדושת היום had been inserted in it, it did not affect the older custom of reciting the Kiddush over the wine, as there was no conflict between the two. At most it was a repetition and, after all, one might repeatedly mention the holiness of the day as long as the day lasts. It was different in the case of the Habdalah which speaks of the separation between the holy and the profane, implying that the Sabbath is just over and that the week day has begun. Such a declaration should be recited at the moment of the separation or at the dividing moment between the holy and the profane. It therefore seemed incongruous or contradictory to declare this separation between the holy and the profane over the cup of wine, at a time when it was already profane time, as it had previously, by the recitation of the prayer service, been declared that weekday time had begun. Hence the question arose whether המבדיל בתפלה צריך שיבדיל על הכוס. To obviate this difficulty or to remove this incongruity, it was suggested that the distinction, not the separation, of the holy from the profane etc. is emphasized in the Habdalah and, of course, the distinction is between the whole Sabbath day and all the week days. And of this distinction — not of the one between light and darkness — one can speak even on Thursday (cf. Yer. Ber. 5.2 (9c)) אם לא הבדיל במוצאי שבת מבדיל אפילו בחמישי הדא דאת אמר במבדיל בין קדש לחול אבל בורא מאורי האש אומרה מיד. And just as one can mention the holiness of the Sabbath throughout all the Sabbath day, so one can mention the distinction between the holy and the profane all week, mentioning that the weekdays are different from the Sabbath מי שלא הבדיל במוצאי שבת מבדיל והולך כל השבת (=שבוע) כולו. מי שלא קידש בערב שבת מקדש והולך כל היום כולו (Pes. 105a). According to this conception, the repetition of the Habdalah over the cup after it had been recited in the prayer is not more incongruous than the recitation of the sanctification of the day over the cup of wine after it had been recited in the prayer. Both are merely harmless repetitions.

tion between the Sabbath day and the six work days of the week
This order was advocated by the school of Hillel, according to
the report of R. Judah b. Ilai, and was later followed in practice
by the people.[22] This order caused little or no disturbance whatever in the older habits of the people. It merely introduced at
the end of their older practices two new features which were
deemed important to emphasize the change in the status of the
night following the Sabbath *day*, signifying that it was no
longer part of the Sabbath. Other people represented, according
to the report in our Mishna, by both the Shammaites and the
Hillelites, seem to have considered it of great importance that
the first ceremony or feature of ushering out the Sabbath should
be the lighting of the light with the benediction recited over it,
which in a concrete manner marks the end of the Sabbath,
since no fire or light could be kindled on the Sabbath day.
Accordingly, they advocated that, as soon as it gets dark, even
before finishing the late afternoon meal, the light should be
kindled and the benediction over it recited.[23] But while the

[22] נהגו העם כבית הלל, אליבא דרבי יהודה (Ber. 52a and Pes. 103a). It should be
noticed that it was a popular decision. For the phrase "the people practice,"
נהגו העם, means that the teachers merely do not object to the people's doing
so but, if consulted by the people, they do not tell them to do so נהגו אורויי לא
מורינן ואי עביד עביד ולא מהדרי ליה (Ta'an. 26b). This popular decision is still the
practice to this day, except that now the Habdalah is completely separated
from the meal and *only* the cup of wine, formerly used for the recitation of
the grace after meal, is left.

[23] The reason why they insisted that the light and the benediction over
it should come immediately as soon as it gets dark, we can only guess. It
probably was to emphasize the idea that, with nightfall, the Sabbath is over
and light could and should be produced. To allow them to continue to sit in
darkness or even to finish their meal in darkness might have lent support to
the opinion of some heretics who maintained that the Sabbath extended
through the following night. We know of such heretics in later times, see
מסעות ר' בנימין ed. Grünhut part I (Frankfort a.M. 1904) p. 23; cf. also S. A.
Posnanski in his introduction to Eliezer of Beaugency's *Commentary to Ezekiel
and the Twelve* (Warsaw 1913) p. 43. But such opinions must have been held
by some people even in earlier talmudic times, since such a position was
merely the logical adherence to the older system of reckoning the day from
morning to morning. The idea that Saturday night was still part of the Sabbath was not completely eradicated from the mind of the people. See Yer.
Pes. 5.1 (30cd) about the persistent practice of the women to refrain from

Shammaites and Hillelites agreed, according to our Mishna, that the light with the benediction over it should be the first in the group of ceremonies performed on Saturday night, they differed in their opinions as to the order in which the other ceremonies should follow it. The conservative Shammaites, wishing to retain as much as possible of the old order of things, seem to have argued that if, for some good reason, the light and the benediction over it had to be put first, even if the meal had to be interrupted thereby, there was no reason why the older order of established practice should be more upset. Hence they argued that, after the light had been kindled, the meal be finished or, if at the kindling of the light it had already been finished, Grace after it over a cup of wine be recited, then there should follow the benediction over the aromatic herbs, בשמים, the *mugmar*-substitute; this was in keeping with the older established practice that the *mugmar* — or the substitute for it — was to come after the meal had been finished and Grace recited (Ber. 6.6). And after the *mugmar*-substitute, there should, in their opinion, follow the recitation of the Habdalah benediction. The order according to the Shammaites, therefore, was: נר מזון בשמים הבדלה (Ber. 8.5). The Hillelites, however, according to our Mishna, advocated a change in the usual order. They argued that, on Saturday night, the benediction over the aromatic herbs should not follow the Grace after the meal as the *mugmar*, for which they were a substitute, always did but that it should come before the Grace, following immediately the benediction over the light. Their order is: נר בשמים מזון הבדלה[24] (*ibid. l. c.*).

In this discussion of the Shammaites and the Hillelites in our

doing any work on Saturday night, which the teachers declared not to be a good custom לאו מנהגא. But, in spite of the objections of the teachers, this practice has persisted among pious Jewish women to this day. In the Middle Ages, pious men would imitate the women in this. See תש״ב״ץ 88 (Warsaw 1875) in הנהות where it says נהגו העולם שלא לעשות מלאכה כל מוצאי שבת. Though נהגו העולם may simply mean נהגו הנשים as given in Abudarham (Lemberg 1857) p. 65. See also לקט יושר ed. Freiman (Berlin 1903) p. 58. Cf. also שערי תשובה to *Šulḥan 'Aruk, 'Oraḥ Ḥayyim*, 300, quoting the disciples of Luria.

[24] Of course מזון means ברכת המזון, the grace after the meal. See especially Alfasi to Ber. *ad loc.* (Wilna ed. 1907) 39a: דהא מזון דקתני במתניתין ברכת המזון היא and cf. *supra*, note 20.

Mishna about the arrangement or the order of the ceremonies at the going out of the Sabbath, there is implicitly attached to the use of aromatic herbs some significance greater than a substitute for the *mugmar*, a merely voluntary act of enjoyment, would justify. It is implied that this act is required for a purpose of its own and is not merely a substitute for the *mugmar*. In fact, since it comes after the light had been kindled, that is, after the Sabbath was practically over and fire could already be made, it would seem rather incongruous to use a substitute for the *mugmar* when the real thing could be prepared, unless it be assumed that there was some special reason for using this substitute for a purpose of its own.[25] Especially is this idea suggested in the arrangement of the Hillelites. For this arrangement emphasizes the independent significance of the ceremony of using these aromatic herbs, in that it removed it from the place which the *mugmar* regularly occupied in relation to the meal and thus changed its character from a mere substitute for the *mugmar*, which customarily came after the recitation of Grace after the meal, to a separate and independent feature, seemingly of some importance, and in a class with the ceremony of kindling the light to which it is put in close proximity. Thus a custom, or mere habit, the original purpose of which was merely to afford some additional enjoyment and enhance the pleasures of the table, was imperceptibly changed and transformed into an independent religious ceremony. How this change was effected we cannot ascertain with accuracy. We can only guess at the process that led to the emergence of this new religious ceremony. And the following suggests itself as most likely to have taken place in the popular mind. There seem to have been current among the people certain superstititious beliefs or mythological notions

[25] Why did they not prepare the real *mugmar* instead of בשמים, since the light had already been kindled and fire could be made? It may be because the *mugmar* substitute, the plants, were brought in during or even before dark, when it was still Sabbath. Probably they used the same plants which had been used at the forenoon meal. Most likely, however, some people assigned to the use of the plants on Saturday night a secondary purpose which the real *mugmar* could not serve; hence they preferred the use of the substitute, i. e., the plants, to the real *mugmar*.

in connection with some of the plants used as substitutes for the *mugmar*, ascribing to them inherent mystic powers and a capability for peculiar functions. This, at any rate, was the case with the myrtle which must have been prominently, if not preponderantly used as a *mugmar*-substitute. And, judging from some manifestations in the later developments of the ceremony to be considered below, it seems plausible to assume that, even while used merely as a substitute for the *mugmar* the myrtle had, in the popular mind at least, a secondary purpose based on or resulting from the mystic powers believed to be inherent in it. And some people, more mystic or more superstitious, attached greater importance to this secondary purpose than to its primary purpose of serving as a substitute for the *mugmar*. This secondary significance of the use of the myrtle may have caused the people to retain it as a substitute for the *mugmar* on Saturday night even after dark, though the real *mugmar* could already be prepared. For, this secondary function, based upon the mystic notion connected with the myrtle, gave the use of it a value of its own, not dependent on its suitability as a *mugmar* substitute.

At any rate, it finally became an established religious ceremony, even recognized by all of the teachers, to use in connection with the Habdalah rite on Saturday night aromatic herbs, especially the myrtle,[26] for a function and a purpose of its own,

---

[26] In one passage of the Palestinian Talmud, Yer. Ber. 5.2 (9c) quoted by Rabiah to Pes. ed. Aptowitzer II, (Jerusalem 1935), 141, it is said הדס של הבדלה ניטל כדרך גדילתו. This sentence was omitted in our texts, perhaps merely, by the fault of the copyist. (See Aptowitzer note 18.) This is the only instance where the Talmud speaks explicitly of the myrtle in connection with the Habdalah ceremony. Otherwise the Talmud speaks only of aromatic herbs, בשמים, in connection with the Habdalah, without specifying that it was the myrtle. Perhaps this was done consciously in order thus to ignore or oppose the superstitions connected with the use of the myrtle. But there can be no doubt that, when used with reference to the Habdalah ceremony, בשמים means primarily the myrtle. This is evident from the fact that the use of the myrtle persisted throughout the ages; and though some authorities objected to it, it was nevertheless considered an established religious custom as a מנהג אבותינו תורה. Thus in *Sefer Ḥasidim*, ed. Wistenetzki 553 (Frankfort a.M. 1924) p. 154, it is declared that the myrtle is absolutely necessary for the Habdalah ceremony, and it is hinted that the purpose of its use is something

besides the one of merely affording the enjoyment of the fragrance. What this special purpose of the ceremony really was,

besides the enjoyment of its fragrance. For it says that even if the myrtle is dry and without any scent, so that it is necessary to use other aromatics or smelling spices for the enjoyment of the smell, the myrtle should nevertheless be used in combination with those other spices. The passage in the original reads as follows: יעלה הדס והיה לה' לשם לאות עולם לא יכרת (ישעיה נ"ה י"ג) שמרו משפט ועשו צדקה (שם נ"ו א') שומר שבת מחללו (שם שם ב') ושמרו את שבתותי (שם שם ד') סמכם לומר לך ששבת צריך להדס כל שומר שבת מחללו מחול צריך הדס כשטבדיל ואם יש לו הדס שהוא יבש ואינו מריח יעטפנו דברים שמריח מהם ועליהם יברך ברכתם. See also Isserles in Š. 'Ar. 'O.Ḥ. 297, 4. I should add that the justification of the use of the myrtle on the basis of the interpretation of the verses in Isaiah, which is also quoted in Ẓedah la-Derek and in Ṭur 'O.Ḥ. 297, seems to have been taken from an old Midrash lost to us.

Likewise in תיקוני הזהר, while it is admitted that some people may use, for the Habdalah, other aromatic herbs, it is emphasized that the mystically inclined prefer the myrtle and for reasons other than its fragrance. It says: ואנן דעבדינן בהדס בגין דאית ביה תלת עלין דאיתקריא תלת הדסים רמיזין לתלת אבהן (ספר תיקוני הזהר, תיקונא שתיתאה (Wilna 1867) p. 329 (=קס"ה). Cf. also Zohar Bereshit 17b. ועל דא הדס במוצאי and Šemot 20a: וישראל עבדי עובדא בהדס וביין ואמרי הבדלה שבת. From the question of R. Judah b. Kolonymos addressed to R. Ephraim: למה מברכים על הדס יותר מבשמים אחרים, quoted in 'Or Zaru'a II, 92 (Zitomir 1862) p. 48, also תשב"ץ 86 (Warsaw 1875) p. 14, it also appears that myrtle was used preponderantly, if not exclusively. R. Ephraim, though, objects to the preference for myrtle and declares that he used a little glass container in which he kept many kinds of spices. But, the majority of the people seemingly still preferred the myrtle. Thus R. Menahem Ibn Zaraḥ (died 1385) in his צידה לדרך (Warsaw 1880) p. פח =175 says: ורנילין רוב ישראל לברך על עצי הדס זכר לדבר כל שומר שבת מחללו וכתוב אחריו תחת הסרפד יעלה הדס. In Ṭur 'O.Ḥ. 297 it is also stated that the established custom is to use the myrtle, and two reasons are given for this preference. The one is the same as given in Sefer Ḥasidim based upon the interpretation of the verses in Isaiah. The other is because the myrtle was used also in another religious ceremony, i. e., in connection with the lulab and etrog on Sukkoth. This would indicate that they would use throughout the year the same myrtle sprigs which had been used on Sukkoth. Cf. Epstein, in קיצור שני לוחות הברית (Lemberg 1863), p. 66. This, at least, suggests that the function of the myrtle in both of these ceremonies is the same (infra, note 58). And though mentioning that R. Ephraim objected to the use of the myrtle and preferred other spices kept in a little glass container, the Ṭur concludes that the use of the myrtle is an established custom followed in all communities: ומיהו נהגו בכל המקומות לברך על ההדס ומנהג אבותינו תורה. See also Joseph Caro in his commentary בית יוסף ad loc. who adds the significant remark that the Cabbalists say that there is a mystic reason for using the myrtle עליו לברך בהדס סוד שיש אומרים הקבלה ובעלי. This mystic reason or what function the popular mind assigned to it, we may discover in our following investigation, but nowhere in rabbinic literature is it clearly indicated. There must have been some hesitancy, to say the least, on the part of the rabbinic authorities to acknowledge the mystic notions on which this special function was based. And when accepting the ceremony and admitting that it has a function of its own, the teachers preferred to interpret it in what to them seemed a more rational manner, and to give it a meaning compatible with their own more advanced thinking. However, our investigation will show that the meaning and purpose of the ceremony as explained by the rabbinic authorities was not the original meaning of the ceremony or, at any rate, not its only meaning. But these very explanations of the post-talmudic teachers,[27] though mere guesses or at best rationalizations, helped the ceremony to maintain itself throughout the generations and, with some slight modifications, to persist to the present day.

will be revealed to us in the course of our discussion in this essay. Isaac Luria, as one of the mystics, also insisted upon the use of the myrtle for the Habdalah ceremony, and his emphasis was not on the fragrance of the myrtle but on the number of the sprigs used, namely, *three*. See נגיד ומצוה (Lublin 1881) p. 51. So much was the use of the myrtle identified with the Habdalah ceremony that, up to this day, the spice box used at the ceremony, although it contains other spices and not myrtle, is still designated by the name *Hadas*, הדס, the Hebrew for myrtle because, in former times, only or preferably myrtle alone was used. *Infra*, note 99 end.

[27] While the Talmud seeks to explain why a blessing over the light is recited at the Habdalah ceremony (Pes. 54a), no explanation whatever is given in the Talmud why a benediction over aromatic herbs is recited at that ceremony. Evidently no explanation was necessary. Since, as we have seen, this ceremony emerged out of the every-day practice of serving *mugmar*, over which people also recited a benediction, there was no need of a special reason why the benediction should be recited over the *mugmar* substitute served on Saturday night. And, although some mystically inclined people may have, already in talmudic times, attached some special significance or assigned a secondary purpose to this ceremony and although the popular mind connected with it some superstitious notions, the talmudic authorities ignored them and preferred to regard the ceremony as what it really or originally was, merely a substitute for the *mugmar* which required no special explanation. After the practice had, for a long time, been accepted and come to be regarded as an established feature of the Habdalah ceremony, separate from

The change in the character of the custom of using aromatic herbs or the myrtle as a substitute for the *mugmar* at the Saturday evening meal had its effect upon the similar custom or

and independent of the last meal of the Sabbath, its original nature as a substitute for the *mugmar* was almost forgotten. It was only then that the post-talmudic rabbinic authorities could begin to ask questions about its purpose and, in answer to such questions, seek to offer some reason why it was introduced. One explanation given by R. Jacob b. Yakar, one of the teachers of Rashi, was that, at the end of the Sabbath, the fire in Hell, which was put out during the Sabbath, is started again, issuing a stench. To neutralize this bad odor, the smelling of herbs was introduced for that particular moment of the going out of the Sabbath. This is quoted in *Vitry* p. 117 and p. 328 as follows: רבינו שלמה בר' יצחק אומר בשם ר' יעקב בר' יקר דטעם בשמים במוצאי שבתות דכל יום השבת שבת אור של גיהנם ולא הסריח כלום ולאלתר כשיוצא שבת חוזר ושורף רע ומסריח לכך מריח בבשמים להפיג ריח רע. See also סדור רש"י 532 (Berlin 1920) p. 266; and *Sefer Ha-Pardes* ed. Ehrenreich (Budapest 1924) p. 29; and *Šibbole Ha-leket* 130 (Wilna 1886) p. 104. This explanation, which may be a reflection of some mystic notion about the connection of this ceremony with the return of the wicked ghosts to Hell on Saturday night (see *Tanḥuma, Ki Tissa* 33), was not very satisfactory even to the rabbinic authorities. Cf. *'Or Zaru'a* II, 92 (Zitomir 1862) p. 48, who dismisses it with the remark: ואין זה אלא דוגמא להראות כבודו של שבת. Probably Tosafot to Pes. 102b s. v. רב had this explanation in mind when they said that there were some wrong explanations, ויש טעמים לא נכונים.

Another explanation quoted by the disciples of Rashi connects the ceremony with the belief (*infra*, note 56) that an additional soul comes to every Israelite on Friday evening and leaves him again on Saturday night. At the loss of this additional soul, the Israelite is sad and depressed on Saturday night and the fragrance of the aromatic herbs is to refresh him and to help him get over his grief. Cf. also Zohar *Vayakhel* (Lublin 1872) p. 416 and *Ẓaw* p. 70. This explanation, which somehow connects the fragrant plants with the additional soul — an idea assumed by the mystics, as we shall see below (note 69), was in itself not so very satisfactory to the rationalistic rabbinic authorities. Hence, they rationalize both about the additional soul and about the refreshing and encouraging effect of the fragrant plants, making the latter merely a part of the strengthening effect exerted by the prayers recited on the occasion. I am quoting here the rabbinic statements, because we can read between their lines that they hesitate to express boldly the crude notion that an additional soul, as an actual spiritual entity, enters the person with the entrance of the Sabbath and departs from him on Saturday night. Thus Vitry p. 117 says שניטלה נשמה יתירה באדם ותהנה הנותרת מן הבשמים ותחזק בצירוף הברכות ותתחזק. The same words are also used in סדור רש"י 542 (p. 262). Even more apparent in its effort at rationalization is the rather verbose state-practice of using the same substitute for the *mugmar* at the Friday evening meal. The thought must have suggested itself, to some people at least, that just as on Saturday night the use of the fragrant plants, especially the myrtle, was not merely a table custom, substituting for the *mugmar*, but rather an important feature of the Habdalah rite and a separate ceremony serving some purpose of its own and suggesting some religious ideas, so also the use of these plants on Friday evening should not be regarded simply as a substitute for the *mugmar*, but as a separate ceremony of some religious significance, in a class with and like the other ceremonies of the evening, the Kiddush and the Sabbath lights.

Accordingly, in imitation of the transformation of the Saturday evening practice, the practice of having fragrant plants on Friday evening was also transformed, and in the minds of some people, at least, was invested with a purpose of its own and gradually emerged as a religious ceremony. This new character, however, was not given to the older practice as a whole, i. e., to the use of all kinds of fragrant plants or aromatic herbs which may have occasionally been used as a substitute for the *mugmar*. It was limited to one part of the older practice, that is, to the use of one special plant, the myrtle, which, as already indicated, figured prominently in the older practice, and which, no doubt, was believed to possess some special quality, and to the use of which the popular mind could assign some special religious or mystic significance.

ment in *Sefer Ha-Pardes* (ed. Ehrenreich) p. 26 which reads as follows: מה טעם
אנו מברכין על הבשמים בברכת ההבדלה מפני שבשבת ניתנה נשמה יתירה באדם והוא שמח
מתוך שאכל נתענג ונח ושקט וכשהיה מבדיל בטלו כל אלו ממנו וניטלה ממנו נשמה יתירה והנה
הוא במחשבה מעתה ובטורח ובעסק ונפשו אינה שמחה כאשר בתחלה ותיקנו הראשונים בשעת
המבדיל להריח בבשמים ותהנה הנותרת ותשמח ותריח בריח טוב ובכך הוא מפיג צערו ולא
יתעצב אל לבו בזוכרו ששת ימי המעשה. וכל זה תיקנו כדי שיהא זכרון שבת בלבו ויהא שמח
אף בצאתו. See also R. Solomon b. Adret, quoted in '*En Jacob* to Ta'an. 27b, (ed. Wilna 1883) pp. 75–76. R. Menahem Ibn Zarah in his צידה לדרך p. 174 merely says: בשמים להשיב ולנחם הנפש שכואבת ומתעצבת בצאת השבת, without in any way connecting the ceremony with the נשמה יתירה. All these explanations and rationalizations are disproved or refuted by the fact that the same ceremony was also observed on Friday evening, the very moment when the additional soul was supposed to come to the Israelite. *Infra*, note 62 and note 77.

Thus, out of the general practice of having fragrant plants at the table on Friday evening there emerged a special religious ceremony performed on Friday evening with twigs of myrtle. This new ceremony seems to have been limited to Palestine and, even there, was observed only among mystic groups or by people with mystic inclinations. It was assigned a peculiar function and associated with some mystic ideas about the Sabbath although, as is usually the case when ceremonies or customs are reinterpreted and given new meanings, the original simple meaning of the practice was not entirely forgotten and the feature of enjoying the fragrance of the myrtle was not abandoned.[28] It was merely pushed into the background or, as we shall see, combined with the newer mystic interpretation of the significance of the ceremony.

The only allusion in the Talmud to such a ceremony is found in Sab. 33b in the story about R. Simeon b. Yoḥai and his son R. Eleazar, who are said to have spent thirteen years in a life of contemplative study and prayer in a cave while hiding from the threatened persecution by the Roman government. When they finally came out of the cave, they were, to put it mildly, upset and, especially Eleazar, provoked when they noticed the people busying themselves with the things of this world rather than with the things eternal. Then, late on a Friday afternoon, so the Talmud reports, they encountered a "certain old man" who was running home carrying two bunches of myrtle. They asked the old man, "What are these for?" and he replied, "To honor the Sabbath." They said to him, "Then one should be enough," to which the old man replied: "One is to correspond to the commandment 'Remember' (Ex. 20.8) and the other is to correspond to the commandment 'Observe' (Deut. 5.12)." Then R. Simeon said to his son, "How precious are the commandments to Israel!" and their minds were set at ease.[29] It is evident from this story that, even though some people may have used the myrtle, among other fragrant plants,

---

[28] *Infra*, note 62.

[29] בהדי פניא דמעלי שבתא חזו ההוא סבא דהוה נקיט תרי מדאני אסא ורהיט בין השמשות אמרו ליה הני למה לך אמר להו לכבוד שבת ותיסגי לך בחד חד כנגד זכור וחד כנגד שמור א"ל לבריה חזי כמה חביבין מצות על ישראל יתיב דעתייהו (Sab. 33b).

as a substitute for the *mugmar* on the Sabbath, it was not the general custom to have *only* myrtle for such a use, or to have a special ceremony performed with the myrtle on Friday evening. For, in that case, there would have been nothing unusual in the sight of a man carrying home bunches of myrtle on a Friday afternoon. And there certainly would have been no cause for R. Simeon and Rabbi Eleazar to stop such a man and ask him for what purpose the myrtle bunches were intended. Further-more, if this had been a generally observed custom, we would find a reference, or at least a casual allusion, to it somewhere else in the talmudic literature. There is no doubt that these myrtle sprigs were not meant by the old man to be merely for the purpose of enjoying their fragrance, as a substitute for the *mugmar*. These myrtle sprigs must have been intended for a special ceremony having some religious significance, since it elic-ited such a highly appreciative remark on the part of R. Simeon b. Yoḥai. Such a ceremony must have been observed only by some particular people or a certain mystically inclined group to which "that old man" belonged.[30] Hence, the old man carrying these myrtle bunches attracted the attention of R. Simeon b. Yoḥai who, being himself mystically inclined, to say the least, was interested in the purpose for which the old man carried home these myrtle bunches. And being told of its purpose, viz. that it was for a special ceremony, he appreciated it as of great religious value. Of course, we are not told any details of this special ceremony and in what its religious or mystic significance

---

[30] Some authorities are inclined to believe that, wherever ההוא סבא "that old man" is mentioned in the Talmud, the reference is to the prophet Elijah. See Tosafot to Ḥul. 6a, s. v. אשכחיה ההוא סבא. However, as Tosafot themselves there declare, the "old man" in our story could not have been Elijah. See also B. M. Levin, *'Oẓar Ha-Ge'onim*, IX, (Jerusalem 1939), 22. He certainly was not a Samaritan either, as Dobsewitz assumes in regard to many instances where ההוא סבא is mentioned in the Talmud. See A. B. Dobsewitz ספר המצרף (Odessa 1870) pp. 34–57. But this old man seems to have been a member of a special group, particular in observing the commandments. And since his practice was so highly approved of by R. Simeon b. Yoḥai, I rather believe that he belonged to a mystically inclined group. It is perhaps not accidental that R. Samuel b. Isaac, who also performed a certain ceremony with myrtle sprigs, is likewise described as סבא "the old man." Ket. 17a cf. *infra*, note 39.

consisted. All that we are told in this talmudic report is that
the old man said that the myrtle bunches were intended for
the honor of the Sabbath and that he also gave an explanation,
if explanation it may be called, of why he needed two bunches.
But it does not explain how and in what way the myrtle was
especially suitable for honoring the Sabbath and for pointing to
or reminding one of the two forms of the commandment about
the Sabbath. "Remember" and "Observe."

This talmudic report certainly does not give full information
about this ceremony. We may suspect that some information
about this seemingly strange ceremony was consciously with-
held or perhaps suppressed in the Talmud, a suspicion which
will find its justification in the following discussion. For, not
only is the information about this ceremony in this talmudic
report very meagre and rather vague but there is, to my knowledge, nowhere else in the talmudic-midrashic literature any reference or even allusion to such a ceremony. And even in post-
talmudic rabbinic literature, with the exception of the passage in
the Zohar to be considered below, there is no mention of such a
ceremony. And up to the sixteenth century, we do not hear of
it or find the least indication of its existence. Such a persistent
silence on the part of the rabbis of the Talmud and of the
post-talmudic rabbinic authorities throughout so many centuries
could not have been merely accidental, and certainly cannot
be interpreted as approval. It rather suggests hostility to the
ceremony and a tendency to suppress it by ignoring it. There
must have been some objections to this ceremony on the part
of the rabbinic authorities, for which reason they would not even
mention it, far less recommend its practice. We can judge and
understand these objections only after we know what ideas or
superstitious beliefs were associated with the ceremony. This we
can learn from a fuller description of the ceremony as it appears
in the sixteenth century in the mystic circle of Isaac Luria.
For, I believe, we are justified in regarding the ceremony, strongly
recommended and fully described by the Lurianic school, as a
continuation of the ceremony so highly appreciated by R. Simeon
b. Yoḥai. We are also justified in assuming that, with perhaps
slight modifications in some details, Luria performed the cere-

mony in the same manner, and for the same purpose, as it had
been performed by certain mystically inclined people ever since
the time of R. Simeon b. Yoḥai,[31] though we have no record
of it in the talmudic and post-talmudic halakic literature. For
there was a transmission through mystic channels from generation to generation of ideas and practices utterly ignored or even
consciously suppressed in the authoritative rabbinic literature.[32]
And the information about our ceremony could well have passed
through such channels from the time of Simeon b. Yoḥai to the
time of Luria. There may even have been some mystic records
about this ceremony available to Luria. In fact, one such mystic
record, though also incomplete and not very explicit, which
Luria no doubt consulted or followed, has been preserved to us
in the Zohar, Ẓaw (Lublin 1872) pp. 69–70, which reads as
follows: "As they (R. Eleazar and his company) were going
along, they came across a man with three myrtle branches in
his hand. They approached him and asked: 'What are these for?'
He replied: 'For the comfort (or enlargement?) of the wandering
(soul?).'[33] Said R. Eleazar: 'That is a good answer. But why

[31] For a parallel to such a phenomenon, namely a ceremony alluded to
or mentioned in the Talmud which, after being suppressed or passed over in
silence for many centuries, eventually turned up again, see Lauterbach,
"The Ceremony of Breaking a Glass at Weddings," in *HUCA* II, (1925),
especially pp. 361–366.

[32] See Lauterbach, *Tashlik* (Cincinnati 1936) p. 30, note 37. In the case
of our ceremony as well as in the case of the custom of staying up the whole
night preceding the Shabuot festival, the Zohar alone mentions the usages
in question, while the halakic rabbinic literature maintains a complete and
persistent silence. This justifies the assumption that the mystics had their
secret channels through which they transmitted their information from
generation to generation, either unknown to and hidden from or perhaps
unheeded by the official rabbinic authorities.

[33] The phrase לרווחא אובדא can have different meanings: it may mean,
"for the comfort of the languishing soul," referring either to the permanent
soul or to the additional soul to whom the myrtle, as part of her native environment in heaven, brings comfort and refreshment. It may also mean, "for the
enlargement of the languishing soul," referring to the permanent soul to whom
the myrtle, as a vehicle for spirits, brings the additional soul, thus enlarging
her. We shall see below which of these two ideas is expressed in this passage from the Zohar. Possibly both ideas are hinted at, as they are not contradictory to one another.

three?' To this the man replied: 'One for Abraham, one for Isaac, and one for Jacob; and I bind them together and smell them, as it is written (Cant. 1.3): 'Thine ointments have a goodly fragrance; thy name is as ointment poured forth.' Because by this smelling the weak soul is kept up, and by this faithful act it is sustained, and thus blessings are drawn down from above.' Said R. Eleazar: 'Happy is the lot of Israel in this world and in the world to come.' "[34]

This story which, in a way, may be regarded as a parallel to the talmudic story is, nevertheless, in very important points different from the latter. In the first place, it does not explicitly assign the ceremony to Friday evening, as it does not fix the time when or on what day the encounter of R. Eleazar with the man took place. But we may take it for granted that it was on a Friday and that the ceremony discussed by them was a Friday evening ceremony. Secondly, we notice that instead of two bunches of myrtle, supposed to correspond to the two versions of the Sabbath commandment as the Talmud reports, the man used for the ceremony three sprigs of myrtle, each one of which he declares to be for one of the patriarchs. It does not, however, explain in what manner these myrtle sprigs served or represented the patriarchs, whether they were intended as offerings to the spirits of the patriarchs or were a means of welcoming them. Nor does it explain how and why these myrtles functioned as special media for welcoming the patriarchs or why they were considered as suitable representatives of or especially acceptable gifts to their souls. It also says that by the smell of these myrtles or, more correctly, by the act of smelling[35] them, the weak soul

---

[34] The passage in the Zohar, Ẓaw, (Lublin 1872) pp. 69–70, reads as follows: עד דהוו אזלו אשכחו חד גברא דהוה אתי וג' ענפי הדס בידיה. קריבו גביה אמרי ליה למה לך האי אמר לרווחא אובדא. אמר רבי אלעזר שפיר קאמרת. אבל נ' אלין למה. א"ל חד לאברהם חד ליצחק וחד ליעקב וקשירנא להו כחדא וארחנא בהו בנין דכתיב (שיר א) לריח שמניך טובים שמן תורק שמך. בנין דבהאי ריחא אתקיים חולשא דנפשא ובהימנותא דא אתקיימא ואתגנידו ברכאן מעילא ותתא. אמר רבי אלעזר זכאה חולקהון דישראל בעלמא דין ובעלמא דאתי. As to the meaning or significance of the phrase ובהימנותא דא "by this faithful act," see following note.

[35] I. e., the feature of bringing the myrtle near to the nostrils, which resembles the act one performs when smelling. But in this case it was not done in order to smell the myrtle, but for the purpose of bringing the vehicle

is sustained and kept up, gets comfort and enlargement. But it does not tell us how this is accomplished, whether the fragrance of the myrtle as such does it or whether the souls of the patriarchs bring with them something of comfort and enlargement for the weak soul or by their mere company comfort it. Thus we see that both of these stories, in the Talmud and in the Zohar, give us neither the full information about this ceremony nor a clear explanation of it.[36] Both, however, unmistakably emphasize that these myrtles were not merely for the enjoyment of their fragrance. For, although the Zohar still speaks of the act of smelling, it is evident that this act was not just for the mere pleasure of enjoyment, but rather to give strength and comfort or enlargement to the weak soul. The main function of these myrtle sprigs was either to remind one of the two versions of the Sabbath-commandment, or to welcome and greet the patriarchs — in either case a rather mystic function.

We therefore have to look for some more specific information to be able to understand fully the purpose of this ceremony. There must have been, in the popular mind at least, certain qualities or characteristics associated with the myrtle, making it suitable for the achievement of the purpose aimed at by our ceremony. In order to find out these popular notions about the myrtle, its qualities and capabilities, we must first ascertain what functions, if any, were implicitly ascribed to the myrtle in its use in other ceremonies and at other occasions.

The oldest use of myrtle in any ceremony that we can find in talmudic literature is the one for making a crown or wreath for the bridegroom עטרות חתנים. This must have been considered very protective and useful. For even after the decree against

---

carrying the additional soul, with the accompanying spirits of the patriarchs, near to the nostrils, the aperture through which souls or spirits can enter the human body, cf. Gen. 2.7.

[36] Perhaps there is an allusion to our ceremony in the phrase שהשבת צריך להדס "the Sabbath needs the myrtle," in the passage from *Sefer Ḥasidim* quoted *supra*, note 26, which implies that, not only for the Habdalah ceremony at the going out of the Sabbath, but for the whole Sabbath, the myrtle was necessary. *Infra*, note 69.

the crowning or adorning of the bridegroom (Soṭ. 9.14), it was still permitted to adorn him with crowns of myrtle.[37] The purpose of such a decoration must have been, just as in the use of crowns made of salt, to keep the demons away and prevent them from doing any harm to the bridal couple. No doubt they adorned the bride also with such a protective crown.[38] We also

[37] See Tosefta Soṭ. 15.8 (Zuckermandel p. 322) אבל של וורד ושל הדס התירו להן. Also the saying of Rab in Soṭ. 49b: אבל של הדס ושל ורד מותר, though, according to the opinion of Samuel (*ibid. l. c.*), even crowns of myrtle were forbidden.

[38] See Lauterbach, "The Ceremony of Breaking a Glass at Weddings," *op. cit.*, p. 357, especially note 3. Conveying the bride to the home of the bridegroom — out of fear that the demons might try to kidnap her — they would carry her in a round covered vehicle made of myrtle branches (see Ket. 17b and Rashi *ad loc.* s. v. תנורא דאסא and cf. '*Oẓar Ha-Ge'onim* VIII, part 2, p. 15. Cf. also Sab. 110a אסא וגידמי לבי הלולא). In one of the מעשיות (Jellinek, *Bet Ha-Midrasch* V, 153), also in מעיל צדקה by Elijah Cohen (1859) p. 21a, it is told that, before the bridegroom went out to invite the guests to his wedding, his father placed in his hands myrtle leaves. This probably was done to afford him protection from evil spirits that might assail him on his way. To protect a new born baby boy, who, before his circumcision, is especially exposed to danger from demons, it was the custom in Palestine to provide, on the day before the circumcision, myrtle twigs and to keep them overnight and then to recite a benediction over them the next morning when the ceremony of circumcision took place. This custom is reported by R. Hirsch b. Azriel of Wilna in his בית לחם יהודה to *Yore De'ah* 265, (Fuerth 1747) p. 95. He says: ונהגו בארץ ישראל לברך על הבשמים בעת המילה ולוקח ההדס ביום קודם המילה ובליל המילה נהגו לרקד ולשמח. Perhaps an additional reason for securing the myrtle on the day before the circumcision was to provide a resting place for the spirit of a departed ancestor or saint [similar to the practice of providing an extra chair for Elijah כסא של אליהו at the ceremony of circumcision. See *Pirke d. R. Eliezer* 29, (Warsaw 1852) p. 66b and *Zohar Lek Leka* (Lublin 1872) p. 93] who is to come on the day before and to rejoice with the parents and to watch with them over the child, throughout the night preceding the circumcision. Probably the custom, introduced by the Gaonim (see *Ṭur Yore De'ah* 305 and *Kolbo* 94 (Lemberg 1860) p. 60c) of using a myrtle and reciting over it the benediction בורא עצי בשמים at the ceremony of the redemption of the first born פדיון הבן also had the purpose of helping to fight off the evil spirits. For, according to the Zohar (Preface p. 14 פקודא תליסר), the effect of the redemption is also that the evil spirit or the angel of death should have no power over the child, וההוא סטרא בישא שבק ליה ולא אחיד ביה. This custom, however, is no longer observed.

read about R. Judah b. Ilai that at weddings he would take up
a sprig of myrtle and dance with it, waving it before the bride.
And R. Samuel b. Isaac would perform a similar dance before
the bride with *three* sprigs of myrtle.[39] No doubt this use of the
myrtle sprig while dancing before the bride was also for the
purpose of driving away the demons. We thus find that one of
the properties believed to be inherent in the myrtle was the
power to drive away the demons, either by its fragrance, as
incense[40] was believed to do, or in any other way. Since the

[39] Ket. 17a. The passage reads as follows: אמרו עליו על רבי יהודה בר אילעאי
שהיה נוטל בד של הדס ומרקד לפני הכלה ואומר כלה נאה וחסודה רב שמואל בר רב יצחק
מרקד אתלת א'ר זירא קא מכסיף לן סבא כי נח נפשיה איפסיק עמודא דנורא בין דידיה לכולי
עלמא וגמירי דלא איפסיק עמודא דנורא אלא אי לחד בדרא אי לתרי בדרא אמר רבי זירא
אהניי' ליה שוטיתיה לסבא ואמרי לה שטותי' לסבא ואמרי לה שיטתי' לסבא. Cf. Tosafot
ibid., *l. c.* s. v. שיטתיה which quotes the Midrash, Gen. Rab. to the effect that
the pillar of fire came down in the shape of a myrtle. The significant passage
in Gen. Rab. (ch. 59, not 61 as given in *Tosafot*) reads as follows: ונחתה שבשבה
דנור ואיתעבידת כמו שבשבה דהדס ואפסיקת בין ערסא לציבורא. This story about R.
Samuel b. Isaac is also told in Yer. Pe'ah I (15d). However, the word דהדס
is omitted there, and it merely reads: ואיתעבידת כמין שבשא דנור בין ערסא לציבורא.
והוון בריתא אמרין חיוי דדין סבא דקמת ליה בישתיה.... Cf. Bacher, *Die Agada d.
Palästinensischen Amoräer* III. (Strassburg 1899), 36, note 6. Perhaps the
angels were coming down in the shape of myrtle.

[40] About the power of incense to drive away the demons, see Lauterbach,
"A Significant Controversy between the Sadducees and the Pharisees," in
HUCA IV (1927), 196, note 21. It seems, however, that the smoke and not
the aroma of the incense had that power. About the smoke as a means of
driving away demons, see also Dr. C. Snouk Hurgronge, *Mekka* II (Hague
1889), 122 ff., and I. Scheftclowitz, *Alt-Palästinensischer Bauernglaube*
(Hannover 1925) pp. 82–84. The practice of midwives, to hold the baby
over smoke prepared by them from some ingredients, mentioned and condemned by Maimonides in his *More Nebukim* III. ch. 37, no doubt was for
the same purpose. Cf. also Gaster, the *Sefer Assufoth*, in *Report of the Judith
Montefiore College*, Ramsgate (London 1893) pp. 60–61, where it is said that
the smoke drives away the spirit that seeks to hinder the delivery of a child.
As a cure against magic spells and as a means of driving away the evil spirits
from a sick person, smoke prepared from some ingredients is still used among
superstitious East European Jews. See Judah Rosenberg ספר רויאל המלאך
(Pietrkow 1911) p. 48 and 49. A rather unusual practice of using smoke to
conjure up a spirit is mentioned by R. David Pardo in his ספרי דבי רב (Saloniki
1799) p. 245b to Deut. 18, 10–11. Of course R. David Pardo condemns the
practice. *Infra*, note 48.

Sabbath is the bride[41] and Israel the bridegroom,[42] who thus celebrate their wedding on every Friday evening, the suggestion offers itself that the two bunches of myrtle were thus brought to the bride and bridegroom, Sabbath and Israel, for the same purpose, i. e., of keeping away the evil spirits, as it was used for any other bride and bridegroom on their wedding day.[43] This may be suggested in the statement "one corresponding to 'Remember'." For, according to the Midrash,[44] the "Remember" was especially addressed to Israel to impress upon him that he was the bridegroom of the Sabbath. And the statement that the other bunch of myrtle was "corresponding to 'Observe'" (שמור), may suggest that it was to remind one of the protection, שמירה, afforded by the myrtle on Friday evening when, according to the belief of some people, the danger from demons was great.[45]

---

[41] The Sabbath is called the queen מלכה and also the bride כלה. See Sab. 119a and Zohar 'Ekeb p. 544.

[42] See Gen. Rab. XI, 9 תני רשב"י אמרה שבת לפני הקב"ה רבש"ע. לכולן יש בן זוג ולי אין בן זוג א"ל הקב"ה כנסת ישראל היא בן זוגך. וכיון שעמדו ישראל לפני הר סיני אמר להם הקב"ה זכרו הדבר שאמרתי לשבת. כנסת ישראל היא בן זוגך היינו דבור (שמות כ) זכור את יום השבת לקדשו.

[43] Isaac Luria in his song for the Friday evening meal (see סדור זוצר התפלות, Wilna 1923, p. 630), says that "the myrtle sprigs are for the groom and the bride that the weak ones may be strengthened" ומדאני אסא לארוס וארוסה להתקפא חלשין which may refer to Israel and the Sabbath or it may refer to the husband and wife in the smallest family. The phrase "that the weak ones may be strengthened" may allude to the power believed to be inherent in the myrtle of increasing sensuality or strengthening the sexual powers. *Infra*, note 46.

[44] Gen. Rab. *l. c.*

[45] On the question whether the Jew need be afraid of demons on the Sabbath, especially on Friday night, there were different opinions. In talmudic times, there prevailed the belief that, on Friday night, the danger of harm by the demons was very great. A *baraita* in Pes. 112b says that on Friday night Agrat, the daughter of Maḥalat, is abroad with a host of one hundred and eighty thousand destructive agents מלאכי חבלה, each one of them having permission and power to do as much harm as he likes or possibly can. See also the statement *ibid.*, 111b בלילי שבת שרו מזיקין עליה and 112a מאי סכנה רוח רעה; also Sab. 24b בשבת משום סכנה which Rashi *ad loc.*, correctly explains to mean סכנת מזיקין. This belief persisted in rabbinic circles even in post-talmudic times and the statement: דשכיחי מזיקין בלילי שבת טפי מבחול or בשבת דשכיחי מזיקין is repeated in *Seder Rab Amram* (Warsaw 1865) p. 25; *Siddur Rashi* (Buber,

There must, however, have been objections to this use of the myrtle on the part of those people who believed that on the Sabbath the demons could not harm the Jews and, hence, there

---

Berlin 1910) p. 240; *Sefer Ha-Pardes*, ed. Ehrenreich (Budapest 1924) pp. 307–8; *Vitry* p. 81; and others. On the other hand, there arose the idea in gaonic times that, on the Sabbath, there was no danger from demons, as they had no power on that day. This idea is expressed in a responsum by R. Hai Gaon, *Responsa* שערי תשובה No. 80 (Leipzig 1858) p. 8, who quotes, in support of this idea, a midrashic saying which probably originated in some mystic work (see S. Hurwitz in *Vitry l. c.*, note 7). Indeed, the same idea quoted by Hai from a saying of Raba in the name of Zera is repeatedly expressed in the *Zohar*. See Zohar *Vayakhel* (Lublin 1872) p. 409, p. 413, and p. 415. Also Zohar *'Ek b* p. 545 ואין מזיק שליט ביומא דשבתא. See also Ibn Yarḥi in המנהיג (Berlin 1855) p. 24 the statement דכתיב מזמור שיר ליום השבת ליום ששובתין מזיקין בעולם which sounds like a quotation from a midrashic work. As a sort of compromise between these two conflicting beliefs, it was suggested that, even though the demons may rove about on the Sabbath and even though they may have רשות להזיק "the power and the permission to harm people," the Jews need not fear them, being protected by their very observance of the Sabbath (*Vitry l. c.*; *Sefer Ha-Pardes l. c.*; and Zohar *Vayakhel* p. 409). This idea gradually came to be more and more accepted, as it was expressed in the Friday evening liturgy where the closing of the second benediction after the *Šema* reads . . . . הפורס סוכת שלום instead of שומר עמו ישראל לעד (see Zohar *Berešit* 48a and cf. סדור אוצר התפלות p. 'ש = 599). There was, however, still the fear of a special class of demons, a fear resulting from other mystic notions. One of these was that Hell is closed on the Sabbath and that its wicked inmates are given a rest and are free to leave the place for the day (see *Tanḥuma Ki Tissa* כי תשא 33; Zohar *Wa'era* p. 31b, *Terumah* 150b–151a and *Jethro* 88b). According to another mystic belief, some demons are the souls of the departed wicked (Zohar, *Aḥare* p. 70a), a belief which is very ancient and which is found already in Philo and Josephus (see L. Ginzberg, Legends of the Jews vol. V, Philadelphia 1926 p. 109). Now, it was feared that those demons, which are the souls of the wicked, might wish to visit their folks on a Friday evening when released from Hell. For, as the demons in general imitate the angels (*infra*, note 95), so also the demons that are but souls of the wicked might like to imitate the souls of the departed patriarchs and saints. And the latter do visit their folks on holidays or on Friday evening, as the spirit of Judah Ha-Nasi did. (*Infra*, note 58.) But the folks here on earth, while they welcome the visits of the spirits of their saintly relatives, are afraid of and dread the visit of the demons, the spirits of their wicked relatives. Gradually, however, this fear was also allayed, and it was declared that the merit of observing the Sabbath protects the Jew against all kinds of demons, even of those that are souls of the departed wicked. See preface to the *Zohar* p. 14b.

was no need of employing such protective measures as the myrtle could afford.

It is also possible that the use of the myrtle for bridal wreaths had something to do with the belief that the myrtle was considered to be the tree of love and to possess the power to stimulate sensuality, for which reason it "was viewed askant by the pious of the ancient world."[46] Hence, it may be that the same function of the myrtle was aimed at by its use on Friday evening when some people considered it desirable to encourage erotic feelings or sensuality.[47] Of course, just for this reason

---

[46] See Charles M. Skinner, *Myths and Legends of Flowers, Trees, Fruits and Plants* (Philadelphia and London 1911) pp. 190–191. Among the ancient Greeks and Romans, the myrtle was believed sacred to Aphrodite and was regarded as a symbol of or a magic charm for increasing fertility. See Pauly-Wissowa *Real-Encyclopaedie* s. v. Myrtos p. 1182. It was forbidden to bring a myrtle into the sanctuary of the Bona Dea (*ibid.*, s. v. Bona Dea p. 687) probably because it was believed to have the power of increasing sensuality and of strengthening the sexual powers. All of these ideas associated with the myrtle in the ancient world could not have been entirely unknown in Palestine. That they were known and even not objected to among Jews in later times is evident from the description given by Leone Ebreo in his work וכוח על האהבה (Lyck 1871) p. 29b or in the English translation of his work: *The Philosophy of Love* (London 1937) p. 149 "... The myrtle ...." Hence, it may be assumed that at least some people among the ancient Jews cherished these superstitions and associated them with the use of the myrtle at weddings. Of course, many pious but rationalistic people objected to these superstitions and hence did not favor the myrtle in connection with some religious ceremonies.

[47] The idea that on Friday night increased sensuality is desirable and a strengthening of the sexual powers even commendable is very old. The Mishnah, Ned. 3.10 assumes that it was an old, characteristically Jewish custom to eat garlic, supposed to have aphrodisiac effects, on Friday evening. This is supposed to have been one of the institutions of Ezra ואוכלין שום בערב שבת (B. Ḳ. 82a). Comp. I. Loew, *Die Flora der Juden* II (Wien 1924) p. 144. The reason given for this custom is that sexual intercourse on Friday night is especially recommended (B. Ḳ. *l. c.* See also Ket. 62b; also Zohar, Preface 14ab; *Bereshit* p. 50, and *Tazria* p. 98).

It is interesting to note that the garlic is also used to keep the demons away so that, although unlike the myrtle in its smell, it is like it in its supposed effectiveness both as an aphrodisiac and as a protective charm in connection with birth, marriage and death. See I. Scheftelowitz, *Das Stellvertretende Huhnopfer* (Giessen 1904) p. 32, especially note 4. Also idem *Alt-Palästin-*

some rationalistic pious people among the ancient Jews, may have objected to such a use of the myrtle.

There is still another function ascribed to the myrtle which, though apparently the opposite of the function above described, namely, that of driving away the evil spirits, may nevertheless have also been in the minds of those who used it for the Friday evening ceremony. For superstitions are not consistent and often combine opposites or extremes. We find that the myrtle was also considered as a possible vehicle for conveying good spirits, souls and angels, or as a resting place for them. And, perhaps,

ensicher Bauernglaube (Hannover 1925) p. 82. It is a custom among East European Jews to carry with them garlic when, on the fast of the ninth of Ab, they go to visit the graves, and to scatter the garlic on the cemetery. The reason for it, is that, according to Luria, the demons seek to attach themselves to a person going to the cemetery. Cf. also Ḥag. 3b and Rashi ibid., s. v. שתשרה עליו רוח טומאה. Hence the garlic is used as a charm to drive them away, for it is a popular belief that the smell of the garlic drives away the demons וסגולה היא ומרגלא בפומי דאנשי שהשום דהיינו ריח השום הוא גם כן מבריח החיצונים. See שער המלך by R. Mordecai b. R. Samuel, part II, 4, chapter 10 end (Dyhernfurt 1797) p. 38d. Cf. also I. Loew, op. cit., p. 147. For the same reason, one of the great Hassidic Rabbis was in the habit of carrying with him garlic whenever he went to visit a sick person (ספר טעמי המנהגים by אי"ש שו"ב part III [Lemberg 1911] p. 171) in order to drive away the demons who according to Ber. 54b (see below note 59) seek to harm the sick. Hirsch Bodek in הלבנון IV (Paris 1867), pp. 228–229 would explain that the custom of throwing garlic when visiting the cemetery was for the purpose of removing the evil odor that comes up from the dead bodies כדי להסב הריח רע מהמתים. But there is no evil odor on the cemetery except the very one brought there by the visitors with the garlic. Joshua Levensohn in an article ישן מפני חדש in הלבנון (ibid., p. 325) argues against Bodek and, in a rationalizing manner, explains the reason for the custom to be that, since garlic is an aphrodisiac we, so to speak, throw it away when at the cemetery, as if to say: Why use these means to make us have more children when the end of man is death? מטעם כי שום מרבה זרע...ובבית הקברות כמו רומזים למה לנו להרבות זרע לקיום המין אם סוף אדם למות. Levensohn (ibid.) also explains the custom of placing myrtle on or carrying it before the bier to be merely a way of indicating that the dead person was a righteous man הדס קודם המטה...הוא לרמז כי איש צדיק היה. All of these are rationalizations, ingenious, but not true. As a means of driving away the demons, the garlic is still used among East European Jews. And it is recommended to hang white onions and garlic on all of the windows and doors and on each of the four walls of every room in the house in times of epidemic, thus to keep out the evil spirits. See Judah Rosenberg ספר רפאל המלאך p. 52.

these two functions, the bringing of good spirits and the driving away of evil ones, do not actually conflict with one another; for the good spirit or angel, conjured up by or resting on the myrtle, might have the precise function of helping to drive away the evil spirits.[48]

Already in the Bible, in the passage: "The angel of the Lord that stood among the myrtle trees" (Zech. 1.11), it is suggested that the myrtle was an abode or resting place for angels or God Himself. This is especially indicated in Lev. Rab. 30.9. Commenting on the symbolic significance of the myrtle and the willow of the brook, the Midrash says וענף עץ עבות [49] (הדס) זה הקב"ה דכתיב בו והוא עומד בין ההדסים וערבי נחל זה הקב"ה דכתיב ביה סולו לרוכב בערבות ביה שמו. Here the הדסים, the myrtle trees, are taken to be a sort of heavenly abode for the Divine Presence, similar to 'Arabot, the name of the seventh heaven where, according to the Talmud (Ḥag. 12b), are found the spirits as well as all the souls destined to be born and the angels and the throne of glory with the exalted God on it. Although the Talmud (Meg. 13a and Sanh. 93a), in a rationalizing manner, seeks to

---

[48] The good spirit needs the help of human beings in fighting against the evil spirit, just as he helps the people to fight off or keep away from them the evil spirit. See Lauterbach, *Tashlik*, p. 245, reference to the story of Abba Jose in Lev. Rab. 24.3. Another instance of the belief in the power of the myrtle to conjure up a good and friendly spirit is perhaps to be found in Maimonides' description of the practice of the magician בעל אוב, which information Maimonides, no doubt, derived from an ancient source. The description reads as follows: "He stands there offering some incense, while holding in his hand a sprig of myrtle and waving it etc." כיצד הוא מעשה האוב. זה שהוא עומד ומקטיר קטרת ידועה ואוחז שרביט של הדס בידו ומניפו והוא מדבר בלאט בדברים ידועים אצלם עד שישמע השואל כאלו אחד מדבר עמו ומשיבו על מה שהוא שואל בדברים מתחת הארץ בקול נמוך עד מאד (*Yad, 'Abodat Kokabim* VI, 1). Apparently the incense was intended to ward off any evil spirit, while the myrtle served to attract and bring up the friendly spirit for consultation.

[49] עץ עבות in Lev. 23.4 was understood to mean the myrtle. Onkelos and Jonathan translate it by הדסין, myrtle; and a Baraitha in Suk. 32b says ענף עץ עבות הוי אומר זהו הדס ... Comp., however, Lev. Rab. 30.15 where this identification of עץ עבות with הדס seems to be questioned, for it is said: וענף עץ עבות מי יאמר שהוא הדס? הרי הוא אומר במקום אחר (נחמיה ח' ט"ו) צאו ההר והביאו עלי זית ועלי עץ שמן ועלי הדס ועלי תמרים ועלי עץ עבות! See R. David Luria in חדושי הרד"ל *ad loc.*

interpret the "myrtle trees" among which God stood, to mean only the righteous ones, אין הדסים אלא צדיקים and to refer specifically to some living righteous men; yet some people, already in talmudic times no doubt, took "the righteous ones designated by the myrtle trees" to mean not the living righteous men, but the souls of the righteous that rest under the throne of glory, כסא הכבוד (Sab. 152b) in the seventh heaven ערבות (Ḥag. *l. c.*). And, indeed, in mystic literature the paradise where the souls of the righteous dwell is a paradise of myrtle trees גן עדן של הדס.⁵⁰ And in the Zohar it is said: "The holy place whence the souls come is the myrtle."⁵¹ Likewise in the סדר גן עדן⁵² it is said that, when the righteous man comes up to the entrance of paradise, the angels provide him with eight sprigs of myrtle and bring him to a place of brooks of water surrounded by eight rose bushes and myrtle trees. From all of these sayings one may safely conclude that the mystics had the notion that not only the place in heaven whence the souls came and whither they returned was full of myrtle trees, but also that a single twig of myrtle by itself might be a resting place for angels and souls, and hence also a vehicle for conveying them to wherever they may want to go. Such an instance in which the myrtle, according to the popular belief, served as a vehicle used by good spirits or souls to move from place to place is recorded in the Talmud (Nid. 36b–37a). Here we are told that two rabbis who had had some differences died on the same day, and their funerals took place at the same time. The people noticed on that occasion that sprigs of myrtle were flying from one bier to the other. Upon seeing this the people remarked that the two rabbis must have settled their differences and become reconciled.⁵³ This clearly shows that, according to popular conceptions, the myrtle,

---

⁵⁰ See מדרש אותיות דרבי עקיבא ed. Wertheimer (Jerusalem 1914) p. 79. In answer to the question where do the righteous who merit the life of the future world dwell, God says: in the Paradise of myrtle היכן דרים כשזוכין לחיי העולם הבא. אמר ליה (הקב"ה) בגן עדן של הדס.

⁵¹ See *Zohar Vayakhel* p. 416: קיומא דאתר קדישא דנשמתין מניה הדס איהו.

⁵² In Jellinek's *Bet Ha-Midrasch* II, 52; also in *Yalḳuṭ Šim'oni* to Gen. §20, and in מדרש תלפיות by R. Elijah Cohen (Lublin 1907) p. 194.

⁵³ חזו דפרח אסא מהאי פוריא להאי פוריא אמרו שמע מינה עבדו רבנן פייסא.

customarily placed on the bier,[54] was in this case, used by the spirits of the occupants of the coffins as a vehicle by which they could go visiting one another.

The custom of placing myrtle upon the coffin was intended for a double purpose. First, it was to drive away the demons who might try to snatch away the departed soul. Secondly, it was to provide a vehicle for the soul by which it could fly up to heaven. Possibly, it was also intended to provide seats or resting places for the angels who come to welcome the righteous man when he departs this world (Ket. 104a). It also might have been to anticipate the act of the angels who, at the entrance of paradise, meet the righteous man and provide him with sprigs of myrtle, when they assign him to his place in paradise.[55] It is therefore evident that, already in talmudic times, mystically inclined people believed in some intimate connection between the myrtle and souls, and assumed that spirits, souls or angels, could and did use the myrtle both as vehicles to move from place to place and as resting places wherever they wished to stay or dwell.

Another rather mystic belief, which was current in talmudic times, was that there comes to every Jew on Friday evening an

---

[54] See Rashi to Nid. 37a s. v. דקא פרח where he says: רגילין היו להניח הדס על המטה. In Beẓ. 6a it is mentioned as one of the preparations for the funeral to cut sprigs of myrtle למינז ליה אסא. An interesting variation of the custom of putting myrtle on the bier is reported by Luria in דרך אמת to Zohar *Vayakhel* l. c., which consisted of putting the myrtle between the legs of the dead person: ומכאן טעם שנמצא בשם ר"י דלא'ריידה שצוה להשים הדסים בין ברכיו לאחר פטירתו וכן צוה לו אביו. This, no doubt, was to provide him with a vehicle on which he could ride up to heaven. Among the ancient Greeks the myrtle was also used at funerals and placed on the graves. See Pauly-Wissowa *Real-Encyclopaedie* s. v. Myrtos p. 1182. Among the Bohemians it is still the custom to use the myrtle at funerals. See Charles M. Skinner *op. cit.*, p. 191. And among Hungarian Jews, there is still observed the custom of placing myrtle on the graves when visiting the cemetery. Dr. Abraham Cronbach calls my attention to the prayer in the Concluding Service for Atonement Day (Union Prayer Book II p. 365) where the phrase: "That from our grave may sprout not the barren thistle but the fragrant myrtle," may perhaps likewise echo the age old belief in some connection between the souls of the dead and the myrtle.

[55] See סדר גן עדן quoted *supra*, note 52.

additional soul, נשמה יתירה, which abides with him throughout the
entire Sabbath day, leaving him on Saturday night[56] (Beẓ. 16a).
A corollary idea, developed by some mystics, was that when
the additional soul comes out from its place in heaven to go
down to earth on Friday evening to enter the body of an Israel-
itish person, there also come out with it certain angels. These
angels remove from the Israelites all sadness and trouble, all
bitterness and vexation.[57]

Now, if the place where the souls dwell in heaven or under
the throne of glory is a place of myrtle, the additional soul that
is ordered to descend and come to every Israelite on Friday
evening with the entrance of the Sabbath, likewise must come
from the same source, the place of myrtle. And just as the soul,
when ascending to heaven uses the myrtle for its vehicle, so
also, it may be assumed, when descending from heaven to so-
journ in man the Sabbath day, it also uses the myrtle as
its vehicle. Likewise, it may be assumed that, when angels or
the spirits of the departed saints come down to visit their relatives, they come riding on a piece of myrtle.[58] At any rate man,

---

[56] נשמה יתירה נותן הקב'ה באדם בערב שבת ולמוצאי שבת נוטלין אותה הימנו. See also
Ta'an. 27b. The author of this saying is R. Simeon b. Laḳish, a Palestinian
Amora of the second generation (third century). The mystics took the phrase
"additional soul" literally, not as a figurative expression for increased spiritu-
ality or ease and comfort, as some rationalizing Rabbis understood it. See
Moses of Przemysl in his מטה משה part IV (Warsaw 1876) p. 122; also Isaac
Lampronti in פחד יצחק s. v. נשמה (Lyck 1864) p. 98, and cf. also R. Solomon
b. Adret's remark referred to above note 27.

[57] See Zohar, *Piḳḳude* (Lublin 1872) p. 511. The passage in the original
reads as follows: כד נשמתא אתוספת מערב שבת לערב שבת ואיהי נפקת כד איהי נפקת
נפקין אילין עמה ומעברי מישראל כל עציבו וכל יניעו וכל מרירו דנפשא וכל רוגזא דעלמא.
Even if one believes the Zohar to be a literary product of the thirteenth century, one cannot deny that it contains older material and embodies ideas
which go back to early talmudic times. In this passage, the angels accompanying the extra soul are mentioned by special names. In later mystic literature
it is merely stated to which group, מחנה גבריאל etc. these angels belong, but
they are not mentioned by name. *Infra*, note 69.

[58] The idea that departed saints can and occasionally do come back to
visit their folks here on earth finds its expression in the Talmud (Ket. 103a)
in the legend that Judah Ha-Nasi, after his death, used to come back to visit
his home every Friday evening. When, however, one Friday evening, he

to be hospitable to his heavenly visitors, whether it be an additional soul, the spirit of a departed saint, or an angel, should supply the vehicle of myrtle by which they may come down and also provide them with a resting place of myrtle somewhat like the one to which they are accustomed in their heavenly abode.

heard the maid telling a neighbor of his presence at home, he discontinued his visits, in order not to cast reflection on the righteous men of former times, as people might say that they were not as worthy as he, Judah Ha-Nasi, to be permitted after death to return to earth and visit their friends. The passage reads, as follows: כל בי שמשי הוה אתי לביתיה ההוא בי שמשא אתאי שבבתא קא קריה אבבא אמרה אמתיה שתיקו דרבי יתיב כיון דשמע שוב לא אתא שלא להוציא לעז על צדיקים הראשונים. In the Zohar, *'Emor* p. 206–207 this idea is expressed in the belief that the Patriarchs, Abraham, Isaac, and Jacob in the company of Joseph, Moses, Aaron and David, come down to visit their people in the *sukkah* during the seven days of the Sukkoth festival. And in the liturgy for the *sukkah* there is provided a special prayer based on this passage in the Zohar, by which the Israelite, every time he enters the *sukkah*, invites and makes welcome these heavenly visitors: סדר האושפיזין (see סדור אוצר התפלות Wilna 1923, pp. 1163–65). But why do these visitors come only on the Sukkoth festival and not on any other festival? Because in their heavenly abode in Paradise, they are accustomed to an environment of myrtle (see above notes 50, 51), and the *sukkah* was made with myrtle. See Neh. 9.15 and Suk. 12a. Even Isserles in Š. 'Ar. 'O.Ḥ. (638 end) still speaks of instances in which myrtle formed the covering of the *sukkah*. And in Safed they made the covering of the *sukkah* of myrtle branches even in the nineteenth century, see Moses b. Menaḥem Mendel Reischer in his ספר שערי ירושלים (Warsaw 1872) p. 39. The *sukkah*, accordingly, was a suitable environment for these heavenly visitors. Furthermore, the myrtle which is used in the ceremony of waving the *lulab* and the *etrog* attracted them and furnished them with the vehicle by means of which they descended. Perhaps the custom of keeping the myrtle sprigs, used for that ceremony, in the home from one year to another — mentioned by R. Joseph Colon in his Responsa, שאלות ותשובות מהרי"ק 41 (Zadilkow 1834) p. 17c — was not, as Colon assumes, for the purpose of making sure that they would have the right kind of myrtle next year, but rather for the purpose of making permanent, as it were, the presence of the good spirits in the home for the entire year. The people may have believed that they might secure thereby protection from evil spirits throughout the year. One is reminded of the Catholic custom of taking home the palms used in the procession of Palm Sunday and preserving them in the home as a sacramental which is believed to have the effect of driving away evil spirits. See *Catholic Encyclopedia* vol. XI p. 433 s. v. Palm Sunday; also *ibid.*, vol. XIII p. 293. s. v. Sacramental.

Now, the idea suggests itself with great plausibility that perhaps the purpose of our ceremony had, in the minds of the mystics, something to do with these beliefs. In other words, it may be assumed that the function of the myrtle in our ceremony was the same as the function of the myrtle on other occasions, and that it combined all these functions. (For a ceremony may, at the same time, serve many purposes if they are not incompatible.) It offered protection against demons[59] and furnished a vehicle by which the additional soul, perhaps with angels or other spirits of departed saints accompanying it,[60] would come down; and it also provided a resting place for these spirits during their visit here on earth.

An examination of the ceremony and all its details as prescribed and explained by Luria and his disciples will confirm this theory and prove that those ideas actually were in the minds of the later mystics who observed this ceremony. And, as already remarked above, they were probably in the main the same ideas which were entertained by the earlier mystics in talmudic times; for the later mystics did not altogether invent these ideas; they received them from earlier generations, though they may have slightly modified them. This may also help to explain to us the objections to this ceremony on the part of the more rationalistic rabbinic authorities who ignored the ceremony or sought to suppress it.

Now let us see how the ceremony was observed by Luria and how his disciples explained its significance. The ceremony as prescribed by Luria was as follows: "A man must be very careful to place on the table (on Friday evening) two bunches

[59] Perhaps the saying מטלטלין עצי בשמים להריח בהם ולהניף בהן לחולה (Beẓ. 33b) also means, not merely waving them in order to refresh the sick person, which function would have been included in the phrase להריח בהם, nor for the sake of cooling the air or of driving away flies which need not be done especially with fragrant plants, but in order to drive away the demons, since a sick person is one of the three categories of people especially threatened by the demons (Ber. 54b). And עצי בשמים in our passage means myrtle. This would be another function in which both myrtle and garlic were believed to be equally effective. *Supra*, note 47.

[60] And the function of bringing good spirits and driving away evil ones are not incompatible. See *supra*, note 48.

of myrtle, and each bunch must consist of three sprigs . . . Then march silently around the table towards the right. Then take the two bunches of myrtle into your hands, hold them close together with both hands, recite the benediction over them and smell them. Then march silently around the table with them a second time and say: ' "Remember" and "Observe" were said in one utterance.' "[61] It is also added that this ceremony, performed before the recitation of the Kiddush, is to be repeated after the meal has been finished and Grace has been recited. It says: "After reciting Grace after the meal you should again smell the bunches of the myrtle, but do not smell them without reciting the benediction over them, and after doing so, say: ' "Remember" and "Observe" were said in one utterance.' "[62] This order for the ceremony is also given by R. Jacob Ḥayyim Ẓemaḥ.[63] It is to be noticed that Luria follows both the report of the Talmud and the one of the Zohar. He combines the different features of each and harmonizes them, by prescribing that there must be two bunches, one corresponding to "Remember" and one cor-

---

[61] See שולחן ערוך של רבינו יצחק לוריא (Wilna 1880) p. כ'ט. The Hebrew text relating to this ceremony reads as follows: צריך האדם להיות זהיר לשום בשולחן שתי אגודות של הדס וצריך להיות כל אגודה משלשה בדי הדס . . . ואח'כ תקיף השולחן דרך ימין בשתיקה ואח'כ קח בידך השתי אגודות של הדס ותחברם בשתי ידך ותברך עליהם ותריח בהם ואח'כ תקיף עמהם השולחן פעם ב' דרך ימין בשתיקה ואח'כ תאמר זכור ושמור בדבור א' נאמרו.

[62] אחר בהמ'ז של שבת תחזור ותברך על אגודות של הדס ותריח בהם ואל תריח בלתי נאמרו ברכה ואח'כ תאמר זכור ושמור בדבור א' נאמרו. We notice that it is insisted upon not to smell without reciting the benediction over spices ולא תריח בלא ברכה which insistence would seem superfluous if the smelling were for enjoyment. See חמדת ימים I. Ch. 8 (Zolkiew 1756) p. 44 where he seeks to give some explanation why it was necessary to mention that the benediction be recited. The real explanation, however, is that since the act was not for the purpose of enjoying the fragrance, but merely to bring the myrtle close to the nostrils, so as to affect a direct transfer of the extra soul (supra, note 35), one might think that it is like the case of one who takes something as a medicine לרפואה and that therefore no benediction is necessary, cf. Ber. 38a. Hence the insistence upon the reciting of the benediction. For, after all, he enjoys the fragrance, even though this is not his real purpose; and therefore, according to the conclusion of the Gemara Ber. l. c., he must recite a benediction כיון דאית ליה הנאה מינה בעי ברוכי.

[63] In his נגיד ומצוה (Lublin 1881) pp. 44, 46, 48. Zemaḥ fled from Portugal in the year 1619. See JE VII, p. 656.

responding to "Observe" as in the Talmud but requiring that each bunch must consist of three sprigs, as in the Zohar. He does not, however, expressly say, as does the Zohar, that the three sprigs are for the three patriarchs. But that this idea of the Zohar was retained in the school of Luria, even if slightly modified, can be seen from an examination of the descriptions of this ceremony given by two exponents of the teachings of Luria; and we shall also learn from them that the function of the myrtle in relation to the patriarchs, hinted at in the Zohar, was similar to the function of the myrtle on other occasions. Thus in the work חמדת ימים, the author[64] of which was an exponent of Luria's ideas about ceremonies and ritual, this ceremony is highly recommended and described as follows: "It is a good custom for those who wish to walk in perfection, to place upon the table on the evening of the Sabbath two bunches of myrtle, each consisting of three sprigs. These two bunches correspond to 'Remember' and 'Observe,' Jacob and Rachel. One must, however, be careful that this myrtle should be the right kind like the '*Abot* prescribed in the Torah[65] . . . And my teacher used to say, 'on the eve of the Sabbath there comes to a man three angels from the world of formation מעולם היצירה, one of the company of Michael representing the "mercy of Abraham". . . and one of the company of Gabriel representing the "fear of Isaac". . . and one of the company of Uriel representing the "glory of Jacob."[66] . . . And, therefore, every man of Israel should arrange to have on the eve of the Sabbath, at least three sprigs of myrtle to serve as a chair or throne for the above mentioned three angels who accompany the additional soul. And, when the additional soul notices that the three angels

---

[64] Supposed to have been Nathan Ghazzati (1644–1680) the follower of Sabbetai Zevi (see JE V, p. 651). Cf., however, David Fraenkel in '*Alim, Blaetter fuer Bibliographie und Geschichte des Judenthums* heft II (September 1934) p. 54, note 1.

[65] *Supra*, note 49.

[66] In ספר ציוני to '*Emor* (Cremona 1560) p. 80b in a note הנה'ה it is also said that the three sprigs of the myrtle, used in the ceremony of waving the *lulab* on Sukkoth, point to or indicate the three patriarchs נ' הדסים רמז לג' אבות, חס'ד, פח'ד, תפאר'ת.

accompanying it have found a place on which to rest until the going out of the Sabbath, then it is glad and joyful. And when, on the night of the going out of the Sabbath, the person recites the benediction (in the Habdalah ceremony) over these three sprigs of myrtle,[67] then the additional soul leaves that person in this very act of smelling and immediately the three angels who have been resting on the myrtle go with it to its (original) place. And therefore one must sniff at these sprigs of myrtle three times (during the ceremony) on Saturday night.[68] And the additional soul, at the moment of its leaving, blesses the person, its host, for the pleasure which it had received. And if one has not prepared these three sprigs of the right kind of myrtle on the eve of the Sabbath, then, when the three angels come and find no place to rest, they move on and go away. And the soul then remains alone, sad of spirit. And when one recites the benediction (at the Habdalah ceremony) over the wrong kind of or 'fool' myrtle הדס שוטה, then an angel from the Other Side, i. e., from the Left Side, attaches himself to the soul (there being no good angels on proper myrtle sprigs to hinder him . . .) and the soul curses the person, its host, who has not troubled himself in its behalf to prepare at least three sprigs of myrtle (as a resting place) for the three angels that were with it.' So far are his (the teacher's) words. Go and learn how doubly beneficial it is for the Israelite to prepare two bunches of the right kind (כשר) of myrtle, so that the beautiful soul may be glad and rejoice with its angels. On the other hand, it is the opposite with one who could have done this thing but neglected it. Such a person causes great harm to himself. Also, if one does

---

[67] He speaks here only of "these three sprigs of myrtle," since he said above that one must have "at least three sprigs of myrtle," that is, actually only one bunch. He thus ignores the requirement of two bunches, corresponding to "Remember" and "Observe." This is also done by Azulai. *Infra*, note 71.

[68] Zemaḥ in נגיד ומצוה p. 51 also says that at the Habdalah ceremony Luria used only one bunch of myrtle: מורי זלה"ה היה מריח על אגודה אחת של הדס דליל שבת כנז' שם והיה נזהר שיהיו בה ג' בדי הדס קשורים בקשר א' ג' הדסים הם סוד נר'ן החול So he also alludes to the significance ותכוין בהם כדי להשאיר מקדושת שבת לימי החול of the three sprigs, as corresponding to נפש, רוח, נשמה as explained by Azulai. See below note 72.

not have the proper myrtle, he should not recite the benediction over the wild myrtle, lest there come upon him a curse and not a blessing. The same is also true with regard to the ceremony on Saturday night."[69]

Abraham ben Mordecai Azulai (1570–1643) in his work חסד לאברהם[70] gives a description of the ceremony practically identical with the one given in חמדת ימים, with one significant variation. He does not mention the feature of two bunches. The idea suggested in the Talmud that this ceremony somehow had the purpose of reminding one of the different versions of the commandment about the Sabbath is entirely dropped; hence, the feature of requiring two bunches of myrtle, supposed to correspond to "Remember" and "Observe," is not even mentioned.[71]

---

[69] The Hebrew text in חמדת ימים I, ch. 4 (Zolkiew 1756) p. 24d reads as follows:

ומנהג טוב להולכים בתמים לתת על השלחן בע"ש ב' אגודות הדס כשר כל אגודה מג' בדים והמה נגד זכור ושמור יעקב ורחל וצריך להזהר שיהא הדס כשר כעבות האמור בתורה שיהיו ג' עלין בגבעול... ומורי נר"ו היה אומר כי בע"ש באים עם האדם ג' מלאכים מעולם היצירה אחד ממחנה מיכאל שהוא נגד מדת חסד לאברהם ואחד ממחנה גבריאל שהוא נגד מדת פחד יצחק ואחד ממחנה אוריאל נגד ת"ת ישראל ולפיכך יש לערוך כל איש ישראל כל ע"ש ג' בדי הדס לפחות שהיו עבות להיות כסא לג' המלאכים הנזכרים הבאים ללוות את הנפש יתירה ובראות הנפש יתירה שג' מלאכים הנלוים אותה מצאו מקום לנוח עליו עד מוצאי שבת אז היא צהלה ושמחה ובאור מוצאי שבת בברכו על ג' בדי הדס אלו אז הנפש היתירה יוצאת באותו הריח ומיד הג' המלאכים השורים על ההדס הולכים איתה עד מקומה ולכן יש להריח בם ג' פעמים במוצאי שבת; והנפש היתירה בעת הליכתה מברכת לבע"הב בעבור הנחת שקיבלה ומי שלא זימן ג' בדי הדס כשרות מע"ש כשבאים הג' מלאכים אינם מוצאים מקום למנוחתם ויסעו וילכו והנפש לבדה נשארה עצובת רוח וכשמברכים על ההדס השוטה מלאך מסטרא אחרא מסטרא דשמאלא מתלוה עם הנפש והנפש מקללת ח"ו לבע"הב על כי לא טרח בשבילה להכין ג' בדי הדס לג' המלאכים אשר איתה אלו דבריו: צא ולמד כמה טובה כפולה לאיש הישראלי בהכין ב' אגודות הדס הכשר והנפש היפה צהלה ושמחה במלאכים שלה וכן בהפכו אשר נמצא אתו והוא מתרשל בדבר גורם רעה לעצמו ח"ו ואשר לא נמצא אתו הדס לא יברך על השוטה פן יבא עליו קללה ולא ברכה וכן במוצאי שבת...

[70] עין הקורא נהר מ"ט (Amsterdam 1685) p. 21b.

[71] While the author of חמדת ימים, although also emphasizing more the importance of the number three of the sprigs, at least mentions and even recommends the requirements of two bunches. *Supra*, note 69 but see also note 67. It seems that, for some mystics, the feature of two bunches lost its significance altogether. It was no longer important to refer to "Remember" and "Observe" and even the significance of referring to the "bride and the groom" or husband and wife, as expressed in Luria's song (*supra*, note 43), was disregarded. It seemed no longer important to emphasize the feature of

The main significance of the ceremony, according to this account, lies in the feature of "the three sprigs" which, while reminding us of or representing the three patriarchs, really are meant for the three angels who come down accompanying the extra soul. צריך לבקש ערב שבת אחר ג' בדי הדס שהם רומזים לג' אבות והכוונה לג' היתירה הנפש את ללוות הבאים הנזכרים מלאכים ג' לג' הדס בדי. And though the idea expressed in the Zohar and modified in the Lurianic school, as represented by the author of חמדת ימים, (that these three angels stand for the three patriarchs) is retained, it is added that there is still another reason for expecting three angels to accompany each extra soul, that other reason being that the extra soul that comes to every Israelite on a Friday night may consist of three parts נפש רוח נשמה.[72] And each of these parts of the extra soul is accompanied by a special angel. Hence, three angels may be needed. It may also suggest that the three sprigs were vehicles for the three parts of the soul themselves. Each one of the accompanying angels may manage to come along with the respective part of the soul on each one of the sprigs, which might accommodate both of them. After the three parts of the soul enter the body through the nostrils, each sprig is left with but one occupant, the accompanying spirit, who abides on it through the whole Sabbath day. On Saturday night when the parts of the soul leave the person through the nostrils, ready to return to the heavenly abode, then, each of the waiting attendant spirits makes room on his respective sprig for one of the respective parts, and thus conveys it back to heaven.

We must notice that both the author of חמדת ימים[73] and Azulai leave out the feature of marching around the table with the

protection of husband and wife against demons, as at weddings, since this would only apply to the smallest family where there is only a husband and his wife. *Infra*, note 86.

[72] See *Zohar Aḥare* p. 140 נשמה ,רוח ,נפש כחד ואתדבקו אינון דרגין ג'. The idea expressed by Azulai *ibid., l. c.*, that the additional soul that comes to a person on Friday night is of the same kind as the soul which that person possesses, is also found in the Zohar *Phinehas*, p. 484, where it says: חד לכל דיליה דרנא כפום יתירה נפש ליה נחית הכי ישראל.

[73] Though the author of חמדת ימים somehow still retains this feature in the discussion of the ceremony at the third meal of the Sabbath (ch. 17, p. 72d) where he says: סעודות בשאר כמו ויקיף, implying that the ceremony

myrtle, prescribed by Ẓemaḥ and by the *Shulḥan 'Aruk* of Luria. This encirclement, הקפה, which no doubt, was to serve as a magic circle keeping away the evil spirits,[74] was not considered so important by these two representatives of the Lurianic school. Not that they did not believe in the presence of the evil spirits, or in the efficacy of the myrtle to keep them away but, for some reasons, they did not feel the need of emphasizing this feature which is the negative function of the myrtle. They merely emphasized the positive function of bringing the good spirits.

In these descriptions of the ceremony by the representatives of Lurianic mysticism, the main function and purpose of the ceremony is clearly stated, though the different descriptions present slight differences in some details. And it is unmistakably plain that this function assumed by the Lurianic mystics is based upon ancient mystic notions about the Sabbath and upon some superstitious beliefs about the inherent powers of the myrtle. Some of these ancient beliefs and superstitions we found indicated in the Talmud. Others we found expressed only in the mystic literature but their origin, no doubt, goes back to talmudic times. The ɪystics of the Lurianic school, or their immediate predecessors, preserved and combined all these mystic notions. They may have modified some of them slightly, but out of them they wove the mystic texture of their explanation of the ceremony. We need not be surprised if we find, in the different presentations, a little confusion and occasionally con-

---

including the marching around the table is to be performed at every Sabbath meal, not only on Friday night.

[74] Marching around in a circle, הקפות, has the purpose of keeping away the demons and is performed when and wherever there is a special fear of demons. Thus, at funerals, it is customary to make such circles either on the way to the cemetery or at the cemetery, and the purpose thereof is explained to be the driving away of the evil spirits רעות רוחות מעליו להבריח (Aaron Berachyah Modena in his יבק מעבר, chapter 17 of רננות שפתי [Wilna 1922] p. 216): Likewise at weddings, when the fear of the demons is especially great, it is customary to march with the bride seven times, or at least three times, in a circle around the bridegroom under the canopy. See המנהגים טעמי by שו"ב אי"ש (Lemberg 1911) part I, p. 112 and part IV, p. 15. See also I. Scheftelowitz, *Das Stellvertretende Huhnopfer* (Giessen 1914) pp. 22–30, and Joshua Trachtenberg, *Jewish Magic and Superstition* (New York 1939) p. 121.

tradictory ideas or slight variations in some details. For, after all, consistent thinking and systematic presentation is not the forte of mystic writers. In the main, however, they all agree as to the chief purpose and function of the ceremony. Their descriptions, notwithstanding the little differences and the occasional omissions of some feature or detail, enable us to trace the development of this ceremony and may also help us to discover the reason why this ceremony was not popular with rabbinic authorities, and the cause of its ultimate falling into disuse.

As our records do not give the exact dates when an idea arose or when it was modified, and as a hint to an idea or notion found in a later source may sometimes actually have reference to earlier times, we shall not be able to document the various stages of this development in their chronological order, but in the main we can trace the course of this development. On the basis of this examination of the various descriptions of this ceremony and the scattered indications of the various notions that entered into the texture of the ceremony or affected its interpretation, I venture to give the following broad outline of the course of its development:

In ancient times, when the myrtle was still used merely as a substitute for the *mugmar*, some people ascribed to it an additional function, based upon the popular beliefs in certain qualities of the myrtle. It was believed to have the effect of exciting or increasing sensuality. This was desirable on Friday nights.[75] It was also believed to have the power of driving away the evil spirits who, according to some people's belief, are especially dangerous on Friday nights.[76] The function of the myrtle then in the ceremony on Friday night was, in both these respects, identical with the functions ascribed to it when used at weddings or for bridal wreaths. The popular superstitions, underlying this conception of the ceremony, of course, were not favored by the Rabbis; but, on the whole, they did not so strongly object to the ceremony. For they could regard the notion that the myrtle on Friday evening had the same purpose as the one used at weddings, merely as a poetic expression and

[75] *Supra*, note 47.   [76] *Supra*, note 45.

and exaggerated presentation of the intimate union between Israel and the Sabbath, picturing it as a wedding in which Israel is the bridegroom and the Sabbath is the bride.

And when the idea that on Friday night every Israelite was given an additional soul that abides with him the whole Sabbath day and leaves him on Saturday night arose and became well-known, the popular mind discovered another possible function for the myrtle used on Friday evening. Remembering the other popular notion that the myrtle was a suitable vehicle or resting place for souls and spirits, some people thought that the use of the myrtle on Friday evening might also serve the purpose of helping to bring down and to make welcome the additional soul. This explanation suited the popular fancy very much, since it was in harmony with the function of the myrtle used in the ceremony on Saturday night when it served the somewhat similar purpose of giving a farewell to the departing additional soul and furnishing it with a vehicle by which it could be transported to its heavenly abode. The people never would countenance the idea that the same means employed on Friday night as a vehicle for or a form of welcome to the extra soul should be used on Saturday 'night to console or refresh the person grieving over the loss of the extra soul, as some rationalizing people conceived it.[77]

Again, the thought also occurred to some people that the extra soul, living in the delightful abode in Paradise among gardens of myrtle, might be reluctant to leave that abode and go down to earth, even if only for a week-end. According to mystic notions, even the regular soul when, at the time of conception or birth it is ordered to enter the human body, pleads with God to let it remain in heaven and not to send it down to earth. It has to be coaxed and forced to enter the human

[77] *Supra*, note 27. From what we have discussed above, it is clear that the purpose of the ceremony was to help the extra soul depart as, on Friday evening, the ceremony helped it arrive. It was not to comfort the remaining soul in its grief over the departure of the extra soul. For, in that case, it would have been entirely out of place on Friday evening when this soul was joyfully anticipating the pleasure of its visitor from heaven.

body.[78] The extra soul, then, presumably no less disinclined to leave its heavenly abode, certainly could not be trusted to proceed to earth by itself. An angel from on high had to be assigned the task of taking it down to earth for the week-end and bringing it back when its visit there was over. Accordingly, the mystics felt, this angelic escort also had to be provided with means of transportation and accomodation for rest. Hence, two bunches of myrtle were required, one for the soul and one for its attendant angel. For originally the people were not so niggardly with their arrangement as to assign but a single sprig for a soul or an angel. They would provide a whole bunch of myrtle in the midst of which, between the single sprigs, the soul or the angel could stand or rest. This was more in keeping with the notion familiar to the people from Zech. 1.9, where the angel "stood among," not on one of, "the myrtle trees."

Some mystics also developed the idea that perhaps it need not be an angel of the regular heavenly hosts who brings down the extra soul. Some spirit of an ancestor or of a departed relative who might wish to return for a week-end visit with his family on earth, as e. g., Judah ha-Nasi used to do for quite a time after his death (Ket. 103a),[79] might take charge of the extra soul and escort it to the place of its assigned destination. In this case, the second bunch of myrtle would serve for the departed spirit in the same capacity as it would serve a regular angel. These superstitious notions connected with the ceremony of using myrtle on Friday evening were even more objectionable to the enlightened teachers. They would never repeat them and would not admit that the ceremony was for such a purpose. Nevertheless, for a time at least, they continued to tolerate, though by no means to recommend, the ceremony and were inclined to consider it as an additional Sabbath pleasure עונג שבת, or a special form of honoring the Sabbath כבוד שבת. And when confronted with an exceptional case of a good and pious man whose intellectual and spiritual attainments could not be

---

[78] See Tanḥuma, *Pikkude* 3; also סדר יצירת הולד in Jellinek's *Bet Ha-Midrash* I, p. 153 ff.

[79] *Supra*, note 58.

doubted, but who was mystically inclined and hence laid special stress upon using two bunches of myrtle for this ceremony on Friday evening, they would, in true rabbinic fashion, judge him on the scale of merit and not impugn to him an indulgence in these foolish objectionable superstitions. They charitably explained that he probably used *two* bunches of myrtle for this ceremony as a symbolic reminder of the two aspects, positive and negative, of the Sabbath laws or, as they put it, corresponding to the forms of the commandment, "Remember" and "Observe." But they would not extend this tolerant attitude, shown in the case of an exceptionally pious person, to the people at large. They could not credit all the people with such ideas of using the myrtle merely as a symbolic reminder. And realizing the impossibility of eradicating from the people's mind the superstitions which were popularly attached to the ceremony, they finally discouraged the ceremony altogether and, in general, were opposed to the use of the myrtle on Friday evening; though they did not object to having other flowers or spices on the table merely for the pleasure of enjoying their fragrance or aroma.[80] Thus, beginning with the later talmudic times, this ceremony came to be suppressed by the rabbinic authorities and no mention of it is ever found in halakic literature.

But the Halakists could not control the private practices of the mystic circles who secretly cultivated their ideas or superstitions and handed them down from generation to generation. Among these mystic circles the ceremony continued to be observed and, in the course of time, some details of it were slightly modified and differently explained. Its main significance was considered to lie in its function of facilitating the coming of the extra soul. This, however, did not preclude the other function

---

[80] *Supra*, note 4. As a form of כבוד שבת or עונג שבת, the custom of having flowers or plants in the home may have continued in some places and in some Jewish homes. In fact, in Palestine today, it is customary to buy flowers for the Sabbath. What the significance of the custom of spreading the aroma of spices in the Synagogue at the entrance of the Sabbath, introduced in German communities about the beginning of the seventeenth century, may have been, I cannot tell. It is interesting to notice, however, that Joseph Juspa Hahn (1570–1637) in his יוסף אומץ 598 (Frankfurt a.M. 1928) p. 127 objected to it.

ascribed to the myrtle, namely of strengthening[81] the bride and the groom on their wedding day or the husband and the wife of the family, by increasing their sensuality and protecting them from harm by driving away the evil spirits. For ceremonies, in the popular fancy, can accomplish more than one purpose and perform different functions at one and the same time.

One change was made in the ceremony which affected the number of the myrtle vehicles required. Instead of two, the mystics required three; but at the same time the extravagance of providing a whole bunch for each spirit was curtailed. It was felt that a single sprig by itself was sufficient as a vehicle or resting place for a spirit. And, instead of two bunches, they required only three single sprigs. The requirement of three sprigs may have come about in the following way: It occurred to some people that two angels or spirits were required for the soul to keep watch over it and to see to it that it stays in the body till the time of its departure, on Saturday night, arrived. For even the regular soul, forced to enter into the body of the child is, while in the womb, watched over by two angels to prevent its getting out from its imprisonment in the womb.[82] Accordingly, three sprigs were required; one for the soul itself and two for the guardian spirits.

Again, some mystics conceived the notion that these guardian spirits were the spirits of the three patriarchs, Abraham, Isaac, and Jacob. And it was felt that these spirits could carry the soul with them on their vehicles, so that there was no need of providing a separate vehicle for the soul itself. All that was necessary, then, was to provide three sprigs for the three patriarchs.[83] Why three guardian spirits were required for each soul was explained by some on the basis of the theory that each extra soul might possibly be a trinity consisting of three parts נפש, רוח, נשמה. The function of these spirits was to bring the additional soul near to the door of its temporary abode for the

---

[81] *Supra*, notes 43, 46, and 47.

[82] See Tanḥuma, *Piḳḳude* 3, referred to above, note 78.

[83] As suggested in the Zohar passage quoted in note 35 above. Cf. also *supra*, note 67.

Sabbath, i. e., to the nostrils where, by inhaling the fragrance of the myrtle, the extra soul is drawn in and thus enters the body. Hence, the smelling or sniffing at the myrtle, originally merely an act for the enjoyment of the fragrance, was still considered necessary. It was still insisted upon that the benediction usually recited over the enjoyment of fine scents be recited; though in this case it was really not an act of enjoying the fragrance but of drawing in the extra soul.[84] As each of the three sprigs, serving as a vehicle for one of the patriarchs, carries one part of the three-fold soul, they must all be brought near the nostrils at the same time, so that the whole trinity may enter the body at the same time. Hence the requirement of tying them together[85] before bringing them near the nostrils for what seemed to be an act of smelling, a requirement which would not be necessary if the apparent act of smelling were merely for the enjoyment of the fragrance. Some of the mystics, respecting the talmudic explanations, wished to retain the number *two*, corresponding to "Remember" and "Observe." They therefore combined it with their own interpretation of the ceremony by requiring *two* bunches, corresponding to the two versions of the commandment, but at the same time insisted that each bunch must consist of three sprigs for the three spirits of the Patriarchs carrying the three parts of the additional soul. While retaining, out of respect for the Talmud, the idea about the meaning of two bunches, some added another significance to the number *two*, namely, Jacob and his wife Rachel, or for "the bridegroom and the bride, that the weak ones may be strengthened."[86] In

---

[84] *Supra*, note 62.

[85] See the expression וקשירנא להון כחדא in the Zohar passage quoted *supra*. note 34.

[86] *Supra*, note 43. Some mystics may have retained the feature of having two bunches, explaining that these bunches, each consisting of three sprigs for the three spirits carrying the three parts of the additional soul, were one for the husband and one for the wife in the smallest family. But since, in a larger family they would require more than two bunches, they dropped this feature entirely, relying upon the three angels on the three sprigs to be able to manage to carry as many additional souls as might be required for any family large or small. Cf. *supra*, note 71.

this manner, they revived or retained the idea that the function
of the myrtle on Friday evening was the same as its function
at weddings.

Again, others ignored this idea that the myrtle was to function as at any other wedding, or be intended for the husband
and wife, the smallest family, since such an idea would not hold
good in the case of a larger family. They, accordingly, dropped
entirely the feature of requiring two bunches. They just required
three sprigs.[87]

How the extra souls came down to the other members of
the family is not explained, but it must have been thought that
souls do not take up much space and many of them could be
accommodated on one sprig; or still better, the three spirits who
carry down the extra soul to the head of the house can, at the
same time with no extra effort, carry along and bring to each
household all the extra souls for all the members of the family.

Another change that was made in the interpretation of the
ceremony was the reversion to the idea that real angels of the
heavenly host, and not the spirits of the patriarchs, had charge
of the task. This was necessary, since it could not be conceived
that the spirits of the patriarchs could manage to be present at
one and the same time in the different localities of the numerous
Jewish homes all over the world. However, these regular angels
were made, in a manner, representatives of the patriarchs.[88] The
soul, it was imagined, would feel better if it knew itself to be
in charge of a representative of the fathers, than if it thought
it were escorted merely by a heavenly officer.

Some mystics seemed also to have retained or revived the
older idea that the myrtle was to drive away the demons. To
emphasize this function, they required a procession around the
table with the myrtle.[89] This feature of the הקפות or encirclement which, as we have seen, had the purpose of forming a
magic circle to keep out the demons[90] was later on dropped

---

[87] Just as, at the Habdalah ceremony, only one bunch consisting of three
sprigs was used. *Supra*, note 68.

[88] See the passage in חמדת ימים quoted *supra*, note 69, where the patriarchs
are expressly identified with certain groups of angels.

[89] *Supra*, note 61.   [90] *Supra*, note 74.

because they no longer wished to emphasize the fear of the
demons. Probably because the idea prevailed and came to be
emphasized, even in the Friday evening liturgy, that on the
Sabbath the demons could not harm the Israelites, there was
no need of any special protection by the myrtle.[91] This was a
sort of concession to the rabbinic law. But all these modifications and reinterpretations did not weaken the silent opposition
of the halakists to this ceremony. The ceremony continued to
be persistently ignored by the halakic rabbinic authorities, and
no work on the ritual and ceremonies of the Sabbath by any
rabbinic author mentions the ceremony.

There is, to my knowledge, but one exception. And this is
Isaiah Horowitz (1565–1630), a great halakic authority, but
also a prominent mystic who was greatly influenced by Luria's
teachings. In his work, *Šene Luḥot Ha-berit*, section Sabbath
(Fuerth 1764) p. 133, Horowitz mentions this ceremony in a
rather simple form without in any way referring to any superstitious beliefs and mystic notions connected with it. He says:
"It is proper that there should be (on the table) at every meal
(of the Sabbath, not only on Friday evening) two bunches of
myrtle for the purpose of enjoying their fragrance."[92] He does
not connect it at all with the "additional soul," and does not
specify the number of sprigs which each bunch should contain;
nor does he mention the feature of marching with them around
the table. He completely ignores all of the mystic explanations
or justifications of this ceremony, which he certainly must have
known, and limits himself merely to mentioning what is said
about it in the Talmud, to which, of course, there could be no
objection. He cites the passage from the Talmud (Sab. 33b)
justifying the requirement of two bunches, as corresponding to
the different expressions 'Remember' and 'Observe' used in
the Sabbath commandment, even though apparently this does
not seem to him to be a completely satisfactory justification.

---

[91] *Supra*, note 45. Those who still retained the feature may have justified
it on the ground that the table was like the altar around which they would
march with the myrtle on the Sukkoth festival.

[92] של"ה. ראוי לכל סעודה להיות תרי מדאני אסא להריח בהם. (Fuerth 1764) p. 133.

He adds: "Although this purpose of referring to or reminding one of the different expressions, "Remember" and "Observe" is already accomplished by lighting two candles,[93] yet a God-fearing person should also observe this custom of having two myrtle bunches." And, as an additional justification, he further says that he had actually seen, no doubt when on his visits in Safed, that "particularly pious people" observe this custom with the two bunches of myrtle because it is mentioned in the Talmud.[94] This closing remark sounds like an apology for mentioning or recommending such a ceremony. It clearly indicates that the ceremony was not at all popular and that only particularly pious people would observe it; and even they would justify their observing it on the ground that it is mentioned in the Talmud. This only proves that the strong objections on the part of rabbinic authorities to the mystic notions and superstitious beliefs associated with this ceremony, continued even to the time when mystic lore in general had gained favor in rabbinic circles and when its study was encouraged and even cultivated by many authorities of the Halakah. The tendency among rabbinic authorities to discourage this ceremony and to seek to suppress its practice remained unabated; with the result that the ceremony could not maintain itself. But what greatly contributed to the complete abandonment of this ceremony, even among more or less mystic circles, was not so much the opposition of the halakists as, strangely enough, another mystic notion which developed as a corrolary to the main idea underlying the mystic interpretation of the ceremony, viz. that the myrtle was the favored vehicle or resting place for angels and spirits. For, in the realm of the spirits there is division, rivalry and competition. Alongside of and opposed to the right party, סטרא דימינא, consisting of the good spirits and angels, there is the party of the left, סטרא דשמאלא, consisting of the evil spirits and demons. These members of the left party are very much like the members of the right

---

[93] Horowitz takes it for granted that the two Sabbath lights are to correspond to "Remember" and "Observe." Rabiah to Sabbath ed. Aptowitzer I (Berlin 1913) p. 265, merely offers it as a suggestion. He says: יש לומר חד כנגד זכור וחד כנגד שמור.

[94] של"ה l. c. וכן ראיתי המדקדקין נוהגין כן בתרי מדאני אסא מאחר שמוזכר בגמרא.

party and imitate many of their habits.[95] Now the notion developed among the mystics that like the angels and good spirits, the demons and evil spirits being, after all, also spirits by nature, might likewise favor the use of the myrtle for vehicles or resting places. This notion engendered great fear of handling the myrtle. For one could never be absolutely certain about the nature of its invisible occupant, whether it be an angel or a demon. Of course, it was assumed that the right kind of myrtle was very particular and would serve only the good spirits and angels, but refuse to let itself be used by the evil spirits. But there is the other kind of myrtle, the wild or "fool" myrtle, הדס שוטה that looks very much like the right kind, but which is not so particular and may readily lend itself to be used by the evil spirits. And we have seen that the author of חמדת ימים as well as Azulai warn against the danger of great harm that could result from the use of the wrong kind of myrtle. They urge great care and precaution in selecting the right kind of myrtle for the ceremony lest, instead of a good angel, an evil spirit, one from the "Other Side" or left party, may come riding on it or be resting on it, much to the harm of the person performing the ceremony. But not every one is expert enough to distinguish between the two kinds of myrtle which look very much alike. Besides, some consider even the right kind of myrtle, after it has become dried up, as being in a class with the "fool" myrtle.[96] Such a myrtle, it was feared, might also be used by the evil spirit. The result was that very few people, even among the mystics, would care or dare to perform this ceremony with the

[95] A baraita in Ḥag. 16a mentions three things in which the demons are like the angels and the habit of riding on myrtle is not one of them. But this baraita may be תנא ושייר and does not mean to exhaust the similarities of demons to angels. See Tosafot ad loc., s. v. כבני אדם who remark that the list of the things in which demons resemble human beings, as given in the same baraita, is not complete either.

[96] See commentary בית חדש to Ṭur 'O.Ḥ. 297 where it is explained that R. Ephraim, who objected to the use of the myrtle at the Habdalah ceremony, considered a dried up myrtle to be "fool myrtle" or הדס שוטה. Whether this was the real reason for R. Ephraim's objection is rather doubtful. It seems that he objected to the use of the myrtle altogether even if it were fresh, for he only used some spices kept in a glass container.

myrtle. And even those who performed it were emphatic in their declaration that they did it merely as a symbolic reminder of "Remember" and "Observe," and because it is mentioned in the Talmud.

In Safed, the place of Luria's activity, the ceremony seems to have lingered on even to the nineteenth century; but even there, its observers, like the מדקדקין referred to by Horowitz, seem not to have emphasized the mystic explanation of it. They merely say that they perform the ceremony because it is an ancient custom mentioned in the Talmud. A report of this ceremony as being still observed in a simple form in Safed in the middle of the nineteenth century is found in the work ספר שערי ירושלים by Moses b. Menaḥem Mendel Reischer, (Warsaw 1872) p. 39, and reads as follows: "It is the custom in Safed to hire a man to bring in sprigs of green myrtle from the fields every Friday and to distribute them in all the synagogues. And on Friday night after the evening service, each person takes home with him two sprigs, one corresponding to the commandment "Remember" and the other corresponding to the commandment "Observe," as is stated in the Talmud; for this is a very ancient custom; and before saying the Kiddush they recite, over these myrtle sprigs, the benediction."[97]

This, to my knowledge, is the last or latest reference to the observance of this ceremony. It is significant that this was in Safed where the myrtle grows plentifully (Reischer *ibid. l. c.*), and where the traditions and memories of Luria were still cherished. But, even there, the ceremony was observed in its simple form without any reference to the mystic interpretations of it. Outside of Safed the ceremony seems either never to have been observed or completely forgotten if ever it had been practiced.[98] For we find no reference[98a] to its being observed outside

[97] The passage reads as follows: מנהג בצפת ששוכרים את א' להביא כל ע"ש הדסים ירוקים מן השדה לחלק בכל בתי כנסיות ובבתי מדרשות ובליל שבת אחר התפלה יקח כל א' שנים א' כנגד זכור וא' כנגד שמור כדאיתא בגמרא כי חוא מנהג קדמון וקודם קידוש מברכין עליהם בורא עצי בשמים ...

[98] H. J. D. Azulai who lived outside of Safed mentions the ceremony in his מדבר קדמות (Lemberg 1864) מערכת שבת אות י"ג quoting the elder Azulai. But whether he himself also observed it or merely quotes it, we cannot tell.

[98a] Dr. I. Sonne called my attention to a MS. work in his possession

of Palestine or even in Palestine in any other place except Safed.[99]

מזמור שיר ליום השבת by Hananiah Eliakim Rieti (b. about 1560 — died before 1623. J. E. s. v.) where, on p. 220, Rieti expresses surprise that the rabbinic authorities who discuss the הדס for Saturday night never mention that such a ceremony was also observed on Friday night, as is indicated in the story of the Talmud, Sab. 33b. He also cites R. Nathan Shapira who, in his commentary to the פיוט מהרש"ל, [see ברכת המזון עם זמירות לשבת למהרש"ל עם פירוש ר' נתן שפירא (Venice 1603) p. 25a] says: לפנים זאת בישראל שהיו משמחין בערב שבת בין השמשות בשני הדסים. Evidently neither Shapira nor Rieti knew that the ceremony was still observed in the Lurianic circle.

[99] We can now sum up and review briefly the development of the ceremony on Saturday night and, comparing it with the development of the one on Friday night, see why and how it succeeded in maintaining itself, even though in a somewhat modified form, to this day, while the Friday night ceremony failed to maintain itself and disappeared entirely.

True, both ceremonies originally served the same purpose and the same superstitions came to be associated with both of them, so that the same objections, on the part of the more enlightened people, could be and were raised against both of them. But certain conditions favored the Saturday night ceremony, helping it to meet the objections better than the Friday night one could. In the first place, as we have seen, the ceremony on Saturday night was the older and was rooted in the habit of the people of serving a *mugmar* substitute even before any superstitious secondary purpose was ascribed to it. Hence, it had a longer time to become firmly established in the practices of the people and to acquire a stronger power of resistance so that, even after some people attached to it certain superstitions, it could withstand any attacks that might have been made against it. The Friday evening ceremony, being the younger one and a mere imitation of the older, did not have such a long time to develop the power of resistance, since the superstitions were attached to it almost at its very emergence as a ceremony. Secondly, as we have seen, the objections to both of these ceremonies were primarily to the superstitions associated with the one kind of fragrant plant, the myrtle, used for these ceremonies, but not to the practice as such. If other fragrant plants, to which no such superstitions were attached, were used, these objections were easily met. And it is significant that in all the talmudic discussion about the ceremony on Saturday night, with the exception of the one reference cited above (note 26) only בשמים, "aromatic herbs" are mentioned and no express reference to the myrtle is found. This would indicate that when the Rabbis acknowledged the well established custom as a religious ceremony, they ignored the one feature or special case of using the myrtle, a usage which entailed objectionable superstitions, and talked only of the use of other fragrant plants, בשמים, in general. And probably they encouraged only the use of the other plants in connection with this ceremony. This, however, did not eliminate the use of the myrtle in the ceremony. The people, as we have seen, continued to use the myrtle and the Rabbis could tolerate the ceremony even with the use of the myrtle among other plants, as long as no special emphasis was laid upon the use of the myrtle in particular. Even after the popular superstition connected it with the belief in the additional soul that comes to a person for the Sabbath and leaves him on Saturday night, the Rabbis could still continue to tolerate the ceremony by reinterpreting it and by giving it a rather harmless and unobjectionable meaning. For the rationalistic people explained this extra soul to mean additional peace of mind and increased spirituality that comes to the Jew on the Sabbath. When, with the going out of the Sabbath, the Jew loses this additional spirituality and faces the worries of the coming week-days, his spirit is rather depressed and needs a little refreshing (supra, note 27). And there was no harm in letting him get this refreshment from the smell of spices or even from the fragrant myrtle, as long as it was fresh and fragrant and its use could be explained to be merely for the purpose of refreshing the spirit, and not for any other superstitious functions. For, after all, the myrtle was also a fragrant plant like any other kind of בשמים and could not be discriminated against, as long as its use was interpreted to be for the same purpose for which other plants could be, and were, used. This reinterpretation of the use of the myrtle as being not a vehicle for the departing extra soul, but merely a means of refreshing the languishing soul facing the troubles of the week, saved the ceremony and caused the Rabbinic authorities to tolerate it. Of course, some of them recommended or preferred the use of spices other than the myrtle, but there could not be or there was not so much objection even to the myrtle. The mystics, as we have seen, preferred the use of the myrtle (supra, note 26) and insisted upon the mystic reason for its use. But gradually the use of other spices became more and more wide spread and the use of the myrtle was not so popular. The fear that the myrtle used might not be of the right kind and, according to the mystic beliefs, that it entailed some danger, as it might have the harmful effect of attracting evil spirits, also discouraged the use of the myrtle, even among mystically inclined people. The mystics could and did find other means of achieving all the purposes, which the myrtle was expected to serve, in other features of the Habdalah ceremony. The feature of pouring out part of the liquor used for the Habdalah ceremony, as an offering to the evil spirits, a sort of bribe, (see מטה משה IV, 504, Warsaw 1876, p. 121 and cf. Lauterbach, "The Ceremony of Breaking a Glass at Weddings" in *HUCA* II, 374, note 35) secured protection which might have been sought against the demons by the use of the myrtle. The feature of burning the part of the liquor which had been poured

out and which thus produced a little ascending flame furnished, in the minds
of some mystics, a vehicle transporting the angels to heaven (see Judg. 13.20)
— another function expected of the myrtle. The third function ascribed to
the myrtle, viz., the stimulation of sexual longing, was not considered desirable on Saturday night. Consequently, even from the point of view of the
mystics, there was no urgent need for using the myrtle as the favorite aromatic
herb in connection with the Habdalah ceremony. The spice box took its
place and also its Hebrew name. For the spice box used on Saturday night
with the Habdalah ceremony is called by the special designation *hadas*,
Hebrew for myrtle.

THE RITUAL FOR THE
KAPPAROT CEREMONY

Of the origin and development of the Kapparot-ceremony itself and its real significance I treat exhaustively in another work, a Study in Jewish Ceremonies,[1] to be published, I hope, in the very near future. Here I limit myself to a discussion of the origin and the development of the ritual of the ceremony, more specifically, the recitations accompanying the performance of the ceremony. The theory about the origin of this ritual to be advanced here will, no doubt, appear to some daring and radical, and some of my statements in this essay may seem rather apodictic. But I ask my would-be critics to suspend their judgment till the appearance of my other work in which the proofs for my theory will be cited in full and the reasons for my opinions, here expressed, stated more elaborately.

The ritual as now found in most of the prayer books does not contain anything like a prayer in form or character. It consists merely of recitations and pronouncements or declarations. Its contents may conveniently be divided into three main parts to be referred to in the following discussion as 1, 2, and 3, respectively, though not all the prayerbooks have all these three parts in exactly the same form and in the same order. These three parts are: (1) Verses from Ps. 107, preceded by the additional phrase or opening words בני אדם "sons of men." (2) Verses from Job 33, accompanied by an additional closing phrase נפש תחת נפש "Life for Life." (3) Pronouncements declaring in various formulas that the rooster is to serve as a substitute for the man and to be taken in exchange for the man, so that the latter may continue to live while the former be put to death.

This ritual is very old but for a long time it failed to receive universal approval. There seems to have been objections to it at its very first official introduction into Jewish religious life. Even among those

---

[1] This work, entitled *Tashlik*, A Study in Jewish Religious Ceremonies, deals with the ceremonies of Tashlik and Kapparot which originally were but one ceremony and only gradually in the course of time developed into two separate ceremonies. Published in *HUCA* Vol. XI, 1936 and in *Rabbinic Essays*.

Reprinted from *Jewish Studies in Memory of George A. Kohut*, 1935.

rabbinic authorities who tolerated, or approved of, the ceremony as such[2] there were some who woud not approve of the original form of the recitations accompanying its performance. They would make some changes in it, modify some expressions, leave out part or parts of the recitations, or add to it verses or phrases which in their opinion would make the formula less objectionable, or more compatible with what they considered correct Jewish belief. Accordingly there were various forms of the ritual for the Kapparot-ceremony offered by various medieval authorities of different times or successive ages. But none of these other versions succeeded in supplanting the original ritual. The latter survived all its would be substitutes and continued to be used by the majority of the people in its original form with but slight modifications which somewhat disguised its real nature and original significance, and thus in a manner or to a certain degree disarmed its critics.

Let us now examine this ritual more closely and find out what changes it experienced in the course of time. I will cite in full the oldest known form of this ritual as given by Sheshna[3] Gaon of Sura in the middle, or the second half, of the seventh century, and then briefly refer to the later medieval authorities, pointing out the changes which each one of them made in it. This ritual of Sheshna is found in the Responsa collection Shaarei Teshubah No. 299 (Leipzig 1858) p. 28, and reads, as follows:

וכך צריך [לעשות] אוחז שליח תרנגול ומניח ידו

על ראש התרנגול ונוטלו מניחו על ראש מתכפר ואומר זה תחת זה וזה חילוף זה זה

מחול [מחולל should read[4]] על זה ומחזירו עליו פעם אחרת ואומרים יושבי חשך

וצלמות כו' ויוציאם מחשך וצלמות כו' אוילים מדרך פשעם כו' כל אוכל תתעב נפשם וגו'

ויצעקו אל ה' ה' בצר להם וגו' ישלח דברו וירפאם יודו לה' חסדו וגו' ויחננו ויאמר

פדעהו וגו' נפש תחת נפש. ועושה כסדר הזה ז' פעמים ואח"כ מניח ידו על ראש תרנגול

ואומר זה יצא למיתה תחת זה ומניח ידו על ראש מתכפר ואומר תכנס אתה פלוני בן

---

[2] As is well known some rabbinical authorities, like Naḥmanides and Solomon b. Adret, condemned the ceremony as a heathen superstition דרכי אמורי, see *Bet Joseph* and *Shulḥan Aruk, Oraḥ Ḥayyim* 605 where Caro urges to refrain from observing this practice יש למנוע המנהג. But even in earlier gaonic times there were some people who objected to and ridiculed the whole ceremony. See the gaonic responsum published by Halberstam in Kobak's *Ginse Nistaroth*, part 3 (1872) p. 4, addressed to people who made fun (ששחקתם) of this ceremony. Halberstam's correction of the text to read שחקרתם as it is found in the collection חמדה גנוזה No. 93 (Jerusalem 1863) 17b, is not correct.

[3] Sheshna was also called Mesharshaya. The latter was probably his official name. See S. Krauss in *Livre d'homage à la Mémoire du Dr. Samuel Poznanski* (Warsaw 1927) p. 136 and V. Aptowitzer, Untersuchungen zur gaonäischen Literatur *HUCA* VIII–IX (Cincinnati 1931–32) p. 437 note 41.

[4] So it is found in *Tur* O. H. 605.

פלוני לחיים ולא תמות. ועושה כסדר הזה ג' פעמים ומניח מתכפר ידו על ראש תרנגול תבנית סמיכה וסומך ידו עליו ושוחטו לאלתר תבנית תיכף לסמיכה שחיטה.
This ritual[5] contains all the three parts of the version found in our prayer books though somewhat differently arranged. Part 1, the recitation from Ps. 107, comprises seven verses, viz. vv. 10, 14, 17, 18, 19, 20, and 21. The expression כו' "all of it" or וגו' "etc." after the part of each verse cited, presumably refers only to the rest of that verse. Part 2, the recitation from Job 33, consists of only one verse, viz. v. 24, the last phrase of which מצאתי כופר "I have found a ransom" is taken to be a statement made by the powers that be, that the rooster has been accepted as a ransom for the man, and the phrase נפש תחת נפש "Life for life" added thereto is to point out that the ransom is adequate.

That this ritual did not meet with the general approval in gaonic times is evident from the fact that about half a century after Sheshna's time the Gaon of Pumbedita, Natronai b. Nehemiah offers another ritual containing only part 3 of our ritual while parts 1 and 2 are entirely left out. This ritual of Natronai is found in a collection of gaonic responsa published by Ch. M. Horowitz in *Halachische Schriften der Geonim* תורתן של ראשונים part I. (Frankfort a. M. 1881) pp. 50–51[6] and reads as follows: ובערב יום הכפורים שוחטין תרנגולין על כל אחת ואחת [should read אחד ואחד] מבני הבית ואומר זה תחת זה זה חילוף זה זה בשביל זה זה מחול [should read מחולל] על זה יוצא זה למיתה ותכנס אתה פלוני בר פלוני לחיים ולא תמות ושוחטין אותו ומחלקין אותו לעניים ויתומים ואומר יהא זה כופר זה כופר כפרה שלנו ויהיה עלינו כפרה. The post-gaonic rabbinic authorities, however, with but few exceptions[7] follow in the main the ritual of Sheshna though

[5] This ritual with a slight change, viz. that the recitation from Ps. 107 includes verse 22, is also found in an anonymous responsum No. 15 in the collection of Ch. M. Horowitz. This responsum (No. 15) is preceded by another responsum (No. 14) ascribed to Natronai Gaon. This would suggest that No. 15 is likewise by Natronai. On the other hand the fact that the responsum No. 16 which follows is again expressly ascribed to Natronai suggests that No. 15 is by another author. Perhaps No. 15 is by Natronai b. Hilai, Gaon of Sura about 853, hence he agrees with and follows Sheshna who likewise was of Sura. But No. 16 is by Natronai b. Nehemiah, Gaon of Pumbedita. The special ascription to Natronai at the head of No. 16 was necessary because this Natronai is not the same to whom Nos. 14 and 15 belong.

[6] Also in the collection of Gaonic Responsa חמדה גנוזה (Jerusalem 1863) No. 93.

[7] Natronai is followed by *Shibbole Haleket* 283 (Wilna 1886) p. 266; *Mordecai*, Yoma 723; and *Mahzor Soncino* II (Casalmaggiore 1486) p. 10. *Tashbaz* 125 (Warsaw 1875) p. 21 follows Natronai partly in that he leaves out the recitation from Ps. 107. He has, however, the recitation from Job consisting of two verses which, significantly enough, he introduces by "that verse which is found in Job," ואומר אותו פסוק שיש באיוב, as if to emphasize that this recitation is a biblical text, found in the book of Job, and not part of an old incantation.

they more or less modify it and make some changes in it. Thus Rashi in ספר האורה (Lemberg 1905) p. 109, also in פרדס No. 186 (Warsaw 1870) p. 69 has Sheshna's ritual with the following significant changes. In part 1, the recitation from Ps. 107, there follows after the words אוילים מדרך פשעם of verse 17 the phrase הפסוק והמזמור וכו' (Pardes ונומר), thus indicating that not only the rest of the verse, or verses 18, 19, 20, and 21 but the entire Psalm is to be recited. In part 2, the recitation from Job, the additional closing phrase נפש תחת נפש is left out in ספר האורה, though restored in פרדס.

Vitry (p. 373) also has this ritual but with more radical changes. In part 1, the recitation from Ps. 107, he leaves out the reference to "those who dwell in darkness bound in iron fetters" (verses 10 and 14), limiting the recitation to five verses, vv. 17–21. He expressly says that only these five verses which he quotes in full are to be recited יאמר עליו חמשה פסוקים הללו. Part 2, the recitation from Job he leaves out entirely, but prescribes instead a prayer both in form and in character addressed to the living God,[8] to be recited immediately after the recitation of the five verses from Ps. 107, לאחר שסיים אלו חמשה פסוקים. Part 3, the declaration that the rooster is to be a substitute for the man, he also has as a separate third part of the ritual. But he also embodies it in the form of a petition in the prayer which he substitutes for part 2. The prayer reads as follows: יהי רצון מלפניך אלהים חיים שתזכרנו ותפקדנו לחיים טובים ויהא תרנגול זה תחת זה וחילופו ותמורתו ויצא תרנגול זה למיתה ויכנס זה לחיים טובים ארוכים ותהא שחיטתו כפרתו וכופר נפשו וינצל מכל צרה וצוקה מכל ינון ואנחה וימצא מנוחה ששון ושמחה אמן אמן סלה ועד.
Kolbo No. 68 (Lemberg 1860) p. 33 also limits part 1, i. e., the recitation from Ps. 107, to the five verses 17–21. Part 3, the declaration or petition that the rooster be the substitute for the man, he has twice, once before the recitation from Ps. 107 as Sheshna has it, and once again after the rooster is slaughtered when the latter is again swung around the head of the person, three times and when verse 23, instead of verse 24, from Job 33 is recited.

Asheri in his *Halakot*, Yoma ch. VIII No. 23 has the ritual as given by Sheshna with the following significant changes. He omits part 2, that is the recitation from Job 33, entirely but retains the words נפש תחת נפש, which formed the closing phrase of that recitation, and puts them right after the words ונפלאותיו לבני אדם, the closing words of the

---

[8] This is to emphasize that the petition is not addressed to Satan or מלאך המות. It is also possible that אלהים here is to be taken in the sense of angel, as in Genesis 32.31 and Judges 13.22. אלהים חיים then simply means מלאך החיים or מלאך הממונה על חיים החיים to whom this petition was addressed. See Isserles in *Darke Mosheh* to Tur O. Ḥ. 605 and comp. below note 20.

recitation from Ps. 107. He also adds at the very beginning of this recitation the word בני (thus in the Bomberg editions of the Talmud, Venice 1520 and 1548) or the phrase בני אדם (thus in the later Talmud editions). His son R. Jacob, the author of the Turim, likewise quotes the ritual as given by Sheshna and like his father leaves out the recitation from Job, retaining merely the closing phrase נפש תחת נפש which he puts at the end of the recitation from Ps. 107. But he omits בני or בני אדם which his father had added at the beginning of this recitation (*Tur*, O. Ḥ. 605). His disciple David Abudarham follows him, in omitting the recitation from Job but again adds the words בני אדם at the beginning of the recitation from Ps. 107. (Abudarham, Lisbon 1489, and all the subsequent editions). This is also done by R. Jacob Möllin in *Maharil* (Lemberg 1860) p. 59b who, however, states that the majority of people do add the recitation of verses from Job 33.

ורובא דעלמא מוסיפין לומר גם פסוק זה מספר איוב וז"ל אם יש עליו מלאך מליץ אחד מני אלף להגיד לאדם ישרו ויחננו ויאמר פדעהו מרדת שחת מצאתי כופר.[10]

The *Maḥzor Romania* (Venice 1527?) vol. II, 326b follows Tur. The *Maḥzor of Rome* (Bologna 1540) follows Abudarham. The *German Maḥzor* (Venice 1567), 132 seems to follow *Kolbo*, in leaving out verses 10 and 14 from the recitation from Ps. 107. It begins this recitation with verse 17 but extends it to include verse 22. It also has the recitation from Job 33, consisting of both verses 23 and 24, as given by *Maharil*, but without the closing phrase נפש תחת נפש. The מחזור כמנהג אשכנז (Wien 1823) again has the recitation from Ps. 107 including verses 10 and 14, with the opening words בני אדם, and the recitation from Job 33, consisting of both verses 23 and 24, but still without the closing phrase נפש תחת נפש. In later editions of the prayerbook this phrase is restored but put at the very beginning of the ritual before the recitations. (See Baer סדר עבודת ישראל Rödelheim 1868, p. 408, and סדור אוצר התפלות Wilna 1923, p. 1078.)[11]

I have cited all these changes made in the ritual from its first introduction into Jewish practice till it received its final and permanent form in the latest editions of the prayerbook, because I believe them to be significant in that indirectly they will help us discover the original significance of the ritual. For these changes are not merely verbal, they are doctrinal or ideological. They are not due merely to preferences of arrangement and they are not accidental. There is method and purpose in these changes and they were prompted by objections

---

[9] See below note 21.

[10] See also Isaac Tyrnau מנהגים (Warsaw 1909) p. 47 who, however, omits the words בני אדם.

[11] See the last page of this essay.

to some ideas expressed or presupposed in the original form of this ritual, if not to the ritual as a whole. For the original meaning and significance of this whole ritual was altogether different from what the rabbinic authorities naively believed, or consciously wished to reinterpret it, to be.

To state briefly what I discuss elsewhere[12] at greater length, there can be no doubt that the Kapparot-ceremony, especially as it was performed in the earliest gaonic time with a horned animal, ram or goat,[13] or with a rooster,[14] was a revival of the ancient ritual of sending a goat to Azazel.[15] And like the goat for Azazel it was a sacrifice to Satan, a sort of ransom or bribe sent to him to persuade him to desist from accusing the people whom he would claim as his prey.

Such an offering naturally had to be accompanied by some message or petition addressed to the party for whom the offering was intended. And so indeed it was. An incantation was recited, composed of appropriate biblical phrases[16] suitable to express the thoughts to be conveyed to Satan and his cohorts, the degraded sons of God, or the fallen angels who had rebelled against the words of God and in punishment for their sins were dwelling in darkness, chained in iron fetters.[17] In this incantation or message, these "dwellers in darkness" were subtly reminded that they themselves, though sons of God, created

[12] In the work on Tashlik referred to above note 1.

[13] See Sheshna's responsum cited above. Another, perhaps earlier, form of the Kapparot-ceremony performed with baskets of beans or vegetables is alluded to in the Talmud (Sabbath 81b, comp. Rashi there s. v. האי פרפיסא). More about this in the work on Tashlik.

[14] Gifts or bribes to Satan are chosen preferably from among animals which resemble him in some features and which presumably he especially likes. Horned animals resemble Satan and the demons. See *Targum Jonathan* to Lev. 9.3, also Rashi to Ber. 62a s. v. שעיר, referring to Is. 13.21. The rooster resembles the devil and the demons in the shape of his feet. See Ber. 6a, also Rashi to Gitin 68b s. v. בדקו בכרעיה.

[15] The similarity in character of the Kapparot-ceremony with the ceremony of sending a goat to Azazel is assumed by Vitry, *l. c.* where the prayer at the performance of the Kapparot-ceremony contains the phrase: ויהא כפרתו כמו כפרת שעיר המשתלח שהיה מכפר על כל ישראל. See also Treves in his commentary קמחא דאבישונא to the מחזור מנהג בני רומא (Bologna 1540) who gives the reason for the Kapparot-ceremony that it recalls the sending of the goat to Azazel which likewsie served the purpose of giving a portion to the demons: שיש בזה רמז לשעיר המשתלח לתת חלק לפורחות ולכחות הטומאה ולהיות ישראל מנוקים ורצוים לאל אלקי הרוחות.

[16] An incantation, consisting of seven biblical verses from Ps. 29, is also prescribed in the Talmud (Pes. 112a) as a means of warding off danger from demons.

[17] See Revelation 20.1–3. Satan-Samael and Azazel or Azael are identical with the fallen angels.

as pure angels, could not resist temptation and "condemned the counsel of the Most High"; hence they ought not to be too harsh upon the
sons of men, who, born in sin and afflicted with the weakness of the
flesh, could not always resist temptation. The wish and the hope was
expressed to them that their supreme Master, the Most High, would
be lenient with them, "bring them out of darkness and the shadow of
death and break their bands in sunder" if they in turn would be lenient
and would show consideration for human beings;[18] if Satan, their chief,
instead of accusing man and claiming him as his prey, a victim for
hell, would rather become a good angel, an intercessor instead of an
accuser,[19] who would vouch for man's uprightness and would "be
gracious and say: 'Deliver him from going down to the pit. I have
found a ransom' " for him in this rooster or horned animal and I accept
"a life for a life." This incantation opened with the words בני אלהים
"Sons of God" thus flattering Satan and his associates and reminding
them of their divine origin and once exalted position.

This was the real nature and original meaning of the recitation
accompanying the performance of the Kapparot-ceremony.[20] Such a
ritual was tantamount to worshipping Satan by offering him a sacrifice and praying to him and could, of course, not be tolerated. It was
incompatible with Jewish teachings, hence the total or partial rejection of it by various rabbinical authorities and the various attempts
at changing or modifying it on the part of those who retained it.

---

[18] The same reminder and veiled threat was suggested to the accusers by the Azazel goat. See Racanati טעמי המצות ed. Abraham Kanaryvogel (Przemysl 1888) p. 16b
where it is said: טעם מצוה זו להודיע למקטרגים שאם יקטרגו עלינו גם עליהם יקטרגו במעשה עזא
ועזאל כשבאו על בנות האדם והתצלות נדולה לבן אדם אם מלאכי עליון שירדו לזה העולם נתלבשו
ביצר הרע מה יעשה יציר חמר מטפה סרוחה אשר בעון חולל.

[19] See Zohar Vayishlaḥ (Amsterdam 1800) p. 174b where the verse in Job speaking
of the One Angel מלאך אחד is interpreted as referring to the accuser who might become
a defender.. Although according to the Zohar it was the Azazel goat that could effect
this transformation of the accuser into a defender, it was believed that the animal
used in the Kapparot-ceremony, another form of the Azazel goat, could likewise
accomplish this task. See Joseph Jospa Kossmann in his commentary מסביר to
סדר סליחות (Amsterdam 1712) p. 108a.

[20] That this recitation was originally an incantation addressed to an angel is evident from statements made by later medieval authorities to the effect that a certain
angel by the name of חתך (indicated in the initial letters of כפרתי (תחתי) חליפתי תמורתי
is in charge of this task of effecting the substitution of the rooster for the man. See
מנהגים by R. Abraham Klausner (ed. Ehrenreich Deva 1929) 11a where it is said:
ונהגו לומר זה חליפתי וזה תחחי וזה כפרתי וכו' לפי שהוא ראשי תיבות חתך והוא שמו של מלאך הממונה
על זה. Comp. also הגהות to מנהגים of Isaac Tyrnau, l. c. and Maharil, l. c. In Darke
Mosheh to Tur O. Ḥ. 605 this angel by the name of חתך is declared to be the "Angel
of Life" מלאך הממונה על החיים. See above note 8.

Natronai and those who follow him eliminate the whole incantation
which actually sounded like a prayer to Satan. They retain the ceremony as such, accompanied by a brief declaration that the animal is
a substitute for the man, but emphasize that it is the charitable act
of distributing the slaughtered animal among the poor and the orphans
that will bring the atonement for the man.

Sheshna retains the incantation but seeks to change its character
somehow. Instead of recognizing it as a petition addressed to Satan
he would interpret it merely as a recitation of biblical verses in a
manner addressed to God, though not in the form of a real prayer.
He, therefore, leaves out the opening words בני אלהים "Sons of God"
and verse 23 from Job 33: "If there be an angel," both of which clearly
indicate that the recitation is addressed to the sons of God, or some
angel. He retains verses 10 and 14 of Ps. 107 but would understand
"those who dwell in darkness" to refer to human beings who might
suffer from poverty or imprisonment. Rashi in ספר האורה follows
Sheshna, but to further change the character of the incantation and
make it appear as a mere recitation of biblical verses, he prescribes
the recitation of the whole Ps. 107 and not merely of those verses
which formed part of the incantation. He also leaves out the closing
words נפש תחת נפש, which had meaning only if "I have found a ransom"
were understood as spoken by the accuser. But if the words are to
be understood as spoken by God, or if the word כופר is to be taken
in the sense of כפרה and the whole sentence "I have found atonement"
as spoken by the man, the words "Life for Life" are either inapprop-
riate, or make no sense. Vitry goes farther in changing the incantation
into a prayer. He leaves out all references to "those who dwell in
darkness," verses 10 and 14 of Ps. 107, fearing that they might be
taken in their original meaning in the incantation, as addressing the
fallen angels, and not as reinterpreted, to refer to suffering human
beings. He also leaves out the entire recitation from Job, and substitutes for it a prayer, both in form and in character, addressed to
the living God.

But the suppressed or eliminated objectionable parts of the incantation were not entirely forgotten and in the course of time the more
the original meaning of the incantation was forgotten and the more
the reinterpretation of it as being a recitation addressed to God was
accepted, the easier it was for some authorities to restore the eliminated objectionable parts. Thus Kolbo reintroduced part of the reci-

tation from Job. Asheri reintroduces the reference to "those who
dwell in darkness" verses 10 and 14 of Ps. 107, adding thereto בני, or,
as in the later editions בני אדם²¹ thus making it clear, that the reference
is to human beings and not to certain angels. This is followed, as we
have seen, by Abudarham and Maharil, the latter adding that the
majority of the people also include the recitation of the two verses
from Job 33. This practice of the majority of the people was adopted
in the majority of the prayerbooks. The additional closing phrase to
the recitation from Job נפש תחת נפש, pointing to the ransom spoken
of in the last sentence of that recitation and characterising it as adequate—which, as we have seen, had also been eliminated because it
no longer fitted that recitation as interpreted by the Rabbis—was
now also restored. But instead of being the closing phrase of part 2,
the recitation from Job, which it no longer fitted, was made the opening phrase of part 3, the declaration that the animal is in exchange of
and a substitute for the man. To avoid any possible mistake of still
taking the words נפש תחת נפש, now made the opening phrase of part 3
for the closing phrase of part 2, the order of the arrangement of the
three parts was changed. Part 3 with its additional opening phrase
נפש תחת נפש was placed before part 1 and 2. See סדר סליחות with commentary מסביר by R. Joseph Jospa Kossmann (Amsterdam 1712) p. 108.

²¹ The words בני אלהים were in some source written in abbreviation ב'א which a later
copyist misunderstood as standing for בני אדם which he accordingly wrote out in full.
Dr. L. Ginzberg has another theory as to how later copyists came to write בני אדם·
His statement follows:
The explanation of בני אדם as a misunderstood reading of the abbreviation בני = ב'א
אלהים angels is, for more than one reason, not tenable. The designation of the
angels as בני אלהים is found in post-Biblical literature only in connection with the
Biblical verses where it occurs (cf. e.g. Pirke R. El. 22) but not otherwise. Hence
even if it were proved that the כפרות were introduced with a prayer to the angels,
their description as בני אלהים would be extremely strange. How is one further to
explain the absence of בני אדם in the old sources like *Sefer ha-Orah* or *Mahzor Vitry*,
though they do not mention the recital of Ps. 106.10 ff. as a part of the ceremony of
Kapparot? As a matter of fact even R. Asher knows only of בני without אדם which
is first met with in the work of his disciple Abudrahim and in the later editions of
רא"ש as well as in the prayer books. It seems to me therefore that בני אדם is a mis-
understtod reading of an abbreviation בנסח ישן which was originally a marginal note
calling attention to the fact that the recital of the following verses is in accordance
with an old text and hence to be considered authoritative though *not* found in the
Responsa of the Geonim dealing with כפרות. The marginal note בני came first into
the text as we find it in the first edition of רא"ש but as it gave absolutely no sense
אדם was later added, an "emendation" suggested by לבני אדם which occurs four times
in Ps. 107 that furnished the recital at the performance of the Kapparot.

This order, however, was not generally accepted. The people some-how felt that the recitations of the Biblical verses, i. e. parts 1 and 2 of the original incantation, must come first. Part 3 then was put back into the third position, but without its additional opening clause נפש נפש חתת. The latter thus remained at the very beginning of the whole recitation. Thus developed the form of the ritual as we have it in the later editions of the prayer books.

THE BELIEF IN THE POWER OF THE WORD

JACOB Z. LAUTERBACH, Hebrew Union College, Cincinnati

THE belief in the effectiveness of the uttered word is common among primitive peoples[1] and was widespread among ancient civilized peoples.[2] The Jewish people were in this respect not different from other peoples. According to this belief, whatever is spoken, even if only casually and unintentionally, comes true and actually happens, that is to say, the word becomes fact. Prevalence of such a belief among the Jews can be traced throughout all the periods of Jewish history. Expressions of it, in various forms, are found in Bible,[3] Talmud and Midrashim,[4] as well as in later Jewish literature. It has survived to this day and still forms part of popular Jewish belief, or folklore.[5] A clear expression or, one might almost say, a formulation of this belief may be found in the enigmatic Hebrew saying, quoted by both

[1] See J. G. Fraser, *The Golden Bough*, Part II, chap. vi, Tabooed Words, p. 319ff. and especially p. 331. Also Robert Briffault, *The Mothers*, (New York 1927) I, p. 12ff.

[2] See Paul Heinisch, *Das Wort im Alten Testament und im Alten Orient* (Münster 1922) about the Word in the Religions of the Egyptians, Babylonians and Persians.

[3] This essay deals with this belief and its underlying ideas as found in Talmudic literature. Hence no attempt is made to trace it through the biblical period. In a few instances we shall refer to manifestations of the belief in the biblical literature. See below notes 49, 53, 55. However, since the Rabbis in most cases base their ideas on biblical passages, (see below notes 46, 47, 42, 50) it is evident that they assumed that their ideas on this subject were derived from the Bible and hence were survivals from biblical times. And we have no reason to doubt the correctness of their assumption. Comp. also Heinisch *op. cit.*, pp. 8–10 and 44–46.

[4] Quotations from Talmud and Midrashim expressing or reflecting this belief would fill a big volume. I content myself with the few quotations cited below in the course of this essay. See especially notes 6, 15, 19, 20, 43, 46.

[5] There is no need to cite proofs from later rabbinic literature. The rabbis of later times to a greater or lesser degree retained, in some instances with slight modifications, most of the superstitious beliefs found in the Talmud.

Reprinted from *Hebrew Union College Annual*, Vol. XIV, 1939.

Palestinian and Babylonian teachers: ברית כרותה לשפתים "A covenant has been made about the lips" guaranteeing that their utterances would not be ineffective.[6] But we are not told who made this covenant or why it was made, or what reasons the people or the teachers had for assuming such a covenant and thus believing in the power and effectiveness of human speech. Whatever may have been the basis of such a belief among primitive people who could not distinguish between words and things,[7] it would not explain the prevalence of this belief among the Jewish people of Talmudic times who were above such a level of primitiveness. Certainly, the teachers of Talmudic times were not so primitive as not to be able to distinguish between a statement or description of a fact and the fact itself, or between an uttered wish or curse and its fulfillment. If therefore we find this belief current in Talmudic times and, in one form or another, endorsed and supported by the Rabbis of different generations, both in Palestine and Babylon, then there must have been underlying it certain ideas which somehow could be made to fit into the theological or philosophical system of the Rabbis and which were in agreement, or at any rate not in conflict with some of their fundamental beliefs. Although it is true that the Rabbis would in some instances tolerate certain popular superstitions,[8] either because they were unable to suppress them or because they themselves, or at least some of them, were not above believing in these superstitions,

---

[6] Comp. the saying in b. R. H. 17b: ברית כרותה לשלש עשרה מדות שאינן חוזרות ריקם. Apparently in our case the Rabbis hesitated to express the saying in full, hence they cited only part of it: ברית כרותה לשפתים. An examination of the context in which this half saying is quoted (b. M. Ḳ. 18a and b. Sanh. 102a) leaves no doubt as to its meaning and implication. See especially Midr. Num. Rab. 18, 10. Commenting on the passage: "And they said: We will not come up" (Num. 16.12), the Midrash says: ויאמרו לא נעלה הכשילם פיהם לרשעים וברית כרותה לשפתים שמתו וירדו לשאול. Here it is expressly stated that their mouths made these wicked people stumble into using the expression "We will not come up" instead of "We will not come," or "We will not go." Hence, since "a covenant is made about the lips" their utterance came true and they actually did go down to Hell. Comp. Num. Rab. 18, 7 and Tanḥuma Buber to Koraḥ 5 (p. 87).

[7] See Briffault op. cit., especially pp. 14f.

[8] See Lauterbach, Tashlik (Cincinnati 1936) pp. 43ff.

they certainly would fight against such superstitions as were in conflict with an essential principle or a fundamental belief and which they would therefore recognize as dangerous to the religious life of the people. In such cases they would seek to combat and suppress these popular notions, or when this was impossible at least to make them theologically less harmful and more compatible with their own advanced ideas and pure beliefs. The aim of this essay is to find out the ideas underlying this popular Jewish belief as far as they are implicitly or explicitly indicated in the Talmud, and to ascertain how the teachers could and did bring them into harmony with their advanced theological ideas.

Ideas and beliefs are not isolationists. They associate freely with others and travel in groups, explaining and motivating, helping and supporting one another. We can understand them correctly only by looking at them in the light of other ideas with which they are associated and by considering the whole complex of which they form but a part. In our case, then, the belief in the power of the word, that whatever is uttered in speech actually comes to happen in fact, can best be understood by considering it in connection with other beliefs concerning the manner in which things or events come to be, and especially in relation to popular notions as to the way in which all the happenings in this world are brought about.

Now, according to Jewish beliefs generally accepted in the Talmudic period[9] and maintained by pious orthodox Jews all through the post-Talmudic times up to the present day, the

9 In the following pages I do not mean to present the theological system of the Talmud. The aim is merely to give a sketch of the popular conception (shared also by some rabbis) of the heavenly management of the affairs of this world as reflected in certain agadic sayings. In many instances other sayings of the Rabbis could be cited objecting to the ideas and beliefs expressed in the sayings cited here. But the latter at any rate prove that such ideas were current among the people and were approved by some of the Rabbis. However, not all of these ideas necessarily formed an integral part of the authentic theological system of the majority of the Rabbis. The Rabbis of the Talmud were not always unanimous in their opinions and were not always consistent in their ideas. They tolerated and even shared in popular fancies and notions which were not always in harmony with their own lofty teachings and advanced beliefs. Comp. S. Schechter, *Some Aspects of Rabbinic Theology* (New York 1907), pp. 30ff.

business of this world in all its details is managed and super-
vised[10] by the heavenly government and nothing happens here
on earth below unless it has been ordered and decreed in heaven
above.[11] Nothing is so small as to be overlooked, and no person
so insignificant as to be ignored.[12] Every person and every action
of every person is observed and watched, recorded and judged
by the heavenly administration.

In some exceptional instances God attends to the details of
the management Himself, personally and directly, not through
any agent or angel.[13] Even in such instances, however, man,
especially the righteous man, can by his word exert some influence upon the management of the world. Thus the righteous
man can, if one may say so, direct the Divine activity, and
modify or even annul the decrees of God.[14] For about the righteous man it is written: "Thou shalt also decree a thing and it
shall be established unto thee" (Job 22.28)[15] and whatever the

[10] See M. Abot II, 1 and III, 15–16.

[11] אין אדם נוקף אצבעו מלמטה אלא אם כן מכריזין עליו מלמעלה, Hul. 7b.

[12] אפילו ריש גרנותא משמיא מוקמי ליה, b. Ber. 58a; B. B. 91b. Comp. also the
saying ציפור מבלעדי שמיא לא יבדא כל שכן בר נשא, p. Sheb. IX, 1 (38b), or, as
Tossafot to Ab. Z. 16b s. v. דימוס quotes it: אפילו צפורא קלילא מבלעדי שמיא
לא מיתצדא כל שכן בר איניש. Comp. to this Matth. 10.29–31: "Not one of them
(the sparrows) shall fall on the ground without your father . . . ye are of more
value than many sparrows," or Luke 12.6–7: "And not one of them is forgotten in the sight of God."

[13] See e. g. Mekilta d. R. Ishmael, Pisha VII and VIII (ed. Lauterbach,
I, pp. 53 and 97) and Sifre Deut., 325 (Friedman p. 139a). Also b. Pes. 118a
where God says to Gabriel that it is proper that He Himself personally should
save Abraham: נאה ליחיד להציל את היחיד.

[14] Not only by appeal or petition but also by utterances which are not
prayers. See b. M. K. 16b where God is represented as saying: אני מושל באדם.
מי מושל בי? צדיק שאני גוזר גזירה ו(הוא) מבטלה. See commentary ad loc. s. v. צור
ישראל where it is explained to mean צדיק מושל בי ומבטלה. Comp. also b. Shab.
63a where it is said: אפילו הק׳ב׳ה גוזר גזירה הוא (הצדיק) מבטלה. In a milder modified form this saying is found in b. B. M. 85a where it reads אפילו הקב׳ה גוזר
גזירה מבטלה בשבילו (של הצדיק) which may mean that God nullifies it because
of the intercession of the righteous man. This modification was prompted,
no doubt, by theological considerations. In the Foreword to the Zohar (Lublin
1872) p. 10, it is expressed in a bolder and more general form: דהק׳ב׳ה גוזר
גזירין וצדיקיא דישראל מבטלין לון דכתיב צדיק מושל יראת אלהים.

[15] דכתיב בהו בצדיקים ותגזר אומר ויקם לך, b. Ket. 103b. This statement is made
to explain that since Judah Hanasi had declared that Hama b. Hanina should

righteous man predicts comes true. What he decrees here below is carried out by God from above.[16] God sometimes nullifies His own decrees because of a countermanding decree of the righteous man.[17] And even an ordinary man, not known to his fellowmen as an exceptionally righteous one, could claim that God would carry out whatever he might decree or ask for.[18] And since we can never really know who is truly righteous, it is advisable not to take lightly the blessing[19] or the curse[20] even

be the head of the Academy it was unavoidable that Ḥama should actually succeed to that high office: כיון דאמר רבי: חנינא בר חמא ישב בראש אי אפשר דלא מליך. Comp. also b. Shab. 59b.

[16] אתה גזרת מלמטה והקב״ה מקיים מאמרך מלמעלה, b. Ta'an. 23a. See also Matth. 18.18: "Verily I say unto you what things soever ye bind on earth shall be bound in heaven; and what things soever ye shall loose on earth shall be loosed in heaven." And compare the comment on this passage by John Chrysostom: "And what priests do here below God ratifies above, and the Master confirms the sentence of His servants." (*On the Priesthood* in *Nicene and Post-Nicene Fathers*, IX [New York] p. 47.) In passing I would remark that Chrysostom's statement (*ibid.*, *l. c.*) that the priests "have received an authority which God has not given to angels or archangels" also reminds one of the saying of R. Joḥanan גדולים צדיקים יותר ממלאכי השרת, b. Sanh. 93a.

[17] הקב״ה מבטל גזירתו מפני גזירתו של צדיק, p. Ta'an. III, 12 (67a). And more explicitly, it is repeatedly stated there when God is represented as saying to the righteous: דידך קיימא דידי לא קיימא.

[18] מצי אמר ליה .... הוה טיקיים בי ותגזר אומר ויקם לך, b. B. M. 106a.

[19] אל תהי ברכת הדיוט קלה בעיניך, b. Meg. 15a. The superstitious belief that uttered wishes will come true is also the underlying idea of the general custom of wishing "good luck." Some of the ancient Talmudic teachers did indeed recognize this as a heathen superstition and objected to it, but to no avail. Thus there must have been objections to wishing "good health" at taking a drink, since the Talmud felt the need of declaring that the expression of such a wish is not to be regarded as a heathen superstition: חמרא וחיי לפום רבנן אין בו משום דרכי האמורי, b. Shab. 67b. And to this day it is customary to wish "life" (לחיים) when taking a drink. Likewise the custom of wishing "life" or "health" (when someone sneezes) was declared a heathen superstition. האומר מרפא הרי זה מדרכי האמורי, Tosef. Shab. VII, 5 (Zuckermandel p. 118). But in spite of this condemnation the custom of saying אסותא, the Aramaic for מרפא, or "life," חיים (Pirḳe de R. Eli'ezer ch. 52.) when one sneezes has persisted among the Jews to this day. And a legendary explanation as to why such a wish should be expressed just when one is sneezing is given in the Midrashim. See Pirḳe de R. Eli'ezer, *l. c.*, and Yalḳuṭ Shime'oni to the Pentateuch § 77 and commentary by Zayit Ra'anan *ad loc.* and comp. also *JE* s. v. "Asusa."

[20] אל תהי קללת הדיוט קלה בעיניך, b. Meg. *l. c.* Also b. B. K. 93a.

of an ordinary person, for he may be one of the few perfectly righteous people, or one of those whose utterances God heeds and fulfills.[21] Hence the utterance of any person may have potential significance.

In the main, however, the heavenly administration of this world and its affairs is carried on by God in conjunction with His court and administrative council[22] through the agency of myriads of angels who are assigned to various kinds of tasks. Some of them are investigators, observers and reporters;[23] others are accusers and prosecutors, or pleaders and defenders[24] at the heavenly court of justice. Still others function as executors of the court orders, inflicting punishment upon convicted evil-doers and bringing rewards to those who have been found in-nocent and righteous.[25] These angels are everywhere. They surround the throne of God and the seat of judgment[26] or stand

---

[21] To this day it is customary among Jews that when one says something of auspicious portent even if it is not said in the form of a wish but is merely a statement, opinion or prediction that such and such a good thing is, or will be, happening, they say to him: "From your mouth into God's ears," i. e. God will, or may, hear your words and carry them out and make them come true.

[22] אין הקב"ה עושה דבר אלא אם כן נמלך בפמליא של מעלה שנאמר בגזירת עירין פתגמא ובמאמר קדישין שאילתא, b. Sanh. 38b, or as it is stated in p. Sanh. I, 1 (18a): אין הקב"ה עושה בעולמו דבר עד שנמלך בבית דין שלמעלה. Also, in contradiction to the Mishnah Abot IV, 8, Juda b. Pazzi, citing 1 Ki. 22.19–23 in proof, says, אף הקב"ה אין דן יחידי, p. Sanh. *ibid.*, *l. c.* Comp. also Gen. Rab. VIII, 3 and 4.

[23] Satan is said to combine many functions. He acts as agent provocateur, reporter, accuser and executor. See b. B. B. 16a: תנא יורד ומתעה ועולה ומרגיז נוטל רשות ונוטל נשמה. Comp. his rôle in Job 1 and 2.

[24] See p. Sanh. *l. c.*: אילו מטין לכף זכות ואילו מטין לכף חובה. Comp. also Gen. Rab. VIII, 8 and b. Sanh. 38b.

[25] See Mekilta de R. Ishmael, Pisḥa I (ed. Lauterbach, I, p. 12) where it is assumed that the angels are sent out to execute both גזירות טובות and גזירות רעות, and in the case of the former they report back about their executions, and the reference is given to Ezek. 9.2–7. Comp. also b. Shab. 88a about the crowns distributed by angels to the Israelites and then removed from them. Also b. B. M. 86b about the one angel sent to bring healing to Abraham and another to destroy Sodom. Also Gen. Rab. 50, 2. For one angel cannot go on two missions: אין מלאך אחד עושה שתי שליחות.

[26] See Isa. 6.1; 1 Ki. 22.19; and Dan. 7.9–10. Comp. also Lauterbach, "A Significant Controversy between the Sadducees and the Pharisees," *HUCA*, IV (1927), p. 185ff.

eavesdropping behind doors and partitions,[27] eagerly waiting to be called in to submit reports of their observations, or to be sent on errands to execute orders. They also accompany every person wherever he may be,[28] observing all his doings and watching his conduct, and are also ready to protect or harm him,[29] i. e. to execute whatever may have been decreed upon him by the heavenly court. There are good and benign angels who delight to go on errands of mercy and to do good. These are the מלאכי רחמים[30] the angels of mercy. There are also, strange to say, bad and malicious angels who find pleasure in making trouble, finding fault, causing harm and bringing destruction. These are the מלאכי חבלה[31] the angels of destruction.

Although all these angels are but subordinate[32] functionaries expected merely to obey orders and to do only what they

[27] See b. Ḥag. 16a. The demons, who are identical with the מלאכי חבלה, are like the ministering angels in that they listen behind the partition שומעין מאחורי הפרגוד. Also b. Sanh. 89b where Satan betrays something to which he had stealthily listened from behind the partition: ואלי דבר יגונב שמעתי מאחורי הפרגוד ...

[28] See b. Ta'an. 11a: שני מלאכי השרת המלוין לו לאדם הן מעידין עליו. Here it speaks of *the* two angels who always accompany a man, not only on the eve of the Sabbath on his way home from the Synagogue, as is said (b. Shab. 119b): שני מלאכי השרת מלוין לו לאדם בע"ש מבית הכנסת לביתו אחד טוב ואחד רע. We learn from the latter statement that of the two accompanying angels one is a good one and one is a bad one. The one reports the good deeds of the person, the other his evil deeds. These two angels are merely the observers and reporters. But man is surrounded by many more good and bad angels. See next note.

[29] In b. Ber. 6a it is said that every person is surrounded by a thousand bad angels or demons on his left side and by ten thousand on his right side. To match these he is also accompanied by a thousand good angels on his left side and ten thousand on his right side. (Mid. Teh. to Ps. 101 [Buber p. 398]).

[30] This designation occurs in Gen. Rab. 50, 1 and elsewhere.

[31] This designation occurs in b. Shab. 88a and elsewhere.

[32] There was considerable disagreement and difference of opinion among the ancient teachers concerning the belief in the existence of angels. (See L. Finkelstein, *The Pharisees*, I, Ch. IV [Philadelphia 1938] especially p. 179ff. and "The Oldest Midrash etc." in *The Harvard Theological Review* XXXI, 4, October 1938 p. 306ff.) Some teachers considered such a belief incompatible with pure Jewish monotheism. A sort of compromise was reached whereby angels were allowed to exist but merely as inferior agents and subordinate beings. Thus modified, the belief in angels found more and more acceptance.

are bidden or say only what is asked of them by their Supreme Master, they sometimes manage to overstep the limits of their subordinate sphere of activity. They sometimes speak up[33] or act[34] of their own accord without any order from God and without having any authority to do so. For, if it could be said, "the earthly kingdom is like the heavenly kingdom"[35] it can just as well be said that the officials and functionaries of the heavenly government are with regard to certain faults and deficiencies not unlike the bureaucratic officials of an earthly government. They are meddlesome,[36] officious and boastful,[37] as if they were acting of their own accord, and not merely carrying out orders. Sometimes they even reveal administrative secrets and have to be disciplined or punished.[38] They have their preferences and

But the angels, once existence was granted to them, revolted against such a degradation and the popular mind sympathised with them and gradually allowed them some share and a deciding vote in the heavenly administration. Comp. Lauterbach, *Tashlik*, p. 46ff. See also A. Kohut, *Ueber die Jüdische Angelologie und Dämonologie in Ihrer Abhängigkeit vom Parsismus*, Leipzig 1866. A more comprehensive treatment of the subject in its independent development in Rabbinic literature is a great desideratum.

[33] Thus when Moses came up to heaven to receive the Torah the angels spoke up and said, "What right has one born of woman to be among us?" (מה ילוד אשה בינינו), and they told God that He ought rather give the Torah to them (b. Shab. 88b). When Akiba was tortured and died as a martyr they protested to God about this injustice by saying זו תורה וזו שכרה (b. Ber. 61b.) They registered a similar protest when God decreed a certain punishment upon Israel. They said: "Should this be done to Israel?" (זאת להן לישראל? — b. Giṭ. 7a). They also cried out and protested when Abraham was about to sacrifice Isaac (Gen. Rab. 56, 5 and Pirḳe de R. Eli'ezer XXXI, p. 71a).

[34] See Gen. Rab. 73, 10, how they helped in the increase of Jacob's flocks, and what they did to the band of Esau (*ibid.* 78, 11). Comp. also p. Sheb. VI end (8d), how an angel came down and smote Nebukadnezzar on his mouth, ירד מלאך וסטרו על פיו.

[35] מלכותא דארעא כעין מלכותא דרקיעא (b. Ber. 58a).

[36] See Gen. Rab. 53, 14 where they wanted to interfere with God's providing a well for the thirsty Ishmael. See also b. Meg. 12b. On the other hand they interfered and interceded in the case of Benjamin the righteous one (b. B. B. 11a).

[37] See Gen. Rab. 50, 9: שנתגאו ואמרו כי משחיתים אנחנו את המקום הזה.

[38] See *ibid.*, *l. c.*: מלאכי השרת על ידי שגילו מסטורין של הקב"ה נדחו ממחיצתן מאה ושלשים ושמונה שנה, and *ibid.*, 78, 2, where the angel, though remembering the disciplinary punishment which his colleagues had received for betraying

their prejudices and allow themselves to be influenced in their official activity by their likes and dislikes. Not only those angels who belong to the heavenly council or are members of the court, but also those subordinates whose functions are merely to execute orders allow their personal preferences to interfere with their functions and to influence their official activity. Thus when some punishment is decreed by the heavenly court upon certain people, angels are dispatched to execute the verdict. If the angels on duty who are assigned to the task happen to be kind and merciful angels, they will be slow in carrying out the order and will delay the execution of the punishment as much as possible. Not that they dare disobey orders or counteract any Divine command. They merely go about their task slowly and hesitatingly, hoping that in the meantime, during their delaying or protracting the execution, the decree may be rescinded. Someone might intercede on behalf of the convicted people and find some exonerating or mitigating circumstance in the act for which they were judged and condemned. The case then, according to Jewish jurisprudence,[39] would be reopened and the heavenly court might reverse its decision.[40]

In other instances the angels show such an eagerness to rush to the assistance of their favorites or to harm those whom they dislike that God has to restrain them from doing so.[41] Furthermore, in their overzeal to be of service to their Master they are prone to indulge in the practice of hurrying to carry out a Divine command even before having heard it fully[42] or understood it

---

secrets, yet upon pressure reveals to Jacob a secret, and even prepares in advance a defence for his conduct in case he should be called to account for his betrayal.

[39] See M. Sanh. VI, 1.

[40] Thus the angels sent to destroy Sodom proceeded very slowly, waiting and hoping that Abraham might succeed in his intercession on behalf of the people of Sodom: מלאכי רחמים היו והיו ממתינים וסבורים שמא ימצא להם זכות (Gen. Rab. 50, 1).

[41] See b. Pes. 118a (cited above) where God restrained Gabriel from rushing to the aid of Abraham and b. Sanh. 103b about the angels who attempted to push Micah aside and were told by God: "Leave him alone" (בקשו מלאכי השרת לדוחפו אמר להם הקב"ה הניחו לו . . .).

[42] See b. Shab. 88a: רז זה שמלאכי השרת משתמשין בו דכתיב ברכו ד' כל מלאכיו גבורי כח עושי דברו לשמוע בקול דברו (Ps. 103.20) ברישא עושי והדר לשמוע.

correctly. This zeal may sometimes lead them to actions which are contrary to the intent of the instructions given to them. For instance, a heavenly decree might be made subject to certain conditions, in which case the angels would be given the order to carry out that decree if, when and as the stipulated conditions ensued. However, the angels, in their zeal, might rush off to carry out the order as soon as they hear it given, without waiting to hear the stipulated conditions attached to it.[43] As a result they perform the task even when the conditions surrounding the case do not warrant the action or are even such as to require the opposite action. In some instances, their eagerness to fly off on their errands causes them not to wait to hear the full description or the right address of the party concerned in the order, and as a result, they rush off to the wrong address and execute the order upon a party other than the one meant by the divine decree.[44]

The most unpardonable negligence of which the angels are sometimes guilty is their failure to pay sufficiently close attention to the source whence issue the orders which they believe to have received; thus they sometimes mistake a human voice for the divine voice.[45] When, while floating around in the air,

[43] See b. Ber. 7a: כל דבור ודבור שיצא מפי הקב״ה לטובה אפילו על תנאי לא חזר בו. By wishful thinking the Rabbis assumed that only when the decree was for something good would the stipulation be ignored. But it could just as well happen that the angel going forth to execute a decree for evil, unlike the angels who went to destroy Sodom (see Note 40), would hurry to carry out the order and would ignore the stipulated condition. See below notes 44 and 46.

[44] See b. Ḥag. 3b–4a about the mistake which the angel of death admitted having made, and comp. Lauterbach, "Naming of Children in Jewish Folklore, Ritual and Practice," in C. C. A. R. Yearbook, XLII (1932), p. 15 and p. 40, note 28. Also ibid., notes 24–26 and 29 about the device used to escape evil, sickness or death by a change of name שינוי השם which is based on the assumption that the angels can make mistakes.

[45] We need not be surprised at this auditory deficiency. Their visual perception is not absolutely reliable either. Thus when they saw Adam, made in the image of God, they mistook him for God Himself and were about to recite before him the invocation: Holy, Holy, Holy, etc. Only after God had caused a deep sleep to fall upon Adam did they realize that he was only a man. See Gen. Rab. VIII, 10: בשעה שברא הקב״ה אדם הראשון טעו בו מלאכי השרת ובקשו לומר לפניו קדוש . . . מה עשה הקב״ה הפיל עליו תרדמה וידעו הכל שהוא אדם.

they hear a voice uttering or reciting words which to them sound like a command, they may erroneously imagine that voice to have come from on high, issuing a command, and without examining carefully whence the voice came or by whom the supposed order was issued, they rush off to carry out the action indicated or implied in the words which they have heard. This particular kind of mistake is described in the Talmud as כשגגה שיוצא מלפני השליט, "a mistaken assumption that it (the voice or command) came from the (Supreme) Ruler,"[46] when in real-

[46] The phrase is taken from Eccl. 10.5 which verse I would render as follows: "There is evil which I have seen under the sun such as when by mistake (it is assumed) that (the order for) it proceedeth from the Ruler." I believe that the biblical author also hints at the belief that the angels make mistakes. (See *ibid.* 5.5: "Suffer not . . . and say not before the angel that it was an error.") He thus ascribes the evil to mistakes on the part of the agent and not to God.

But whatever the interpretation of these biblical verses may be, there can be no doubt that the Rabbis, when using — not quoting — this biblical phrase, used it in the sense and with the meaning given here in the text, and most likely they understood the biblical verse also in this sense.

Ten instances are cited in Talmud and Midrashim in which after a man had made an utterance of some evil import, the evil actually happened. This coming into being of the evil suggested in the utterance is assumed to be the result of the utterance and is explained with the phrase כשגנה שיוצא מלפני השליט. The instances cited are found in p. Shab. XIV, 4 (14d); p. Shab. XVI, 1 (15c); p. Soṭah IX, 16 (24c); b. M. Ḳ. 18a; b. Ket. 23a; b. B. M. 68a and in Midrash Koh. Rab. to 10.4. In all these instances the phrase can have no other meaning than that the mistake or error was on the part of the agent or angel who brought about or executed the evil suggested in the utterance. In b. M. Ḳ. the context shows unmistakably that the idea expressed in the phrase כשגנה שיוצא מלפני השליט is intimately connected with and explanatory of the idea expressed in the phrase ברית כרותה לשפתים (see above, Note 5). The case of Rachel's premature death cited in Koh. Rab. *l. c.* and Gen. Rab. 78, 6, said to have been caused by Jacob's saying that whoever had Laban's gods should not live (Gen. 31.32) is especially significant. While in Koh. Rab. and Gen. Rab. the connection between Jacob's utterance and the fact of Rachel's untimely death is explained by the phrase כשגנה שיוצא מלפני השליט, in Pirḳe de R. Eliʻezer ch. 36 (p. 84b) it is explained by the phrase מפי והיוצא צדיק כיוצא מפי המלאך, and in Midrash Ha-gadol to Gen. 31.32 (ed. Schechter, Cambridge 1902), p. 492, by the phrase וכל היוצא מפי הצדיק כיוצא מפי הגבורה. These two variants clearly show that it was believed that Jacob's words had been erroneously assumed to have come from on high, i. e. from an angel in the name of God or from God Himself. Comp. also Lauterbach, *op. cit.*, p. 39,

ity it was but the voice of a human being entirely unauthorized to give such an order and even innocent of any intention of doing so. To this misunderstanding concerning the source of the words they sometimes add other misunderstandings such as taking a statement, description, or even a mere quotation, for an order. And — this is especially the case with the malicious angels — even when they fully recognize the source of the voice as human and can identify the person who uttered the words, they would not infrequently take a quotation cited by a person for his own statement. Further, especially in the case of the malicious angels, they may take the words out of their context and construe them as self-accusations or admissions of guilt on the part of the person, who, however, had spoken or quoted these words in an entirely different sense and in a context which would not admit of their being interpreted as proving anything against the person who uttered them.

All these possible misunderstandings or misinterpretations on the part of the angels, benign or malicious, give a wide scope to the potential effectiveness which all speech, read, quoted or uttered in any form or in any context by any human being, may have in bringing about the thing or the act which the words, taken literally and out of their context, may indicate. Hence excessive precaution is to be observed in human speech in order to prevent any resultant unpleasant consequences not intended by it.

There are two main classes of words or kinds of utterances of which one must beware in conversation as well as in loud reading[47] or recitation, lest they bring evil results upon the

---

note 20. The hope expressed there that I would deal more exhaustively with this subject is only in part realized in this essay.

[47] This belief in the potential effectiveness of the uttered word controls the arrangement of Bible readings in the Synagogue. The division of the sections read is so arranged that every section closes with a felicitous word or phrase. The passage אל תעמוד בדבר רע (Eccl. 8.3) is interpreted to mean, not: "Stand not in an evil thing" as our translations have it, but: "Do not stop at, or close with, an evil word." This is clearly stated in an old Baraita cited in Midrash Zuṭa to Kohelet *ad. loc.* (ed. Buber, Berlin 1894), p. 117, which reads as follows: הפותח פותח בדבר טוב והחותם חותם בדבר טוב. בברכות קורא ומפסיק, בקללות קורא ואינו מפסיק. למה אין מפסיקין בקללות ר' איבו אמר משום אל תעמוד

speaker himself or upon the person spoken to or spoken about.
1) Any utterance containing an incriminating phrase which
might indicate an accusation or imply an admission of guilt
of some sort is to be strictly avoided. In such cases there is
danger that Satan or any of the other spy-angels who accompany every person might misunderstand the words or take
them out of their context and misconstrue them as incriminating evidence against the party concerned.[48] The angel might
then report them as such to the heavenly authorities who might,
on the basis of such evidence, issue a verdict of guilty against
the people concerned and decree some punishment upon them.
2) Words connoting evil and suffering, sickness or death, and
phrases containing allusions to any catastrophe that has be-
fallen, or which was merely threatening to befall any people
anywhere should not be uttered lest the floating angels or
heavenly agents mistake the human voice for a voice from on
high, and taking the words out of their context, construe them
as a command from the heavenly Ruler. In their hasty zeal
these agents, especially the angels of destruction, might hurry
to carry out the supposedly divine command and bring upon
the people speaking or spoken to the evils indicated in the literal
meaning of the words which had been uttered for an entirely
different purpose and in a different sense.

In cases of necessity when an utterance of either one of these
two classes has to be made and phrases or words alluding to

בדבר רע. When reading Lamentations on the ninth of Ab they do not stop
with the last verse of the book which reads: כי אם מאוס . . . קצפת עלינו עד מאד
but they repeat the preceeding verse (v. 21), thus finishing with חדש ימינו
כקדם. The same precaution is also taken when studying the Mishnah. All
tractates close with felicitous words. In the Tractate Yadayim which properly
ends with the quotation from Ex. 5.2, "Who is the Lord that I should hearken
unto His voice?," another sentence is added quoting Ex. 9.27, "The Lord is
righteous." And Bartinoro in his commentary remarks כדי שלא להשלים המסכת
במי ד' אשר אשמע בקולו משום אל תעמוד בדבר רע. Comp. also Tossafot Yomtob
ad. loc. which explains away the apparent exception to this rule in the closing
of the Tractate Peah.

[48] This is expressed in the Talmud by the saying: אל יפתח אדם פיו לשטן,
"A man should not open his mouth for Satan" (b. Ber. 19a; M. Ḳ. 18a and
elsewhere.) Comp. הכותב to 'En Ja'aḳob, Ber. 19a, who explains it as follows:
פירוש, שלא יתן פתחון פה לשטן לקטרג ולומר הודאת בעל דין הוי כמאה עדים . .

suffering or guilt have to be cited or quoted or even read aloud from a book, certain precautions must be taken to prevent any evil consequences which might otherwise result from them. These precautions are of two kinds.

The one consists in some form of circumlocution. The expression denoting the evil is disguised in some euphemistic form, or is not clearly stated, or is entirely suppressed, as when it is said יבא עלי, "May there come upon me,"[49] without stating what should come. Or the sentence is couched in the third person while the first or second person is actually intended,[50] as in the phrase תיפח רוחיה דההוא גברא, "may the soul or life of that man be extinguished"[50a] (p. Ber. IX, 7 [14b]), instead of "thy soul" or, if taken as an oath of affirmation, "my soul"; or in the saying of Rab Hamnuna to his disciple: "Does that man wish to bring suffering upon himself?," יסורים בעי ההוא גברא לאתויי אנפשיה (Ber. 60a) instead of "Do you wish" etc.[51] Or the enemies of the people are mentioned and referred to when the people them-

---

[49] See p. Sheb. IX, 1 (38d) יבא עלי אם לא שמעתי, "May (such and such a punishment) come upon me, if I have not heard." This method of suppressing the evil word has its prototype in the biblical formula: כה יעשה לי אלהים "The Lord do so unto me" (1 Sam. 3.17; Ruth 1.17 and many other passages). This is a form of an oath not expressed in full, for fear that the angel might hasten to bring about the punishment even before listening to the condition on which it is dependent. Hence the fear among Jews of taking an oath even to affirm a true statement. See Tanḥuma Vayikra 7: אמרו רבותינו אפילו על שיהא הין שלך צדק ולאו שלך צדק, b. B. M. and the saying האמת אינו יפה לאדם להשבע 49a and Sifra Ḳedoshim 8 (Weiss 91b). Comp. Matth. 5.33–37: "Swear not at all . . . But let your speech be yea, yea, nay, nay." All these sayings are based not upon high ethical principles but upon fear of the evil consequences which the utterance, even though made conditional, might bring.

[50] This method is described in the Talmud (b. Soṭah 11a) as כאדם שמקלל עצמו ותולה קללתו בחבירו, and it is traced back to the Bible. For the Rabbis (ibid., l. c.) interpret the passage in Ex. 1.11: "And get them up out of the land," to mean that Pharaoh really intended to say — but was afraid to say so — and get us, the Egyptian people, out of the land.

[50a] J. M. Sabludowski in his משען מים (Wilna 1868), p. 42, in his explanation of this phrase misses its significance. Comp. however his remarks ibid., pp. 45–46.

[51] Comp. also Rab's saying: ברעות נפשיה לקטלא נפיק וכו', b. Sanh. 7b and Rashi's remark there s. v לקטלא, that Rab was speaking about himself: ועל עצמו היה אומר כן.

selves are meant. Thus e. g., when something evil is to be said about Israel "the enemies of Israel" are mentioned, as in the phrase סימן רע לשונאי ישראל "it is a bad omen for the enemies of Israel."[52] When a condemnation of the teachers is to be expressed, "the enemies of the teachers" are referred to, as in the phrase חרב על שונאיהם של תלמידי חכמים (b. Ta'an. 7a).[53] In this manner the possible evil effects resulting from any mistakes on the part of the angels are forestalled, or at any rate are diverted to other people who are only indefinitely mentioned.

The other form of precaution consists in a qualifying remark or protective phrase added to the evil words, indicating that these ominous utterances should not be taken as applying to the persons speaking or spoken to, such as the phrase שלא תבא . . . על, "may it not come to"[54] or "happen to . . .", or לא עליכם, "let it not come unto you,"[55] or לא עלינו "let it not come unto us." Or a little prayer is uttered invoking the powers that be that no evil may come as a result of the speech, like the phrase חס ושלום, "Have pity and let there be peace" or "God forbid."[56]

Viewed in the light of these explanations this belief in the potential effectiveness of the uttered word does not ascribe any magic power to the human voice as such and is certainly not

[52] Mekilta de R. Ishmael, Pisḥa II (ed. Lauterbach I, p. 19). The circumlocution שונאיהם של ישראל is found in numerous passages of the Talmud. I will cite here only two: b. Ber. 32a and Yoma 77a. These instances are significant in that although they refer to what long ago in the past might have happened, but actually did not happen, to the Jewish people, yet the precaution is taken of using the circumlocution "enemies of Israel" instead of "Israel."

[53] Such a form of circumlocution is also found in the Bible. See 1 Sam. 20.15–16 where, when referring to David, the expression אויבי דוד "enemies of David," is used, and Rashi ad loc. correctly remarks כנה הכתוב, "Scripture circumlocutes."

[54] See e. g. M. Ta'an. III, 8 the phrase על כל צרה שלא תבא על הצבור.

[55] This is also found in the Bible, Lam. 1.12.

[56] B. Ber. 28a and 63b and in many other passages in the Talmud. A similar protective phrase is רחמנא ליצלן, "May God save us," which is more frequently used in later Rabbinic literature. In the Talmud it is not used when something evil is expressly mentioned but only when it is implied, as רחמנא ליצלן מהאי דעתא, "God save us from holding such an opinion" (b. Shab. 84b and b. Ket. 45b) which, however, may mean, God save us from being considered guilty of holding such an opinion.

incompatible with Jewish teachings. On the contrary, it rather stems from generally accepted Jewish doctrines and orthodox beliefs. It is the logical consequence of the doctrine concerning Divine Providence and the manner in which the affairs of this world are administered by the heavenly powers — carried perhaps a little to the extreme by the popular mind. On the one hand, the belief in the possible good effects of the human word is but an expression — a naive popular expression to be sure — of the belief that God sees, hears and knows all, and that He who listens to the prayer of the humblest, may also hear and heed even the casual utterance of an unimportant person who in His sight may be a truly righteous person, although he does not appear as such in the eyes of his fellow men. On the other hand, the belief in the potential evil effects of the human utterance and the dangers that might result from it, is but a popular expression of doubt concerning the absolute reliability of the angels and of a suspicion of their accuracy and absolute faithfulness and impartiality in the discharge of their functions as God's agents and messengers. And doubting the perfection of the angels and considering the servants of the One on High as not altogether infallible and as subject to error, is not an unjewish attitude and may even be considered as good Jewish belief. For we are told in sacred Scripture that God Himself "putteth no trust in His servants and His angels He chargeth with folly"[57] (Job 4.18).

---

[57] The idea that the angels and the whole host of heaven may sometimes be tried and judged is expressed in Isa. 24.21. In the meditation ונתנה תוקף recited in the Synagogue Service on New Year's Day and the Day of Atonement, the confusion among the angels in fear of the Day of Judgment is described as follows: "The angels are dismayed; fear and trembling seize hold of them as they proclaim, Behold the Day of Judgment! The host of heaven is to be arraigned in judgment, for in Thine eyes they might be found not innocent when judged."

THE ATTITUDE OF THE JEW TOWARDS THE NON-JEW

The greatest injustice which has been done to the Jewish people throughout the ages and which has been the cause of all the horrible crimes and outrages committed against them, has been the tendency among the gentiles to consider the Jew a stranger instead of a brother, an enemy instead of a friend. This attitude is not based upon correct information and sound conclusions; it is simply the result of ignorance as to what the Jew and Judaism stand for. Even in the manner in which he is judged, the Jew is discriminated against, in that people allow themselves to judge him without a hearing and to form opinions about his religion without knowing anything of it. The opinions of the majority of the gentiles on Jews and Judaism are based mostly on traditional hearsay and false rumors. Even many of the learned and educated of the non-Jews who, in any other case, would recognize the claims of scientific methods in collecting data of information and examining them carefully before passing judgment, seem to think, that in the case of the Jew and Judaism, they can ignore all rules of scientific exactness and abandon the usual standards of evidence.

Instead of collecting correct data and discriminatingly sifting the facts in order to get at the truth, they content themselves with references to some stray instances in Jewish life or to some casual remarks in Jewish literature on which they base their sweeping generalizations. The casual saying of one teacher, even though he be not prominent and not representative, uttered at one particular time, under peculiar conditions and with a special purpose, is represented as being the authoritative opinion of Judaism, accepted by all the teachers and valid for all times and

Reprinted from *Central Conference of American Rabbis Year Book*, Vol. XXXI, 1921.

under all conditions. The exceptional act of one individual Jew, even if committed under certain trying circumstances in an exceptional frame of mind, is frequently declared to be typical of how the Jew in general would always act even under the best of circumstances. Such willful misinterpretations, or even unintentional misunderstandings, of Jewish conduct and Jewish teachings are necessarily bound to result in false conceptions about Jews and Judaism.

With those people who willfully seek to misinterpret facts and misrepresent Jews and Judaism it is of no use to argue. It would be futile to try to convince them of their error, for they are merely seeking an excuse for their hatred and prejudice, and their errors are really willful misstatements. They do not wish to be enlightened. Any attempt to prove to them the incorrectness of their views would be a useless effort. These people merely seek pretenses and false excuses for their campaign of hate, "and he that seeketh, findeth". Fortunately, however, these intentional misinterpreters of Judaism are comparatively few. The majority of those people who are prejudiced against the Jew are merely misguided by some misinterpretation of Judaism and by false rumors about Jews. They are easy prey to anti-semitic propaganda, because they lack knowledge as to what Jews and Judaism stand for. But they are open-minded and could be freed from their prejudice and made to give up their wrong opinions, if we would convince them of their mistake by giving them correct information and an authoritative presentation of what the Jewish attitude really is and what Judaism demands of the Jew in his relation to the non-Jew. Such a presentation on the part of an authoritative body of Jewish teachers and rabbis as represented by this Conference, is not only a duty towards the Jews who should be defended against slander and false accusation, but is also a patriotic duty which we owe to our non-Jewish fellow-citizens. The majority of the American people are liberal and fair-minded. They are true to the lofty ideals and noble traditions of this great republic. They do not wish to misjudge their fellow-citizens of the Jewish faith; they rather wish to know them better and to appreciate them. By giving them correct information about Jews and Judaism we render them the great service of clearing away any possible misunderstanding and preventing them from doing an unintentional wrong in misjudging their Jewish neighbors.

But above all, it is our sacred duty to truth to expose falsehood, and to remove misunderstandings, to help the people to a true knowledge of the ethical principles of Judaism and its teachings in regard to the relations between man and man by giving them an adequate presentation of these authoritative teachings of Judaism. Such a presentation of the teachings of Judaism in regard to the attitude of the· Jew towards the non-Jew, I shall attempt to give in this paper.

Limitation of space prevents me from going into a detailed discussion of all the minutiae of the Jewish religious laws about the conduct of the Jew in his dealings with the non-Jew and his relation to him. I must content myself with stating the general attitude of Judaism towards the followers of other religions and presenting the principles in regard to dealings with non-Jews and the treatment of them by Jews, as formulated by representative teachers of Judaism and accepted as authoritative Jewish teachings by the majority of Jewish teachers in the various periods of Jewish history. For only such teachings which have been formulated by representative and responsible Jewish teachers and indorsed by the majority of the people, as represented by their teachers, throughout the various periods of Jewish history, can be considered as the true authoritative Jewish teachings.

Our method, therefore, will be both historical and critical. The teachings on a certain point or the sayings bearing upon a special question, as held by the teachers of successive generations will be stated in their chronological order: and, whenever necessary, these sayings will be compared with whatever apparently different statements or contradictory utterances may be found in Jewish literature, and then critically and carefully examined, and an objective decision will be sought as to which of these sayings are authentic Jewish teachings and which are merely momentary outburst of individual Jews of a certain temper or a peculiar state of mind, produced by particularly unfavorable conditions, by sad personal experience or harsh treatment and cruel oppression, received at the hands of the non-Jewish people of a particular time or in a particular country.

For, surely, it could not be expected that the Jew who finds his house burned, his property destroyed, his children murdered, his wife outraged, and himself cruelly beaten and tortured by a fiendish enemy, would embrace that enemy and say to him: "Thou art my brother, made in the image of my God and I love thee as myself." This would be unnatural and untrue. The Jew could not see in his savage persecutor the image of God! In the agony of his suffering, he would naturally utter harsh words against his brutal tormentor or even curse him. And if such harsh words, uttered by the Jew, when suffering in distress and agony, were occasionally preserved in the records of Jewish literature, they did not thereby become Jewish religious teachings and are not to be considered as authoritative expressions of Judaism.

The Jew has a right to justice. And justice demands that the Jew be judged only by the acts of the majority of his people, by the rules of conduct recommended and approved by his representative leaders, and by the dicta of his authoritative teachers, expressed in all normal times and under normal conditions, but not by some of his passionate outcries made in moments of excitement and in an abnormal state of mind, produced by extreme pain and suffering.

It should also be understood that when we speak of the attitude of the Jew, we mean the attitude of the Jew, as a Jew. as one guided in his conduct and controlled in his life by the principles of the Jewish religion, and not the attitude of one who may be racially a Jew or belong to the Jewish people, but yet may hold views diametrically opposed to Jewish teachings, or conduct himself in utter violation of all Jewish religious principles. For there are some so-called Jews who are guilty of transgressing the Jewish religious laws not only in their relation to God but also in their dealings with their fellowman, Jew or non-Jew alike. Such individuals do not represent the Jewish people. And the Jewish people or the Jewish community cannot be held responsible for any act committed by such individuals, or for any view held by them. Our theme, therefore, correctly formulated, is the Jewish attitude toward the non-Jew, or the attitude of Judaism toward the followers of other religions.

And we must keep in mind and insist upon distinguishing the religion of Judaism from the religion of the Old Testament. Judaism is not identical with the Old Testament religion. This fact, which Christian theologians persistently refuse to acknowledge, has been known and accepted by every professing rabbinic Jew ever since the doctrine of the authority of the traditional law has been proclaimed, which was a long time before Christianity came into the world. The Old Testament contains simply the foundation of Judaism but the superstructure is larger than the foundation. Furthermore, the Old Testament, besides containing the principles upon which Judaism is built, contains also, especially in the Pentateuch, the constitution and the civil and criminal codes of law, intended for the ancient Kingdoms of Judah and Israel. And whether some of these laws, found in this statute book of the ancient Jewish states, can meet with the approval of modern conceptions of just and humane state laws or not; whether they compare favorably or unfavorably with the laws on the statute books of modern civilized states, discriminating in their legislation between their own citizens and those of other countries, these are questions with which we are not now concerned. What concerns us in our present discussion is the fact that the laws for the ancient Jewish state, like so many other laws found in the Pentateuch, do not form part of the Jewish religion as such. They have never been considered as Jewish religious laws in the sense that they must be observed by the followers of the Jewish religion in other countries outside of Palestine, or even in Palestine since the time that an independent Jewish state ceased to exist. Consequently, any of these ancient *State* laws of Judea, comparatively few in number, which may have made some slight distinction between citizens and foreigners in Judea, could not, and actually did not, determine the attitude of the Jew, as a follower of Judaism, towards the non-Jews in all the countries in which the Jews for the last eighteen hundred and fifty years have lived merely as a religious people obeying the laws of the land in civil and political matters.

And one more preliminary remark should be made. We must keep in mind, if we want to judge the Jewish attitude fairly and correctly, that Judaism has been constantly developing and there has always been progress and evolution in Judaism, even before the modern reform movement. With the ever-broadening of the Jewish conscience and the unfolding of the religious genius among the Jews, the Jewish religious authorities, as they grew in the understanding of the fundamental principles of the Bible, have discarded or modified many a law or ritual practice, prescribed in the Pentateuch, if it no longer harmonized with their higher religious conceptions or advanced moral standards. Such discarded views are no longer considered as the adequate expression of Jewish religious teachings. As illustration of such advanced teachings, one could cite all the instances where for the sake of קדוש השם or in order to avoid חלול השם the rabbis went beyond the law and demanded of the Jew higher ethical standards in his dealings with the non-Jew.

With these ideas in mind, we can now proceed to the discussion of our theme. We begin with the general charge brought against the Jews and Judaism. It is the oft-repeated false accusation that Judaism is a religion of particularism and separateness, that it teaches the Jews to be a separatistic and unsocial people, to consider themselves as the favorites of God and hence, despise, hate, and keep aloof from all other peoples. This charge, originally made by Greek and Roman heathen writers, and repeated by Christian theologians and anti-semitic writers up to this day, is absurd. It is both false and stupid. It is based partly upon ignorance and misunderstanding, but mostly upon intentional misrepresentation and wilful misinterpretation of facts. It endures only through the narrowminded persistency of those who repeat it, in stubbornly refusing to seek and obtain correct information, or, when such information is offered, in wilfully ignoring the facts and rejecting all proofs that speak against their cherished preconceived notion.

Every unbiased and open-minded student, conversant with Jewish religious literature, cannot fail to recognize that Judaism, as a religion, is universalistic in essence and character as well as in its ultimate aim and purpose. It extends its endeavors for human welfare to every human being and includes all mankind in its plan of salvation. For, although Judaism, the product of the religious genius of the Jew, recognizes in the Jewish people a distinct and separate group, it does not mean to discriminate against other peoples. Judaism insists upon the religious separateness of the Jews from other people not because of hatred or contempt for the rest of humanity, but on the contrary, out of love for humanity. Judaism makes the Jews a distinct people and assigns them a sacred task to fulfill. It imposes upon them special historic obligations, prescribes for them special rituals and religious institutions, demands of them that they preserve their identity and maintain their unique character by being loyal to their sacred traditions and by cherishing and cultivating their great spiritual heritage, in order that they may be better fitted for achieving the special task assigned to them in the economy of nations.

This task is to become a blessing unto all the families of the earth and to benefit humanity. The Jew must therefore avoid anything that might impair his usefulness in that direction or hinder him in the accomplishment of his noble task. He must keep himself separate in religion only, in the sense that he should not give up his religious teachings and practices for the sake of becoming like the others. He is, however, to associate and mingle freely with other peoples, live with them in neighborly friendliness and brotherly love and thus be enabled to teach them the principles of his religion and to give them an opportunity to appreciate and follow his ethical teachings. In other words, the Jew must be separatistic in order to be truly universalistic. His separateness is not an end in itself, but merely a means to an end; the end being to spread the true knowledge of God among all people and raise all mankind to the high standard of holiness and ethical morality set up by the Jewish prophets of old. This view as to the position of the Jew among other people is shared by all religious Jews, no matter what their special theological bias may be. The universalistic tendency gives the fundamental tone to all Jewish religious literature, it echoes from all the Jewish liturgy, it forms the special theme of the choicest prayers recited by the Jews on the most solemn occasions;[1] it has always been, and still is, the hope and the aspiration of every Jew, no matter to what group or party he may belong.[2]

It is true, Judaism teaches that the Jewish people are the chosen people. But there is a fundamental difference between the conception of the selection of Israel, as taught by Judaism, and the notion of being a chosen people as entertained by other ancient and modern nations. While the latter considered themselves as better and superior peoples and hence looked down with contempt upon the rest of humanity as being inferior, the Jewish people, in regarding themselves as chosen, consider themselves merely as the older, more responsible, brother of the other nations. Israel is called the first-born son of God (Ex. IV, 23) which clearly indicates that the other nations are also children of God, younger brothers of Israel. It is the duty of the older brother to be kind, considerate, helpful and loving to his younger brothers. Hence, Jewish literature has no such opprobrious epithet for the other nations, as the term "Barbarian" applied by the Greeks and Romans to all other people.[3] For the Jew knows, because he has been taught so by all his teachers from the prophet Amos down to the rabbis of our own days, that he has been chosen not for special privileges but for special service, that as the older brother, with more responsibility, he has the duty and the obligation to be an exemplar to his younger brothers, a helpful influence and a blessing to all the peoples of the earth. Thus, the very doctrine of the selection of Israel, far from making the Jew particularistic and unfriendly to other people, has made him universalistic, broad-minded, tolerant, and friendly towards all other people. For, if he is to help in the education of the younger children of his Father in heaven, he can do so successfully only by loving kindness and sympathetic understanding of the younger children and not by an overbearing and unfriendly attitude. For "an impatient and ill-tempered person cannot be a successful teacher".

And the relation of Israel to the other nations, according to this very doctrine of the selection of Israel, is precisely the relation of teacher and pupil. There can be no enmity or ill-will on the part of a teacher to his pupil, especially when the teacher undertakes to teach voluntarily and without any compensation. Naturally, even such a teacher may occasionally get a little impatient with his pupils. He may, at times, be provoked to anger and righteous indignation by the indifference and lack of appreciation manifested by some pupils or by the misbehavior and bad conduct exhibited by others. At times, he may even wish to see such pupils disciplined and punished, but he does not wish them any real harm. He cannot think ill even of the worst of them. He never considers them hopelessly bad. If he did, he would surely give up the thankless job of trying to teach them, especially since his compensation is nothing but grievous disappointments and ingratitude. Yet, he does not abandon his task because he still loves his pupils in spite of their temporary indifference and their occasional display of bad manners and ill conduct. He persists in believing in the essential goodness and the potential nobility of his pupils whom he recognizes to be fashioned by the same Maker and of the same clay as himself. He knows well that he himself has attained to the position of teacher only by receiving the precious doctrine his great teachers gave to him and by assiduously training himself to follow the instructions and carrying out the commandments of his Master. And he feels assured that his pupil could do likewise. Hence, he never ceases in his efforts to help and benefit his pupil. Patiently and untiringly he labors at his task to impart to his pupil all the noble teachings and precious doctrines which it has been his own good fortune to acquire. He ignores the disappointments and swallows the humiliations and even disregards the insults which are occasionally heaped upon him, for he believes in the potential good qualities of even the most refractory pupil. He hopes and is convinced that his efforts will ultimately be crowned with success and that, sooner or later, he will have the joy and satisfaction of welcoming his pupils as his colleagues, collaborating with him in his sacred task. Could such a teacher be possibly suspected of hating, despising or wishing harm to and seeking to take advantage of his pupils? Only maliciousness or stupidity could bring such charges against him. And the Jewish people in their relation to other peoples are exactly in the position of such a self-sacrificing, struggling teacher.

Of course, as a "teacher-people" Israel considers himself better trained in a moral-religious sense. If, out of a sense of false modesty, Israel should pretend that he is in no respect superior to his pupils, that he does not know any more than they do, and that he has actually nothing to offer them that they do not already possess, he would make a very poor teacher. He would be guilty of a betrayal of his sacred trust and a neglect of duty; he would practically be abandoning his task of being a teacher- or a priest-people. As a "priest-people" or "teacher-people", Israel properly believes himself to be in certain respects superior to his pupils. He claims to excel them in the things which he sets out to teach them, for he has received a longer training and a more thorough instruction along these lines. But he recognizes that his pupils are his equals in other respects and possibly even superior to him. In fact, even in his specialty, he believes them capable of being his equals if they would receive from him the instruction and the high teachings which he so gladly offers them. At any rate, this is certain. He can have no ill-feeling or con- tempt for them even while they have as yet not accepted his teachings. For these very teachings, which he proclaims, pre- vent him from discriminating against other people because of their different beliefs. His very religion, which he would like others to accept, teaches him to consider all men as equals and to have the same friendly attitude towards the stranger as towards one of his own people. This attitude of the Jew towards the non-Jew is taught in the very principles of the Jewish religion and is repeatedly expressed in numerous sayings by various Jew- ish teachers of all generations.

The most fundamental principle of Judaism is, according to the rabbis, the doctrine that all men are brothers, children of one father and one mother, as stated in the opening chapters of the Torah. Said Ben Assai, "This is the book of the generations of Adam (Gen. V, 1) is the most comprehensive rule of the Torah".[4] It is, so to speak, at the root of the Torah. It has been put right in the beginning of the Torah to teach that the basic principle of the Torah is, that all human creatures are alike, made in the image of God, descendant from the same first human pair, hence peace, equality, and brotherly love must prevail among men, for no one can claim to be of nobler birth and hence better than his fellow-men.[5]

The second great principle of Judaism, which is but a logical consequence of the first, is declared to be the commandment (Lev. XIX, 18) "Thou shalt love thy fellow-man—not thy fellow-Jew only, but thy fellow-man—as thyself".[6] For, declared the same Rabbi Akiba, who quotes this great principle, "Every human being—and not only the Jew—is beloved by God since he is a creature of God, made in His image",[7] and therefore he should also be beloved by the Jew whose religious ideal is the *imitatio dei*,[8] to imitate God and to love whom God loves.

It is, therefore, a fundamental belief and the great hope of Judaism that there will come a time, the Messianic era, when all men will recognize these great principles and follow them and live together in brotherly love as behooves members of one family. It is the task of Israel to work for the realization of this ideal. This task involves a long educational process and only if the teachers are faithful in their endeavors and do their work creditably will God hasten the coming of that glorious time, the golden age of humanity.[9] Israel, accordingly, must teach by precept and example, and hence he cannot in any way discourage or discriminate against his younger brothers, even though he may notice their shortcomings and find fault with some of their actions. If he did in any way discriminate against his brother, he would be a poor example and would bring his fine teachings and high principles into disrepute, and thus fail in his efforts to make the other people recognize and accept these principles. But above all, his religion, as we have seen, expressly teaches him that he has no right to discriminate against his younger brothers, made in the image of his Father; he has no reason to think himself essentially different from and better than the others.[10]

Human beings, so the Talmud and the rabbis teach, are afflicted with certain weaknesses or evil proclivities, because, although

made in the image of God, they are also made of flesh and in
the form of an animal. They can overcome these weaknesses
and suppress these evil proclivities only by training and discipline, by cultivating the spiritual or divine element of their being
and making it rule over and control their animal nature. Or, to
use the words of the Talmud, (*Kiddushin,* 30b) the Torah furnishes the antidote for the poison of sin and evil passion. The
Jewish people who have received the Torah from Sinai, have, to
a certain extent, by their training and their discipline, gotten
rid of some of these weaknesses. The other nations, who did
not accept the ten commandments, are more subject to the bane-
ful influence of that original evil tendency, lodged in man's
animal nature.[11]   But those of them who accept these principles of the Torah are no longer in any way inferior to the
Jew. In fact, these principles of the Torah were *meant* for
all peoples. There was no partiality shown to Israel in giving
them the Torah. It was offered to the other nations who
refused to accept it. Israel, prepared by the family traditions from Abraham, Isaac, and Jacob to appreciate such teachings, had the good sense to accept it.[12] But God did not give it
to them as their exclusive possession. On the contrary, it was
intended to be the common possession of all peoples. For this
reason, say the rabbis, the Torah was not given in Palestine, in
order that the Jews should not be able to claim it as their
monopoly and say to the other nations, you have no share in it.
The Torah was intentionally and purposely revealed on Sinai in
the wilderness, in "no man's land," so that any person of any
nation can acquire it. (*Mekilta Bohodesh,* I. Friedmann 62a).
Furthermore, in laying down these principles, the Torah addresses
itself, not to priest, levite, or Israelite, but to mankind, and
whenever any one of the other nations occupies himself with the
principles of the Torah and practices them, he is fully equal to
the highpriest who officiated in the Temple at Jerusalem.[13] The
Jew has but the duty to help all the other nations in acquiring
those high principles of the Torah. In imitation of God who
went around with the Torah among all nations, asking them to
accept it, the Jew is also to seek to bring a knowledge of the

Torah to all the nations. One of the purposes aimed at by the Divine Providence with the dispersion of Israel, was that the Jew might thus be in position to spread the knowledge of God and His Torah among a larger number of men of various races and nations.[14] No race or nation is to be excluded from this privilege.[15]

The great teacher, Hillel, who so admirably summed up the whole of Judaism in the saying, "What is unpleasant to yourself, do not unto your fellowman", has also given the following maxim: "Love all human creatures and thus bring them nearer to the principles of the Torah".[16] That is to say, show your love and good will to all human beings and, in doing so, you will bring them near to the Torah and make them realize and appreciate its high teachings. In other words, not by forceful conversions and missionary enticements are we to carry out our mission, but by spreading the knowledge of the Torah and conducting ourselves according to its teachings.[17]

The non-Jew can be morally and ethically like the Jew and have all the spiritual advantages accruing from the Torah, even without formally accepting all the laws and rituals prescribed in the Torah. For, says the Midrash, (*Lev. R.* III, 7) "if the gentiles follow a wise course of ethical knowledge and moral understanding, they get the very essence and reach the fundamentals of the Torah and they love God with a complete and perfect love, no matter whether he sends them sorrow or happiness." And, says the Talmud, "the righteous among the gentiles will have a share in the future world."[18] And just as it is not necessary for the gentile to become a Jew in order to share equally in the future world, so it is not required of him to be a Jew in order to share in the rights, privileges, and courtesies of this world, as far as it is in the hands of the Jews to bestow such privileges and courtesies. Nay, more. In this world, even those gentiles who cannot be classed as "righteous gentiles" are entitled to our consideration and friendly and honest treatment. There is nothing in the religious teachings of Judaism that would allow or justify any unjust discrimination against the non-Jew. The "fellowman" whom our religion teaches us to love as ourselves need not be exactly like ourselves. Whatever his race, creed, or nationality may be, we are to treat him as we would like to be treated by him; we must respect him, extend to him our courtesies and refrain from taking any undue advantage of him.

Judaism does not impose upon the Jew the task of seeking to convert all the world to the whole system of Jewish religious law and practice, or to make them all members of the Jewish congregation. Judaism demands of us only to spread the knowledge of God and the fundamental principles of Judaism among all peoples. We can therefore not discriminate against those who do not formally become Jews and do not fully accept the whole system of the Jewish religion. The Jewish religious attitude towards conversion of the non-Jew is as follows: If the non-Jew sincerely wishes to become a Jew and join the Jewish community as a full member, he is welcome to do so, and after his attention has been called to the difficulty of the task which he is to undertake and to the possible material disadvantage that might result to him from such a step, he will be received most cordially.[19] But the Jew is never to persuade him to do so, for there is really no need for the non-Jew to become formally a convert to Judaism. If he does not feel like doing it, he is not to be discriminated against and he is none the worse for it. He can nevertheless attain to spiritual heights and be like the best of the Jews, provided that he lives up to the moral teachings of his own religion and observes the so-called Noahitic laws, i. e. the seven commandments which the rabbis believed to have been given by God to Adam or to Noah, and thus made obligatory upon the children of the entire human race.[20] By observing these seven laws he is classed among the "righteous of the gentiles" and is equal to the best of Israel, for he observes the dicta of his religion and fulfills the commandments given to him, just as the religious Jew observes the laws given to him. Each one of them, then, is doing his duty and no distinction is to be made between them.[21] Such righteous gentiles are considered members of the priest-people, and to them the rabbis apply the scriptural verse: "Thy priests are clothed with righteousness", (Ps. XXXII, 9)[22] for, like the Jews, the priest-people, such gentiles are also helping to spread the knowledge of God among the peoples of the earth. Of course, they are not regarded as Jews in such matters as are simply historic obligations or special religious laws incumbent upon the Jews as members of the house of Israel and upon all those who *formally* join their congregation. The gentile who does not believe in these laws and observances and is not a member of the house of Israel or of the Jewish congregation cannot, of course, function in a religious capacity in the performance of any such Jewish religious ceremony or ritual practice. But in all other respects, especially in matters of relations and dealings between man and his fellowman, no distinction whatever is made between such a gentile and a ⁻ew. In fact, such a gentile, while, of course, he can not be regarded as a perfect and formal proselyte to Judaism, is considered by the Jewish religious teachings as being in a sense actually a proselyte. The rabbis have a special name for such a proselyte; they call him *Ger Toshab*.[23]

To this class of proselytes or *Ger Toshab,* belong also the Mohammedans and all the Christian sects, since they believe in and worship the One God and they embody in their religious principles all the seven commandments given to Noah.[24] In fact, in some very important points the followers of these religions come much nearer to Judaism than the ordinary *Ger Toshab.* For, as pointed out by the great medieval rabbinical authorities, the Christians and Mohammedans acknowledge and believe in the divine origin of the Jewish Bible which is the foundation of Judaism, and in other fundamental teachings of Judaism.[25] Although in the case of most of the Christian sects, their belief in God is not identical with the purely monotheistic belief, as taught by Judaism, yet it cannot be doubted that they believe in and worship the one, true God, even though they associate other beings with Him. Their associating other beings with God, as giving him a son whom they worship like the father, is, of course, according to the Jewish teaching a false notion, and an incorrect theological conception. But it cannot be considered as idol-worship on their part. For, in reality, they do believe in the One God, only they have not reached the true conception of His absolute unity and oneness. They are mistaken but not ill-intentioned.

Their heart is directed towards the true God alone, even when
they mention another being with Him, and according to a general
talmudic principle (*Berakot,* 15a) "their words must be understood according to the intention of their heart."[26]This view that
the non-Jew who associates another being with God is, nevertheless, to be regarded as a worshipper of the one, true God, not as
an idolater, is held by practically all the rabbinic authorities.[27].
Hence, all rabbinic authorities agree that the attitude of the Jew
towards the non-Jew of the Mohammedan faith or of the Christian denominations must be the same as the attitude towards the
Ger Toshab. This means that with the exception of religious
matters of a purely ritual character and congregational activities,
we make no distinction whatever between Jew and Christian or
Mohammedan. We consider the Christian and the Mohammedan
as brothers fully our equals, so that in all human activities, as in
questions of law, business relations, social welfare work, neighborly duties and mutual helpfulness, we would treat them as we
would treat the Jew. Moreover, even in questions of traditional
beliefs, historic obligations, or forms of worship and religious
ritual, we teach mutual respect and tolerance. Let each seek to
find God in his own way, express his religious ideas in his own
forms, train his children in the ways of his fathers and cherish
the traditions of his people or of his religious group.

Having described in broad outline the general attitude of the
Jewish religion towards the people of other religions and especially towards the Christians and the Mohammedans, we shall
now take up the discussion of individual questions bearing upon
the various relations between Jew and non-Jew and ascertain
the teachings of Judaism concerning these questions.

Let us begin with questions of social and neighborly relations.
The Jewish religion teaches that in all activities of social welfare
work, in acts of mutual helpfulness between man and man and
of kindness to neighbors, the gentile should be included as well
as the Jew. Thus, according to the talmudic-rabbinic law, the
gentiles are to share in the gifts of the poor which according to
the law, (Lev. XIX, 9-10 and Deut. XXV, 19) are to be left in
the field at harvest time,[28] and furthermore, we must support the

non-Jewish poor together and equally with the Jewish poor,[29] and even appoint non-Jews together with the Jews as officers and administrators of institutions carrying on such works of charity.[30] We should also visit and attend the sick among the non-Jewish people, bury their dead and comfort their mourners, just as we would do to Jewish people.[31] We should also offer protection to their property and help in the safekeeping of any articles belonging to them if such be in danger of being lost, stolen, or damaged, precisely as we would do for a fellow-Jew.[32] We should also offer them assistance and encouragement in their work, even if the work is of a kind which the Jew would not be allowed to do for himself, e. g. agricultural work on the Sabbatical year.[33] Since the non-Jew is not prohibited to do this work, the Jew should be friendly and neighborly and offer him encouragement.

As a general reason for all these regulations, the Talmud gives the motive: מפני דרכי שלום "in order to further peace and good-will among all men alike." This phrase, מפני דרכי שלום has been ignorantly or wilfully misinterpreted by some Christian theologians, and taken to mean, merely to avoid the enmity of the non-Jewish population in whose midst the Jews lived.[34] This interpretation is absolutely false. The Talmud is quite exact in its definitions and terminology. When in the case of some other laws, it wishes to give the reason of the law as being in order to avoid the enmity or the ill-will of the heathen, it says so expressly and uses the phrase משום איבה for the sake of avoiding enmity or hatred on the part of the heathen (Abodah Sarah 26a and passim).[35] But the phrase מפני דרכי שלום expresses a positive ideal and a definite tendency to promote good-will among men. That this is the meaning of the phrase, מפני דרכי שלום is evident from the fact that it is used also as the reason for other laws and regulations which deal exclusively with relations between Jew and Jew in which case it certainly cannot mean "to maintain peaceful relations with the gentiles". But above all, we must let the Talmud itself explain the meaning of its phrases. And the Talmud (Gittin, 59b) unmistakably gives us the meaning of this phrase as being the furthering of peace and good-will among all men. For the

Talmud there says: כל התורה כולה מפני דרכי שלום
דכתיב דרכיה דרכי נועם וכל נתיבותיה שלום   "The entire
Torah has the aim and the purpose of furthering ways of peace,
as it is written, (Prov. III, 17) 'Her ways are ways of pleasantness, and all her paths are peace.' "[36] This certainly cannot mean
that the purpose of the entire Torah is merely to avoid the enmity
of the heathen, or to maintain peaceful relations with them.
And Maimonides, when quoting these regulations from the Talmud, together with their motivation, adds the following explanatory remarks: "for behold it is said, 'The Lord is good to all, and
His tender mercies are over all His works' (Ps. CXLV, 9) and
again it is said, 'Her ways are ways of pleasantness and all her
paths are peace.' "[37] This clearly shows how he understood the
phrase   מפני דרכי שלום.[38] Most of these regulations commanding the Jew to perform acts of kindness and friendliness
towards the non-Jew, were formulated and enacted in Palestine
not later than the second century of the common era, probably
even earlier. And all these regulations together with their motivation, to further peace and good-will among all men, have been
embodied, by Maimonides, Jacob Asheri, and Joseph Caro in their
respective codes,[39] and are repeatedly quoted and emphasized in
other standard works by Jewish authorities, which proves that
these regulations are generally accepted as authoritative Jewish
teachings.

The Jew is not only to be helpful and kind towards the non-
Jew when the latter is in need of assistance and encouragement,
he is also to extend to him all the social courtesies customary
among neighbors, and be considerate of his feelings. The Jew
must have regard for the honor and the human dignity of the
non-Jew and show consideration for his cherished beliefs. Thus
Shammai, about 30 B. C., taught: "Receive every man, not only
every Jew, with a cheerful countenance." (Abot I, 15) and R.
Mathithiah b. Ḥeresh, a Tanna of the second century taught:
"Be first in the salutation of peace to all men" (Abot IV, 15).
Of Rabbi Johanan b. Zakkai it was said that he was always the
first to offer greetings to whomsoever he met on the street even to
a heathen. A later talmudic teacher taught that a man must

be friendly, offer greetings and good wishes to every human being even to a heathen whom he meets on the street (*Berakot, 27a*).[40] These greetings and wishes of success and happiness should be offered to the heathen even during the season of their religious holidays.[41] We should honor the old men among the gentiles, stand up before them and show them all the respect due to old age according to the law (Lev. XIX, 32).[42]

All these laws are commanded to the Jew because of the honor and respect which, according to Judaism, we must have for every human being made in the image of God; and because, as the Midrash puts it, the Israelites are commanded to be kind at all times and on all occasions, and to be helpful to every one who comes along,[44] be he Jew or gentile. Hence, it is also forbidden to speak evil of or slander the non-Jew. Commenting upon the passage, "Thou sittest and speakest against thy brother; thou slanderest thine own mother's son" (Ps. L, 20), the rabbis say, "If you accustom your tongue to talk evil of, or speak against your non-Jewish brother who is not of your nation and race, you will also slander and find fault with the brother who is of your nation".[45] Or, to quote another comment, "If you speak evil of Esau, *i. e.* the non-Jew, who is your brother you will also talk against the greatest son of your nation, *i. e.*, Moses, the master of all the prophets".[46]

And it is most emphatically forbidden to deceive in any way or mislead the non-Jew by giving him the false impression that we have done something specially for him and thus cause him to consider us undeservedly his friends and think highly of us when we know that we do not merit it. We should not say flattering and friendly things to him, which we do not mean, intending thereby to make him believe that we think highly of him. Such a practice of insincerity, the rabbis term as גניבת דעת "stealing the good opinion of your fellow man", or receiving undue credit for our own selfish purpose. Such a practice of "stealing the good opinion" of the non-Jew is strictly forbidden in social relations, *e. g.* to lavish upon him our invitations, or to offer him our services whenever we know that he cannot and will not accept them, as well as in business relations *e. g.* to make him believe that we have given him preferential treatment, or that we have let him have a special bargain or gone out of our way to accommodate him, when it is not so.[47] And this brings us to a discussion of the laws regulating the dealings of the Jew with the non-Jew in all business relations. The charge that the Jewish law permits the Jew to do business with a gentile on a different basis and according to different standards than those observed in dealings with a fellow Jew is, I emphatically declare, a malicious falsehood. The Jewish religious law in its regulations about business transactions and standards of business ethics does not discriminate against the non-Jew.

No distinction is made by the Jewish religious law between Jew and non-Jew with regard to the duty to deal honestly and refrain from taking any undue advantage. In fact, there is one distinction made in favor of the non-Jew in that any sharp practice or unfair dealing in any transaction with him is considered a graver sin and is more severely condemned than a similar offense committed against a fellow Jew, because in the former case there is added to the sin of dishonesty, the offence against the good name of the Jew and Judaism. Such a practice against the non-Jew may lead to a profanation of the name of God and bring the Jewish religion into ill-repute among the non-Jews. The ancient rabbis knew well that honesty knows no creed nor nationality, and that he who is dishonest with the stranger will be so also with his own people. Hence, they said, a man shall keep far from robbery or cheating whether he deals with Jews or gentiles, for he who steals from a gentile will also steal from a Jew, and he who robs the gentile will also rob the Jew, and he who swears falsely to the gentile, will also swear falsely to the Jew, and he who falsely denies the claim of a gentile will also falsely deny the claim of a Jew, and he who sheds the blood of a gentile will also shed the blood of a Jew (*Seder Elijahu Rabba* XXVI, Friedmann, p. 140).

The following general principle about business is therefore laid down by the rabbinic law, embodied in the standard codes of Maimonides and Joseph Caro, and accepted by all rabbinic authorities: "The Jew is forbidden by law to cheat people in business, whether they be. Jews or idol worshipers. If the Jewish merchant knows that the article which he sells is of inferior quality or has some defect unknown and unnoticeable to the non-Jewish buyer, he must call the latter's attention to it".[48] And the principle is repeatedly stated by mediaeval Jewish authorities, that the Jew in his dealings with the gentile must conduct himself with the same honesty and faithfulness which he is to observe in his dealings with his fellow-Jew, and he should never play a trick nor do an injustice to or deal falsely with the non-Jew.[49] These are general principles. To be more specific, let us take up the various aspects of honesty in business and see what the Jewish law teaches about these questions as regards transactions between Jew and non-Jew.

It is strictly forbidden by the Jewish law to force the non-Jew to give up some of his legally acquired property, to rob him of any of his possessions, and to take anything from him by violence or by cheating. The rabbis derived this law from the biblical law concerning a Jew who is sold as a slave to a non-Jew. The law in Lev. XXV, 47-52, reads: "And if a stranger who is a settler with thee be waxen rich and thy brother be waxen poor beside him and sell himself to the stranger who is a settler with thee . . . . after that he is sold, he may be redeemed, one of his brethren may redeem him. . . . . And he shall reckon with him that bought him, from the year that he sold himself to him unto the year of jubilee; and the price of his sale shall be according unto the number of years; according to the time of a hired servant shall he be with him. If there be yet many years, according unto them he shall give back the price of his redemption out of the money that he was bought for. And if there remain but few years unto the year of jubilee, then he shall reckon with him; according unto his years shall he give back the price of his redemption." Commenting upon this biblical law, Rabbi Akiba remarks that it teaches us that it is forbidden to rob or cheat the heathen. For in this law the Bible expressly tells us that the Jewish people, even when they have the power and the jurisdiction over the heathen who is a settler among them, cannot free without compensation the Jew who has sold himself as a slave

to the heathen stranger. The law expressly states: "After that
he is sold he may be redeemed", but he may not be just taken
out of the house of the stranger and set free, without compen-
sating the owner. And lest you think, continues Rabbi Akiba,
that the Jews might fix an arbitrary price for the Jewish slave and
force the heathen to accept it, or try to cheat the heathen in
figuring up the compensation due to him, therefore, the law
expressly states: "And he shall reckon with him", etc., that means,
be exact in figuring up the years of service which are still due
the heathen owner and according to the value of these services
fix a fair and exact compensation which the heathen should get
for giving up his Jewish slave. (*Talmud B. K.*, 113ab. comp.
Tossafot ad. loc. s. v. יכל). This talmudic law, forbidding
the robbery or the cheating of the heathen, has been accepted by
the rabbis of the Middle Ages. It is embodied in the standard
codes of Jewish law, and is frequently repeated and quoted by
the great rabbinic authorities.[50]

It is also strictly forbidden to steal anything from the gentile,[51]
to defraud him by giving him short measure or poor weight,[52] or
to sell him inferior goods, without calling his attention to it[53] or
to deny his just claim, or to seek to avoid the payment of debts
owed to him, or to make a false statement to him. Above all, we
are to call his attention to any error or mistake which he himself may have happened to make in our favor,[54] we are to remind
him of anything he has forgotten and left with us and to restore
to him any article of his which he lost and we happened to find.[55]
In what spirit this is to be done, and was done by the Jew, can be
seen from the following story, told in the Palestinian Talmud
(*B. M.* 11, 8c). A rabbi once came to visit Rome. While he
was there it happened that the Empress lost a very valuable
bracelet and the rabbi found it. A proclamation was made by the
government to the effect that whosoever found this bracelet
should return it within thirty days and receive a reward. Should
he delay more than thirty days in returning it, he would be punished by death. The rabbi waited till the thirty days were over
and then returned the bracelet which he had found. The Empress
asked him, "Were you in the city all these thirty days?" The

rabbi said, "Yes". "Did you hear the proclamation"? asked
the Empress. The rabbi said, "I did". "What did the proclamation say"? the Empress asked. "It said," answered the rabbi,
"that he who returns the bracelet within thirty days would receive
a reward, but he who returns it later, his head will be cut off".
"Why then did you not return it within the fixed time"? asked
the Empress. To this the rabbi answered, "In order that you
should not think that I returned it because I care for the reward
or am afraid of the punishment. My only motive for returning
it was a religious one. I have returned this article lost by you
because I fear my God". The Empress then exclaimed, "Praised
be the God of the Jews."[56]

Not only are we to restore to the gentile any lost article, but
we should even seek to protect his property and prevent him
from incurring any loss. We should give him correct information about reliable firms with whom he may deal, and warn
him against any person who might take undue advantage of him
in business, even if that person should happen to be a Jew.[57]
In other words, we should protect the non-Jew from any unfair
treatment on the part of an unscrupulous Jew. It was, therefore, an established institution and common practice in many
Jewish congregations, that the leaders of the community would
see to it that no injustice or wrong be done to the non-Jew. They
would accordingly publish the names of such Jewish persons
who might be suspected of ordering goods on credit or borrowing money without the intention of paying, thus warning the
non-Jew against dealings with such people. (*Beer Hagoloh* to
Shulhan Aruk, Hoshen Mispat 388, 12.)

The laws cited above are to be observed by the Jew even in his
dealings with heathens. Needless to say that they are to be even
more strictly observed in dealings with Christians and Mohammedans who, as we have seen, are considered as *Ger Toshab*,
and are treated exactly like Jews in all business transactions. In
discussing some of the above-mentioned laws about business
transactions between Jew and heathen, R. Menahem Meiri of
Perpignon (1249-1306) expressly states, that those non-Jewish
peoples who are controlled by some religious laws or ethical

principles and, in some form or another, worship the Deity, even though their religious beliefs be far removed and different from our own belief, are in respect to these matters to be considered fully equal to the best of the Jews, and no distinction whatever should be made between them and Jews in our business transactions or other dealings with them. [Quoted by R. Bezalel Ashkenazi in his *Shittah Mekubezet* (to *B. K.* 113) Lemberg, 1876, p. 94a]. Furthermore, the Jew is taught to observe these rules of business conduct not merely as laws of equity but as *religious* laws, as laws which God wants him to observe, and he must always think of the name of his God whenever he deals with his non-Jewish fellowman. Hence, even when according to the law, the Jew might have the right to take special advantages, he must, from a purely religious motive, refrain from so doing. He must go beyond the letter of the law, avoid doing anything which, although legally permitted, might lead to a profanation of the name of the God of Israel and cast unfavorable reflection on the higher principles and ethical standards taught by Judaism.

It need hardly be stated that besides the above-discussed specific regulations and positive Jewish religious teachings concerning dealings with non-Jews, the general talmudic-rabbinic principle, *dina de malkuta dina*—that the law of the country is the law by which the Jew must abide—declares it a religious offence and a grave sin on the part of the Jew, to make any unfair discrimination against his non-Jewish fellow-citizen or to follow any practice in business or in other dealings with the non-Jew which would be forbidden by the law of the land.

This brings me to the discussion of one more question which is closely connected with the laws of business conduct, namely, the law about lending money on interest. This question will be discussed here at greater length. Such a discussion, I hope, will show the fallacy of identifying Old Testament laws, intended for the ancient Jewish state, with Jewish religious teachings, and will also prove to us that we cannot correctly understand the Jewish religious law without taking into consideration the course of its development and the changes and modifications to which it was subjected at the different periods in its evolution by its authoritative interpreters. It is just this confusing of state laws in ancient Judea with principles of the Jewish religion, and the disregarding of the development of Jewish law, that caused so many people to make the mistake of believing that the teachings of the Jewish religion make unfair discriminations against the non-Jew in permitting the Jew to charge him interest on loans.

It is true, the biblical law, while prohibiting the Israelites from lending money on interest to a fellow Israelite, permits[58] the charging of interest on loans to a foreigner. The law in Deuteronomy (XXIII, 21) reads as follows: "Unto a foreigner thou mayest lend upon interest but unto thy brother thou shalt not lend upon interest". As a state law in ancient Judea, protecting its citizens, as we shall see, from exploitation by foreigners, this was a just and wise rule, and compares favorably with modern laws regulating business relations between citizens of different nations. Special concessions or the privileges of favored nations are exchanged by modern nations on the basis of mutuality. Nationals of one country cannot claim any special protection or privileges in another country, if their own country does not accord the same privileges and the same protection to the citizens of that other country. This principle is underlying the biblical law permitting the Israelite to lend to a non-Israelite money on interest. For the foreign citizen or non-Israelite who was not subject to or did not accept the Judean law prohibiting its citizens to charge interest to one another, would, of course, charge the Israelite interest on loans. Had the law of the Jewish state forbidden the Israelite to take interest from the non-Israelite in cases when the latter was borrower, it would have been an unfair and unjust discrimination against the Israelite, who had to pay interest when he borrowed from the foreigner. It would have exposed the Israelite to unfair competition and exploitation on the part of the foreigner. Hence, this law is by no means a discrimination against the non-Israelite; it is merely a protection for the Israelite, securing for him the same rights in dealing with foreigners which the latter according to their own laws enjoy when dealing with Israelites.

After the Jewish state ceased to exist, the real significance of

this ancient state law, as a protection for its citizens, was no
longer fully realized by the rabbis. The rabbis of the Talmud
considering the law from the ethical and religious point of view
and not from its practical side as a state law, came to look upon
the taking of interest no matter from whom, as wrong in itself.
They were mindful of the fact that when Ezekiel (XVIII, 8, 13,
17) and the Psalmist, as well as the author of Proverbs, condemned the practice of usury, they made no distinction between
exacting usury from the native or from the foreigner. Accordingly, the rabbis of the Talmud, also condemned the practice of
lending money upon interest even to a non-Jew. Hence, they
interpreted the saying: "He that augmenteth his substance by
interest and increase, gathereth it for him that is gracious to the
poor," (Prov. XXVIII, 8) as applying even to one who takes
interest from a non-Jew (*Talmud, B. M.* 70b). And Ps. XV, 5:
"He that putteth not out his money on interest", they interpreted
as referring to him who has not lent on interest even to non-
Jews (*Makkot,* 24a). And they actually forbade lending money
on interest to non-Jews (*B. M.* l. c.; see Maimonides, *Yad Malwe
Welove,* V, 2).[59] Only in exceptional cases, as when the Jew
absolutely has no other means of getting subsistence or earning
a livelihood, would they permit the Jew to take interest from a
non-Jew and even then only to the extent of getting subsistence
כדי חייו but not as a business for acquiring wealth. This talmudic decree was accepted as a rabbinic law by the mediaeval
Jewish authorities. Only when in the Middles Ages, the Jews
were deprived of all other means of earning a livelihood and
were actually driven into the money-lending business, the majority of the rabbis considered it a case of necessity, coming under
the category of כדי חיי and hence, they were more lenient
and would not enforce this rabbinic law which prohibited Jews
from lending money on interest to non-Jews. But some great
authorities persisted in objecting to it. Thus R. Nissim Gerondi (about 1340-1380) expresses his great surprise at the action
of the people in lending money on interest to non-Jews which
is contrary to the talmudic law (*Responsa* No. 56, edition Warsaw, 1882, p. 94). And Isaac Abravanel, expressly states that

Christians and Mohammedans, being considered as brothers to
the Jews, are included in the biblical injunction, "But unto thy
brother thou shalt not lend upon interest".[60]   The only excuse
that the rabbis later on could find for permitting this practice was
that the same considerations which originally prompted the enactment of the biblical law to protect the citizens of the Jewish
State, might equally hold good now in the case of members of
the Jewish group in other countries.   Since the non-Jews, if
they lend money to Jews, charge them interest, the Jew must
equally charge interest if he lends money to the non-Jew.   But
in countries where interest rates are regulated by the state law
for all citizens alike, all authorities agree that the Jew besides
being in duty bound to obey the law of the land, is forbidden by
his religious law to discriminate against the non-Jew and charge
him a higher rate of interest than the one fixed by the law of the
state, which he would also charge to his fellow-Jew.

The above discussion will convince any fair-minded intelligent
person that the Jewish religious teachings do not permit the Jew
to do business with a non-Jew on a different basis than with
his fellow-Jew; but that, on the contrary, the Jewish religion
makes it the sacred duty of the Jew to observe the standards of
honest dealing and fair treatment with Jew and gentile alike.

Let us now consider a few isolated sayings in the Talmud
which have been cited by anti-Semites as proof for their charge
that Judaism teaches a hostile attitude towards the non-Jew.
One of these sayings is the oft quoted remark of R. Simon b.
Johia, "The best of the heathen should be killed", (p. *Kiddushin*
IV, 66b).   This is taken by anti-Semites to be one of the teachings of Judaism, expressing hatred for the non-Jew.   Now, I
have already stated in the opening of this paper that an isolated
saying, quoted in the Talmud in the name of an individual
teacher, cannot be considered as Jewish religious teachings unless
it is approved by the other teachers and accepted by the rabbis
after the talmudic period and embodied in their codes—which
is not the case with this saying.   But aside from this, and even
considering such a saying as the private opinion of the individual
teacher who uttered it, it is wrong to ignore the conditions under

which it was said, and to take it out of its context and misquote it, as is constantly done by the anti-Semites.

R. Simon b. Johai, the author of this saying, who witnessed the cruel persecutions of the Jews by the Romans under Hadrian and who personally suffered greatly from the Romans, being compelled to hide in a cavern for thirteen years to escape his persecutors, naturally could not, and actually did not, have any too good opinion of the heathen Romans and could not entertain any friendly feelings towards them. So, we could well understand and pardon him if, in a moment of bitterness, he had uttered an unqualified general condemnation of all the Romans. But as a matter of fact he did not do so. He did not make the statement in such an unqualified form in which it is frequently quoted. Those who quote his saying leave out two very imporant words. His full saying was תוב שבגוים הרוג בשעת מלחמה "The best of the heathen should be killed in time of war."[61] These words: "in time of war" בשעת מלחמה are usually left out from the quotation, but every one will realize what a tremendous difference these words make in the meaning of this harsh saying. For we of the present generation know very well to what exaggerated expressions of hatred even very good and kind-hearted people can be driven by the excitement during time of war. But above all, the saying should not be taken out of its context. It should be given the same value as the other exaggerated statements, given there in the same passage of the Talmud, e. g., "The most pious of women practice witchcraft", or "The best of the physicians is doomed to hell". Any one who, ignoring all the numerous teachings commanding kindness and helpfulness to the heathen which we have quoted, would take this saying of Simon b. Johai seriously and consider it as Jewish religious teaching, would also have to believe that Judaism condemns even the most pious women, notwithstanding the fact that Jewish religious literature is full of praise for the pious and virtuous woman. He would also have to assert that Judaism condemns to eternal damnation all its great religious teachers of all the generations who in addition to being teachers of religion also practiced medicine. I doubt very much if even the most malicious anti-Semite will be stupid enough to make such assertions.[62]

Another such isolated haggadic exaggeration is a saying by the same R. Simon b. Johai, who so thoroughly hated the Romans, to the effect that the heathen people do not deserve to be properly called "Adam" or "man" (*Yebamot*, 61a). Aside from the fact that this is merely an *haggadic* interpretation of a biblical passage (see *Tossafot Yomtob* to *M. Aboth*, III, 14) and has absolutely no bearing upon *Halakic* practice or upon the conduct of the Jew towards the heathen, it is contradicted by numerous other statements in the Talmud, absolutely refuting such a definition of the term "Adam" or "man". But, even the author of this saying merely meant to say that only people who observe ethical or moral laws, and thus live up to the dignity of man, can properly be called "man". But those heathens who disregard the law of God and man, do not maintain their human dignity. Consequently, they do not deserve to be dignified by the title "man" (see Guedeman, *Juedische Apologetik*, Glogau, 1906, p. 240). But above all, who could ever think seriously that such exaggerated expressions by an individual teacher represent Jewish teachings. In the same talmudic tractate (*Yebamot*, 63a) there are found two sayings by another individual teacher to the effect, that he who has no wife, or does not possess land is not to be considered as an "Adam" or "man". And there always have been, and there still are, rabbis and teachers in Israel who are unmarried and the large majority of Jews do not own land. Yet we have never heard and not even the anti-Semites could claim, that the Jews discriminated against or held in contempt these unmarried teachers or those among them who were not landed proprietors.

To the same class of isolated and exaggerated expressions belongs also the saying of R. Johanan. "A heathen who studies the Torah is deserving of death". (*Sanhedrin*, 59a). Aside from the fact that on the same page of the Talmud is found the saying of the rabbis extolling the heathen who studies the law and declaring him to be like the highpriest, and that the rabbis themselves have taught the Torah to the heathens, and were very anxious for the non-Jew to study the Torah and learn the Jewish religion, no intelligent person could think that the author of this saying, R. Johanan, really meant it to be understood literally. The same R. Johanan said that a student on whose garments is found any stain or spot is deserving death, (*Sabbath,* 114a) and also that the student who yields to an ignorant priest the honor of reciting first the benedictions is deserving death (*Megillah,* 28a) which, of course, is not to be taken literally.[63] It is just an emphatic way of expressing his disapproval of certain actions. It would hardly be necessary to discuss such isolated expressions which are contradicted by the whole tenor of Jewish teachings, were it not for the fact that it is the method of the slanderers of Judaism to ignore its authentic sayings and generally accepted true teachings, and pick out just such isolated sayings, uttered by an individual teacher under peculiar conditions or for a special purpose, to search out in the vast store of Jewish literature just such exceptional sayings and to represent them as if they were genuine Jewish teachings accepted by all Jewish teachers. It is, therefore, necessary to point out the fallacious methods of those false accusers of the Jewish religion. And who knows but that R. Johanan in strongly objecting to the heathen studying the Torah and in expressing his objection in such an emphatic manner, had in mind just such heathen slanderers and enemies of the Jews who with malice and evil intent were trying to study the Torah merely in order to misinterpret its teachings so as to lend a semblance of truth to their false accusations and libellous charges against the Jews and Judaism!

Another charge of unfriendliness and unsociability often brought against the Jew is based upon the law which forbids the Jew to walk in the ways of the heathen. And yet there is not the least justification for this charge. The law prohibiting the Jew to walk in the ways of the gentiles, has nothing to do with friendliness, sociability or mutual respect, which according to the Jewish religion should prevail between Jew and non-Jew. This law was not directed against foreign customs in general; it was directed originally against the immoral practices of certain heathen nations of antiquity. The law reads as follows: "After the doings of the land of Egypt wherein ye dwelt shall ye not do; and after the doings of the land of Canaan whither I bring

you shall ye not do; neither shall ye walk in their statutes."
(Lev. XVIII, 3). The law-giver then goes on to specify some
of these incestuous and immoral practices which are thereby forbidden (verses 4-23) and concludes with the words: "Defile not
ye yourselves in any of these things; for in all these the nations
are defiled which I cast out from before thee." (verse 24). It
is evident from this closing statement that the practices of the
Canaanites were forbidden to the Israelites, not because they were
foreign practices, but because they were immoral and abom-
inable practices. The rabbis of the Talmud have included in
this prohibition all heathen and superstitious practices designated
by them as דרכי אמורי "ways of the Amorites"[64] which are
incompatible with the moral teachings and pure beliefs of Judaism, but did not include in it any practice of the heathen which
could not be characterized as superstitious and was not of an
immoral character (see *Abodah Zarah*, 11a and *Tossafot* there
s. v. ואי חוקה). There has never been any objection on the
part of the rabbis of the Talmud to imitating or adopting non-
Jewish customs merely on the ground that they were non-Jewish.
On the contrary, the rabbis of the Talmud urged upon the Jews
to imitate what is good and noble in the conduct of other peoples
(*Berakot* 8b, *Kiddushin* 31a, and parallels). Commenting upon
the apparent contradiction in the words of Ezekiel, who, in one
passage, says that God will punish the people because "they
have not done after the ordinances of the nations that were round
about them (V, 7-8) and in another passage, he rebukes them
for having done after the ordinances of the nations that were
round about them (XI, 12), the Talmud explains that the prophet
reproaches the people for imitating only the bad practices of
their non-Jewish neighbors, while neglecting to imitate and
adopt their good customs כמקולקלים שבהם עשיתם כמתוקנים שבהם
לא עשיתם (*Sanhedrin* 39b). And the post-talmudic-rabbinic
authorities have repeatedly stated that the Jew is to refrain from
following practices or observing ceremonies of the non-Jew, only
if such practices or ceremonies suggest a special belief, or symbolize an idea peculiar to the particular creed of the non-Jew
which the Jew does not share.[65] The Jew who does not follow

the religion of the non-Jew and does not subscribe to his creed, should therefore not perform any ceremony prescribed by that religion or expressive of that creed.

I have endeavored, as far as it is possible within the limited scope of this paper, to give faithfully and accurately a concise presentation of the teachings of the Jewish religion as to the attitude of the Jew towards the non-Jew. I believe I have succeeded in showing that the principles of the Jewish religion in their broad universalism, aiming at embracing all humanity, cannot and do not countenance any hostile attitude towards any nation or group of the human family. I have also shown that the teachings of the Jewish religion in their specific rules of conduct in daily life do not contain any laws or regulations discriminating against people of other creeds who recognize and observe some system of laws of morality and justice, and that the Jew is not allowed to deal unjustly with them or treat them unfairly. Especially, in the case of the Christians and Mohammedans who are regarded as being, in a sense, proselytes to the Jewish religion, Judaism teaches that they are to be considered as brothers and equals. They are, of course, different from us in that they do not share all our beliefs and cherished traditions. Hence, we are strictly separate from them in matters of ritual and forms of worship, in specific congregational activities and in the fulfillment of all historic obligations resting exclusively upon members of the house of Israel and upon all those who formally joined themselves to it. But in all other matters of human relations, as in business transactions, general educational, cultural, and social welfare work and in neighborly helpfulness, they are to be treated exactly like Jews. For they certainly are included in the fundamental commandment: "Thou shalt love thy fellowman as thyself" and consequently, are entitled to all considerations, kindnesses, and courtesies which are to be extended to the fellowman.

We have also found that the biblical laws, unfavorable to certain nations of antiquity, were merely of the character of state laws of the ancient Jewish commonwealth, discriminating against foreign citizens, and are not to be considered as religious teachings, imposing duties of corresponding actions upon the Jew living outside of Palestine or even in Palestine after it was no longer an independent Jewish state. Most of these laws have been practically abrogated by all Jewish authorities in that they have been unanimously interpreted to have been intended or directed only against the idolatrous nations of antiquity, especially the morally corrupt Canaanitic peoples or the so-called "seven Canaanitic nations", who, in the course of time, have entirely disappeared from the scene of history. If some of the early rabbis of the Talmud occasionally observed that among the nations of their times there were some morally corrupt and idolatrous people who might have been considered to be in a class with the ancient Canaanitic nations and to whom, therefore, some of the ancient discriminatory laws of the Bible could equally apply, and if Jewish literature has preserved the text and the wording of such dead-letter laws, and theoretically discussed, quoted, and commented upon them, it has at the same time been expressly and repeatedly stated by the great rabbinic authorities, that such laws do not apply to the nations of their times, and that such casual expressions of some ancient teachers no longer represented the Jewish religious attitude towards the non-Jewish people of later days.

In every age and generation and in every country where there were Jewish settlements and centers of Jewish culture, the great Jewish religious authorities have repeatedly made solemn declarations, asserting their friendly and well-intentioned attitude towards the non-Jew. It would fill volumes to cite these authoritative statements. For, there is hardly a book written by a Jewish teacher on subjects of law and ethics in which the author, either in the course of his discussion in the text of his book, or in his introduction, or in a special prefatory remark, does not affirm that when he occasionally brings a quotation from ancient sources, containing some deprecating remark or speaking in derogatory terms about the ancient heathen people, such remarks are not to be taken as referring to the peoples of subsequent ages who have abandoned the abominations of the ancient heathen nations. These emphatic general declarations on the part of all Jewish teachers are more expressive of the real attitude of the Jew towards the non-Jew than any law or dictum in favor of the Gentile, found in Jewish literature, which I may have quoted. The fact that these declarations have been made by Jewish teachers in all ages and in all climes and under all kinds of conditions proves them to be the expressions of the real character of the Jewish teaching. It shows that they are common to all the Jewish teachers and accepted by all the groups of Jews of the most varied shades of opinion and theological differences. And all these statements are genuine expressions of Jewish doctrine. They were made in all sincerity and with the honest conviction on the part of their authors that, in making such statements, they correctly interpreted the teachings of the Jewish religion. For those statements were addressed to Jews. They were intended to impress the mind of the Jews with the true spirit of the teachings of Judaism. They were not intended to give the gentile a false impression of the real Jewish attitude, as our slanderers would have the world believe. Such statements were made by authors who never could have expected that their Hebrew works would be read by non-Jews. Such statements, expressing high regard for Mohammedans, were made by rabbis who wrote and published their works in Christian countries, and similar declarations, abounding in words of appreciation of the Christians, are found in works by authorities who lived in Mohammedan countries. So these statements were not made merely for the purpose of favorably impressing the non-Jewish people among whom the rabbis lived. Further, to make such statements is practically identical with giving a decision on a religious question and interpreting the Jewish law. To make such a statement without meaning it would, therefore, be tantamount to giving a false decision on a religious question and knowingly misinterpreting the Torah. Such an act is considered by the rabbis tantamount to denying the Torah, for it would actually deny the Torah in its true sense. And such an untrue decision, according to the rabbis, should not be rendered even when facing the dangers of persecution,[66] for it would mean denying one's religion to escape oppression, a practice with which not even their worst enemy would charge the rabbis. But above all, considering how severely the Talmud and all mediaeval Jewish scholars condemn גניבת דעת "the stealing of the good opinion of the Gentile", the attempt to make a false impression upon them, is it conceivable that all the rabbis were guilty of a practice which they so strongly condemned? Is it possible to believe that while preaching against גניבת דעת and so utterly abhorring it, all these rabbis and teachers conspired to make such false statements about the attitude of the Jewish law towards the non-Jewish people of their times, merely in order to deceive the gentiles, "to steal their good opinion" and make them believe that the Jews were friendly to them, when actually they were not? Is it possible that such a practice could have been agreed upon by all the rabbis without even one of them at any time protesting against it? It would seem almost impossible that even the most stupidly credulous could believe in such a secret agreement among all the Jewish teachers of all the ages. And only malicious slander could bring such a charge against religious teachers who have given numerous proofs of their readiness to die for the truth of their religion.

CLOSING STATEMENT

In the presentation of the Jewish religious teachings in regard to the Jewish attitude towards the non-Jew given above, I have considered only such Jewish authorities who lived before the beginning of the modern liberal movement in Judaism. I have purposely refrained from citing statements by authors who lived later than the eighteenth century. For, it might be argued, though there is, of course, no justification whatever for such an argument, that those modern teachers had an apologetic purpose in their liberal utterances and in their interpretations of Jewish teachings. But, considering that there has always been progress and development in Judaism, and that according to the talmudic principle אין לך אלא שופט שבימיך (*Tosefta, Kiddushin* II, 3) the teachers of every generation are the sole arbiters to decide for that generation what is authoritative Jewish teaching, are not the modern teachers, the only authorities who have the right to declare what constitutes Jewish religious teaching? And who, I ask in all fairness, is better qualified to interpret Jewish religious law and state what the Jewish religion teaches? Is it the anti-Semite who with malice and evil intention sets out to find in the vast storehouse of Jewish literature such sayings which he can possibly distort and misinterpret so as to give them a meaning which would serve his purpose of hate, or is it not rather the rabbi who has made a special study of Jewish literature and devoted his life to teaching and preaching Judaism?

With all due modesty, I may say that no one can deny me the right and the authority to interpret Jewish law and to decide what is and what is not Jewish religious teachings. I have received my rabbinical training and my rabbinical ordination from great European rabbis of the strictest orthodox school. I now belong to the liberal progressive party in Judaism and am a member of this Conference, representing a body of rabbis and teachers who did not hesitate to discard some beliefs, formerly held by Jewish teachers, when such beliefs were no longer compatible with their advanced thoughts, and to abrogate and abolish some older Jewish laws and practices when such were no longer expressive of the true spirit of Jewish religious doctrine as understood by them. If I had found that the Jewish religion, according to the orthodox interpretation, teaches something against the non-Jew which is incompatible with my liberal views, I would not hesitate to say so and to declare that we of the reform group no longer share such views. But I have not found this to be the case. I have found, on the contrary, that on these questions we all agree, and I can speak on behalf of the orthodox as well as the reform group in Jewry. To the best of my knowledge and in honest scientific search for the truth, I have gathered my material from sources older than the nineteenth century and examined the expressions of opinions by recognized authorities of past ages as to the Jewish attitude toward the non-Jew. I have presented these authoritative opinions in this paper, quoting the statements from the original sources and giving the exact references where these statements are found. I feel convinced that every one who will examine the material presented, will agree with me that the following is the attitude which, according to the authoritative teachings of our religion, we Jews, orthodox and reform alike, are to observe toward people who follow other religions. We of the House of Israel are united by the bond of common blood, common history, common sufferings, and common traditional beliefs which naturally make us feel near and close to one another as members of one family. But these feelings of close relationship to our co-religionists do not prevent us from having similar sentiments of brotherly love and friendship toward people of other faiths. We consider ourselves also as members of the larger human family whom we also must love, just as the greater love which one naturally feels for his blood-relatives and brothers in the flesh does not prevent him from also loving his friends and brethren outside of his immediate family circle. And, certainly we have no hatred or ill-will towards people of other faiths or other races. For we are mindful of the fundamental principles of our religion, that we all have one Father in heaven, that every human being is made in the image of the Father and that we sin against God if we harm any man. We consider it, therefore, our sacred religious duty to be honest, kind, considerate, friendly, and helpful to any human being of whatever race or creed he may be, and to treat him as we wish to be treated by him. Thus, we endeavor to live up to the great commandment of our religion: Thou shalt love thy fellowman as thyself, as interpreted by one of our greatest teachers, "not to do unto others, what we would not wish others to do unto us." This, we declare with our great teacher, Hillel, is the sum and substance of our religion, the Jewish Torah.

זו היא כל התורה כולה

NOTES

[1] See the prayer offered by Solomon at the dedication of his Temple (I K. VIII, 41-43) which Josephus (*Ant.* VIII, 4, 3) paraphrases in the following words: "Nay, moreover, this help is what I implore of Thee not for the Hebrews only when they are in distress, but when any shall come hither from any ends of the world whatsoever and shall return from their sins and implore Thy pardon, do Thou then pardon them and hear their prayer. For hereby all shall learn that Thou Thyself wast pleased with the building of this house for Thee and that we are not ourselves of an unsociable nature, nor behave ourselves like enemies to such as are not of our own people, but are wishing that Thy assistance should be communicated by Thee to all men in common and that they may have the enjoyment of Thy benefits bestowed upon them". And the anonymous prophet in speaking of the Temple says: "For My house shall be called a house of prayer for all peoples" (Isa. LVI, 7). The seventy bullocks which were offered in the Temple at Jerusalem on the Succoth festival were intended as an atonement for the seventy nations, says the Talmud (*Sukkah* 55b; compare also R. Moses Hagiz, Palestinian rabbi, (1671-1750) in his work *Eleh ha-Mizwot* (Amsterdam, 1713, p. 107). And in the ancient as well as modern service of the Synagog for New Year's day and Day of Atonement we hear repeatedly such strains, as: "May all creatures worship Thee and may they all form one band to do Thy will with a perfect heart" or "Shine forth in the majesty of Thy strength over all the inhabitants of Thy world that every form may know that Thou hast formed it and every creature understand that Thou hast created it" (comp. also R. Jacob Emden in his *Responsa Sheilat Yabez*, No. 144). And in the adoration, recited three times daily, the Jew prays for the time when "the world will be perfected under the kingdom of the Almighty and all the children of flesh will call upon Thy name."

[2] Jewish nationalists and political Zionists also aim through their plans to benefit not only Israel but all mankind. The hope for the coming of the Messiah and the restoration of the Jewish state has always been conceived as tending to help in carrying out the Jewish mission of teaching the world ideals of justice and righteousness. By setting up an ideal government of righteousness and truth the messianic state will be a model of true democracy and all nations will come up to Mount Zion and learn to walk in the ways of the Lord. The Messiah will be the arbiter between many nations and from Zion shall come forth the true doctrines of universal peace and the brotherhood of man.

[3] The term   גוי   in the Bible simply means "people" or "nation" and is applied to Israel as well as to any other nation. In postbiblical Jewish literature it has been used to designate a person from any other people

but the Jewish. It is exactly equivalent to the word Gentile. It has no
evil connotation at all and casts no aspersion upon the character of those
thus designated. See M. Guedemann, *Juedische Apologetik* (Glogau,
1906) p. 47; compare also A. Berliner, *Randbemerkungen zum taeglichen
Gebetbuch*, II. (Berlin, 1912) p. 33ff. and p. 72ff.

[4] בן עזאי אומר זה ספר תולדות אדם זה כלל גדול מזה *Sifra Ḳedoshim*, IV (Weiss 89b). The reason for this principle of Gen. V, 1, being
considered greater than the one of Lev. XIX, 18, is given by R. Aaron
Ibn Hayyim (a Moroccan rabbi, d. 1632) in his commentary *Korban Aaron*
(Venice, 1609) p. 306b, in the following words: משום דקרא דואהבת לרעך
הוא מחייב האהבה מצד הרעות לבד אבל זה ספר מחייב אותה מצד האחוה
שהוא חיזב יותר גדול ועוד כי בזה הראה לנו שכלנו בצלם אחד ובחותם אחד
והיא הצורה האלהית שהיא תחייב אותנו להתאחד בכל דברינו כשם שאנו
אחדים בצורה האלהית.

[5] ומפני שלום הבריות שלא יאמר אדם לחבירו אבא גדול מאביך
(*M. Sanhedrin*, IV, 5). Here it is evident that the term הבריות
as well as אדם and הבירו mean human beings Jew or non-Jew alike;
see the following note.

[6] ואהבת לרעך כמוך רבי עקיבא אומר זה כלל גדול בתורה *Sifra* l. c.
compare Midrash *Gen. R.* XXIV, 7, where this rule of R. Akiba is repeated and given the following specific application: אמר רבי עקיבא זה
כלל גדול בתורה שלא תאמר הואיל ונתבזיתי יתבזה הבירי עמי הואיל ונתקללתי
יתקלל חבירי עמי אמר רבי תנחומא אם עשית כן דע למי אתה מבזה בדמות
אלהים עשה אותו. Here, again, it is evident that under the
term רעך is understood every human being made in the image of God.
The reason for the equality of all men is that one God made them all;
compare *P. B. K.* VIII 6c where R. Joḥanan gives the same reason for
treating his slave as an equal. See also my *Ethics of the Halakah*, p. 22.
It is significant that in the entire Midrashic literature not one comment can
be found which would limit or qualify the meaning of the term רעך
in this verse so as to exclude the non-Jew. Evidently it was understood
by all the rabbis to mean "fellowman," Jew and non-Jew alike. This is
further proved by the fact that Hillel, who a long time before R. Akiba
expressed this great principle in a negative form (*Sabbath*, 31a), also
commanded the love for all human creatures (see below note 16).
Speaking about the duty of loving one's fellowman, R. Phinehas Elija
Hurwitz in the second part of his *Sefer ha-Berit* (Bruenn, 1797) in the
treatise אהבת רעים Ch. IV remarks, as follows: והתורה מתייבת אותנו
זאת באר היטב כמה שבתוב ואהבת לרעך כמוך ואין הכוונה בו לישראל דוקא
... אבל הכוונה בן לרעך שהוא אדם כמוך ועוסק בישובו של עולם כטוף וכל
האומות במשמע.

[7] Abot III, 14. חביב אדם שנברא בצלם חבה יתירה נודעת לו שנברא
בצלם שנאמר בצלם אלהים עשה את האדם
It is evident that under אדם here are meant all descendants of Adam, Jew

and non-Jew alike. This is further proved from the context. In the same
sentence R. Akiba speaks of another distinction which he says is peculiar to
the Jews, hence the distinction of being beloved because being made in the
image of God, is common to all mankind. In this sense R. Akiba's statement has been understood by mediaeval Jewish authorities who quote and
comment upon it. Only a few need be cited here. R. Jacob Anatoli
(1194-1256) in his *Malmad ha-Talmidim* (Berlin, 1866) p. 25ab. R. Oba-
diah Sforno (1475-1550) in his commentary to the Pentateuch, commenting upon the passage "Yea, He loveth the people" (Deut. XXXIII, 3)
quotes the statement of R. Akiba in support of his interpretation of the
passage to mean that the entire human family is God's precious treasure.
He says: ובזה הודעת שכל המין האנושי סגולה אצלך כאמרם ז'ל חביב
אדם שנברא בצלם   Compare also his remarks to Exod. IX, 19 and
XIX, 5. R. Yomtob Lipmann Heller (1579-1654) in his commentary
Tossafot Yomtob ad loc. remarks: ובכל אדם אמר רבי עקיבא וכמו שהיא
הראיה שממנו הביא שהיא נאמר לבני נח לא לישראל לבדם ורצה רבי עקיבא
לזכות את כל אדם אף לבני נח

[8] *Sifre Deut.* 49, Friedmann, 85a. Comp. also K. Kohler, *Jewish Theol-*
ogy, p. 477ff.

[9] זכו אחרישנה *Sanhedrin*, 98a.

[10] It is interesting to note that according to the rabbis the Genesis story
also teaches the equality of all men as regards their moral and religious
responsibilities. Thus the *Tosefta* (*Sanhedrin*, VIII, 4) says: ולמה נברא
יחידי בעולם שלא יהו הצדיקים אומרים אנו בניו של צדיק ושלא יהו הרשעים.
אומרים אנו בניו של רשע   In other words a man's religious and moral
character is not determined by his birth and does not depend on the race
or nationality to which he belongs. It depends solely upon his self-
determination and his free choice whether he shall be righteous or wicked.
For, although man is afflicted with evil inclinations, and may be born with
evil passions, God has provided for him religious teachings by which he
can train and discipline himself, so as to overcome all evil inclinations,
as the Talmud says (*Ḳiddushin*, 30b) : בראתי יצר הרע ובראתי לו תורה
תבלין ואם אתם עוסקין בתורה אין אתם נמסרין בידו.

[11] Some of these inherent weaknesses are ascribed by the rabbis to the
poisoning of the human race by the serpent in his intercourse with Eve.
By receiving the Torah, Israel freed himself from the effects of this poison.
This is expressed by the Talmud (*Sabbath*, 146a) as follows: בשעה שבא
נחש על חוה הטיל בה זוהמא ישראל שעטדו על הר סיני פסקה זוהמתן עובדי
כוכבים שלא עמדו על הר סיני לא פסקה זוהמתן   This is an echo of
the idea of the original sin. Judaism has suppressed this idea as tending
to paralyze human efforts at religious and moral improvement. Hence
it is but rarely mentioned in Jewish literature. Where it is mentioned,
as in this passage, it is made harmless by the declaration that the

acceptance of the Torah counteracts the evil effects of that poisoning. Not only the Jew but also the gentile can, by accepting the Torah, free himself from these human weaknesses. This is expressed in the Talmud (*ibidem, l. c.*) in the following discussion: אמר ליה רב אתא בריהדרבא לרב אשי גרים טאי אמר ליה אף על גב דאינהו לא הוו מזלייהו הוה דכתיב את אשר ישנו פה ' ' ' ואת אשר איננו פה

In other words, any person who accepts the Torah gets the same whole-some benefit from it, whether his ancestors stood at the foot of Mount Sinai or not.

[12] כשנגלה המקום ליתן תורה לישראל לא על ישראל בלבד הוא נגלה אלא על כל האומות וכו' (*Sifre Deut.* 343, Friedmann, 142b, compare also *Abodah Zarah*, 2b). The meaning of the midrashic statement in *Sifre* that the other nations refused to accept the Torah, is simply this that due to their inherent weaknesses which were their national characteristics and to their lack of training, since they had not observed even the seven commandments given to them, they were not prepared to accept the Torah. The Israelites, on the other hand, were prepared, because they had been trained in the observance of the seven commandments and even practiced other virtues which they inherited from the patriarchs. This is clearly expressed in the midrashic saying (*Pseudo-Seder Elijahu Zutta*, ed. Friedmann, Wien, 1904, p. 56) that when God asked the Israelites whether they would accept the Torah they answered and said: עד שלא שמענו התורה שמרנו את מצות התורה - "We have practiced many of the laws of the Torah even before we heard of the Torah." This is but another way of saying we have been trained in its practice and conse-quently are ready to receive it. Compare my article on *Jewish Theology* in the *Jewish Encyclopedia*, XII, p. 136.

[13] אתה אומר מנין אפילו גוי ועושה את התורה הרי הוא ככהן גדול תלמוד לומר אשר יעשה אותם האדם וחי בהם וכן הוא אומר. וזאת רתורת הכהנים והלוים וישראלים לא נאמר כאן אלא- וזאת תורת האדם ה' אלהים. וכן הוא אומר פרתחו שערים- ויבא כהנים ולויים וישראלים לא נאמר אלא. ויבא גוי צדק שומר אמונים. וכן הוא אומר זה השער לה'-כהנים לויים וישראלים לא נאמר אלא-צדיקים יבואו בו. וכן הוא אומר-הטיבה ה' לכהנים ללויים לישראל לא נאמר כאן אלא-הטיבה ה' לטובים הא אפילו גוי ועשה את התורה הרי הוא ככהן גדול. *Sifra Aḥare Mot*, XIII, Weiss, 86b, com-pare also *Sanhedrin*, 59a and 77a.

[14] לא הנלה הקדש ברוך הוא את ישראל לביו האומות אלא כדי שיתוספו עליהם גרים *Pesahim*, 87b, comp. also R. Moses of Coucy (first half of 13th century) in his *SeMaG, Commandments*, 74, and R. Raphael b. Gabriel of Norzi (16th century) in his סאה סלת Amsterdam, 1757, p. 8b.

[15] In ancient times some restrictions, based upon the biblical law, were put upon members of certain nations, when they joined the Jewish people. They were admitted into the Jewish fold and could join the congregation but were refused the right of intermarrying with those of pure Jewish

descent. These restrictions were removed at the beginning of the second century, C. E. when R. Joshua declared in the assembly at Jabneh that the nations in question, although called by the same names and inhabiting the same countries as those against whom the biblical prohibitions were directed, could no longer be considered as absolutely identical with the nations mentioned in the biblical law, hence its prohibition was not to be applied to them. See *M. Yadayim*, IV, 4. This, by the way, shows how the rabbis of the Talmud could and actually did, declare biblical laws, discriminating against certain nations, as no longer binding for their times. As a result of this decision of R. Joshua which was accepted as law, no restriction whatever is put upon the members of any race or nation if they wish to join the Jewish community. They are given full equality with those born in the Jewish fold.

[16] הלל אומר הוה מתלמידיו של אהרן אוהב שלום ורודף שלום אוהב את הבריות ומקרבן לתורה *Abot* I, 12. It is evident that under the term בריות here are meant people who are not of the Jewish faith, not yet under the Law, but are to be attracted to it. Compare also R. Hayyim Vital (1543-1620) in his *Shaare ha-Kedushah*, I, 5, (Sulzbach, 1758), p. 8b, where he expressly teaches to love all human creatures Jew and non-Jew alike. לאהוב את כל הבריות ואפילו כותים

[17] Because the Jew is to teach his religious principles by precept and example, Judaism considers any act on the part of the Jew whereby the reputation of the high standard of the Jewish religion is maintained as of the greatest religious merit, as an act of קדוש השם "glorification of the name of God." On the other hand, any act on the part of the Jew whereby the Jewish religion is brought into disrepute, is regarded as the gravest sin for which no forgiveness can be obtained. It is considered a חלול השם a "profanation of the name of God and His Torah." See K. Kohler, *Kiddush ha-Shem* and *Hillul ha-Shem* in *Jewish Encyclopedia*, VII, p. 484ff.

[18] יש צדיקים באומות שיש להם הלק לעולם הבא *Tosefta Sanhedrin*, XIII, 2 and *b. Sanhedrin*, 105a. Compare also *Midrash, Tehillim*, IX, 15, ed. Buber, p. 90.

[19] *Yebamot*, 47a; Maimonides, *Yad, Melakim*, VIII, 10 and *Issure Biah*, XIV; *Shulhan Aruk, Yore Deah*, 268, 2.

[20] These seven commandments are: (1) to establish courts of justice, (2) not to blaspheme the name of God, (3) not to worship idols, (4) not to commit adultery, (5) not to commit murder, (6) not to commit robbery and (7) not to eat flesh that had been cut off from a living animal (*Sanhedrin*, 56ab). The first six had been commanded to Adam and then repeated to Noah with the addition of the seventh one. Compare J. H. Greenstone, *Laws Noachian* in *Jewish Encyclopedia*, VII, p. 648ff. The

gentile who accepts these seven laws is considered as one of the
חסידי אומות העולם the pious ones among the gentiles who will
have a share in the future world (Maimonides, *Yad, Melakim*, VIII, 11).

21 The Talmud (*Sanhedrin*, 59a) interprets the saying נכרי ועושה את
התורה הרי הוא ככהן גדול(see above, note 13) to mean that the gentile who
practices the seven commandments is like the highpriest. Compare also
Midrash Tanḥoma Ekeb, 3, where it is stated that the gentiles in their way
observe the commandments and glorify the name of God.

22 כהניך ילבשו צדק . ... כהניך אלו צדיקי אומות העולם שהם כהנים להקדוש
ברוך הוא בעולם הזה *Seder Elijahu Zutta*, XX, (Warsaw, 1880), p.151.

23 גר תושב כל שקיבל עליו בפני שלש חברים שלא לעבוד עבודת אלילים דברי
רבי מאיר וחכמים אומרים כל שקיבל עליו שבע מצות שקבלו עליהם בני נח
(*Abodah Zarah*, 64b, comp. also tractate *Gerim*, in R. Kirchheim's *septem
libri Talmudici parvi Hierosolymitani*, Frankfurt a. M. 1851, p. 41). Maimonides, *Yad, Issure Biah*, XIV, 7, accepts the opinion of the חכמים
though some medieval authorities accept the opinion of R. Meir, that the
mere resolution not to worship idols makes one a *Ger Toshab* (R. Isaac
b. Sheshet, *Responsa*, No. 119, and R. Raphael of Norzi in his
סאה סלת p. 7b). The formal promise in the presence of three
members בפני שלשה חברים was necessary only during the time when
there was an independent Jewish state, see Isaac Baer Levinsohn in his
Zerubabel, III (Warsaw, 1901), pp. 16-18, and D. Hoffman, *Der Shulchan
Aruch und die Rabbinen ueber das Verhaeltniss der Juden zu Anders-
glaubigen*, (Berlin, 1894) pp. 151-152. Indeed the words, בפני שלשה
חברים are omitted in tractate *Gerim*. Such a *Ger Toshab* is to be
helped and supported, ransomed from captivity and saved from any danger
exactly like a Jew, see R. Moses b. Nahman in his comments to Maimonides, *Book of the Commandments*, commandment 16 (*editio*, Warsaw,
1903), p. 43; R. Eliezer Askari of Safed (16th century) in his
ספר חרדים commandments ch. V. (*editio*, Lublin, 1889), p. 18a, and
R. Raphael of Norzi *op. cit. l. c.* In tractate *Gerim* there is also stated
that it is forbidden to lend to him or borrow from him money on interest
ולא מלוין אותו ולא לוין ממנו ברבית compare Kirchheim note 11
and see below note.

24 Compare Responsa, *Zera Emet* by R. Ismael ha Kohen (Leghorn,
1796), part II, No. 112; Levinsohn, *op. cit.* II, p. 90; Hoffman *op cit.*, p. 152.

25 Maimonides, *Yad, Melakim* XI, 4 (*editio*, Amsterdam, 1702-03) declares that Christianity and Mohammedanism are preparing the way for
the messianic era expected by the Jews; R. Joseph Jabez (15th and 16th
century) in his *Maamar ha-Aḥdut* III, (Altona 1794, p. 4) says, כי האומות
היום מאמינים בחדוש העולם ... מודים בעקרי אמונתנו ובמעלת אבותינו
ושנתנה התורה אלינו Don Isaac Abravanel in his commentary to Deut.
XXIII, 21 states that Edom, i. e. Christians, and Ishmael, i. e. Mohamme-

dans, cannot be considered as strangers but are to be regarded as brothers to the Jews. R. Moses Alshech (Rabbi in Safed, Palestine, second half of 16th century) in the preface to his *Torat Moshe,* a commentary to the Pentateuch, declares that Christians and Mohammedans, although differing in many points are alike in that they believe in God the Creator and they honor the Torah and it is one of the wonderful plans of the Divine wisdom, thus to include others in the covenant with the holy people Israel:

הצד השוה שבהם ששניהם יודו ויאמינו בה' קונה שמים וארץ ... ומבלעד

נצחיות התורה כל יקר ראתה עיניהם והמה נותנים כבוד לתורתנו הקדושה ...

והוא מפלאי ההכמה הריבונית להכנים בברית עם קודש ישראל גם את הזולת.

Compare also the letter addressed to the leaders of the Council of Four Lands, *Waad Arba Arazot,* by R. Jacob Emden, printed in the latter's edition of *Seder Olam,* Hamburg, 1757.

²⁶ See Maimonides' *Letters* (Leipzig, 1859), p. 23: ומה ששאלת על האומות

הוי יודע דרחמנא לבא בעי ואחר כוונת הלב הם הדברים.

²⁷ Compare Hoffman, *op. cit.,* p. 144ff, where the authorities holding this opinion are cited.

²⁸ *Gittin,* 59b.

²⁹ *Gittin,* 61a; *Tosefta Gittin,* V, 4-5; p. *Demai,* IV, 5, 24a.

³⁰ p. *Gittin,* V, 9, 47c.

³¹ *Tosefta Gittin,* l. c. b. *Gittin,* 61a.

³² p. *Gittin* l. c. compare *Tur Ḥoshen Mishpat,* 266.

³³ *Gittin,* 62a compare Rashi *ad loc.;* M. *Shebiit,* IV, 3 and V, 9 and p. *Shebiit,* 36a.

³⁴ Compare A. Bertholet, *Die Stellung der Israeliten und Juden zu den Fremden* (Leipzig, 1896), p. 347.

³⁵ Where the rabbis wish to express merely the idea, for the sake of peace or to avoid quarrels, they use the expression בשביל השלום or בדבר השלום or לעשות שלום but not the phrase מפני דרכי שלום.

³⁶ Philo, *De Virtutibus (De Humanitate)* Mang. 395 (Translation, C. D. Yonge, III, p. 439) expresses the same idea when he says: "And this is an object which the most holy prophet is endeavoring to bring to pass throughout the whole of his code of laws, studying to create unanimity and fellowship and agreement and that due admixture of different dispositions by which homes and cities and altars and nations and countries and the whole human race may be conducted to the very highest happiness.

³⁷ *Yad, Melakim,* X, 12.

³⁸ See also Hoffman *op cit.* p. 49; Guedemann, *op. cit.* p. 78, and my *Ethics of the Halakah,* p. 35, note 83.

³⁹ Maimonides, *Yad, Matnot Aniyyim,* I, 9; *Abodat kokabim,* I, 5; *Melakim,* X, 12; *Ebel,* XIV, 8; *Shemittah ve-Yobel,* VIII, 8; *Tur Yoreh Deah,*

151, 335, 367; *Shulḥan Aruk, Yoreh Deah*, 151, 12-13; 251, 1 (*Isserles*); 335, 9; 367, 1.

[40] Compare also *Seder Elijahu Rabbah*, XVIII, Friedmann, p. 104.

[41] שואלין בשלומם ואפילו ביום אידם מפני דרכי שלום *Kallah Rabbati*, III, compare also b. *Gittin*, 62a.

[42] *Kiddushin*, 33a, decision of Issi b. Jehudah, declared by R. Joḥanan to be the accepted Halakah; Maimonides *Yad, Talmud Torah*, VI, 9, *Shulḥan Aruk, Yoreh Deah*, 244, 7.

[43] גדול כבוד הבריות שדוחה לא תעשה שבתורה *Sabbath*, 81b, compare *Ethics of the Halakah*, p. 20.

[44] מצווין הן ישראל לעשות חסד לכל מי שיבא *Midrash Tehillim* to Psalm LII, Buber, p. 286, compare Buber's remarks *ibidem*, note 33.

[45] אמר רבי יוהנן אם הרגלת לשונך לדבר באחיך שאינו בן אומתך סוף בבן אומתך תתן דופי *Midrash Debarim*, R. VI, 9. R. David Lurja in חדושי הרד"ל *ad loc.* remarks to this passage, as follows: ומבואר מכאן שאסור לספר לשון הרע על עובדי כוכבים

[46] רבי יהושע בן לוי אמר אמר דוד אם דברת בעשו שהוא אתיך סופך לדבר בבן אומתך זה משה רבן של כל הנביאים *Tanhoma Pikkude*, 7, (Lublin, 1893) p. 223.

[47] אסור לגנוב דעת הבריות ואפילו דעתו של עובד כוכבים Hullin, 94a; Maimonides, *Yad, Deot*, II, 6; *Mekirah*, XVIII, 1; *Sefer Ḥassidim*, 51; *Shulḥan Aruk, Ḥoshen Mishpat*, 228, p.

[48] Maimonides *Yad, Mekirah*, l. c. R. Moses Coucy in his *SeMaG, Prohibitions*, 170; *Shulḥan Aruk, Ḥoshen Mishpat*, l. c.

[49] *Sefer Ḥassidim* (editio Wistinetzki, Berlin 1891) 1232, says: אל יעשה אדם ישקר אפילו לנוי and in the older editions 395 and 1080, it is said: כשם שאתה צריך להיות נוהג באמונה עם ישראל כך ארתה צריך להרתנהג עם הנכרי R. Jonah Girondi (13th century) in his *Sefer ha-Yirah* (Königsberg) p. 4a says: ואף עסקו עם הנוי יהיה באמונה: This principle is also expressed by R. Bahya b. Asher (13th and 14th century) in his *Kad ha-Kemah*, Warsaw 1870, p. 17b; by R. Jacob b. Isaac Luzzatto in his *Kaftor va-Ferah*, Amsterdam 1709, p. 30; by R. Raphael Norzi op cit. p. 6b and R. Moses Hagiz in his *Zikkaron libne Israel*, No. 20.

[50] Maimonides, *Yad, Gezelah ve-Abedah* I, 2; *Shulḥan Aruk, Ḥoshen Mishpat*, 359, 1. To rob the Non-Jew is considered even a graver sin than to rob the Jew because the former act may lead to a profanation of the name חמור גזל הנוי מגזל ישראל מפני חלול השם (Tosefta *B. K.*, X, 15); compare also *Seder Elijahu Rabbah*, XVI, Friedmann, pp. 74-75; Bahya b. Asher *op cit.*, p. 17; and R. Samuel Edels (1555-1631) in his *Novellae* to the Talmud *Ketubot*, 67a, who strongly condemns the cheating of a Non-Jew and declares it to be a חלול השם a desecration of the name.

[51] R. Eliezer b. Nathan (first half of the 12th century) in his *Eben ha-Ezer*, (Prague 1610) p. 91b; Maimonides *Yad, Genebah* I, 1; *Sefer Ḥassidim*, 661; *Shulḥan Aruk, Ḥoshen Mishpat*, 348, 2.

[52] Maimonides *Yad, Genebah*, VII, 8; *Shulḥan Aruk, Ḥoshen Mishpat*, 231, 1; compare also *Seder Elijahu Rabbah*, XVI, Friedmann, pp. 74-75.

[53] *Tosefta Ḥullin*, VII, 3; b. *Ḥullin*, 94a; Maimonides, *Yad, Mekirah*, XVIII, 1; *Shulḥan Aruk, Ḥoshen Mishpat*, 228, 6.

[54] See p. *B. M.* II, 8c, story about Simon b. Shetah; R. Eliezer b. Nathan, *op. cit. l. c.*; Maimonides, *Yad, Genebah*, VIII, 8; *Sefer Ḥassidim*, 358; R. Menaḥem Meiri quoted by R. Bezalel Ashkenasi in his *Shittah Mekubezet* to *B. K.*, 113b, and R. Moses Ribkes (17th century) in his *Beer ha-Golah* to *Ḥoshen Mishpat*, 348.

[55] In the case of people who have no laws of their own and do not respect property rights, the Jew is by the letter of the law not bound to make an effort to restore to them their lost articles, since they on their part would not restore to the Jew any of his lost article, if they should happen to find them. However, for the sake of avoiding a חלול השם the Jew is commanded to restore even to such people their lost article (*B. K.*, 113b, compare especially marginal note in Talmud, edition Wilna); *Maimonides Yad, Gezelah ve-Abedah*, XI, 3; *Shulḥan Aruk, Ḥoshen Mishpat*, 266, 1. But in the case of people who have laws of their own and respect property rights, the Jew is commanded by the strict letter of the law to restore to them their lost articles. See *Sefer Ḥassidim* and R. Menaḥem Meiri *l. c.* and *Beer ha-Golah* to *Ḥoshen Mishpat*, 266; compare also Hoffmann *op. cit.*, p. 61ff.

[56] This is but one of many instances. A similar story is told there in the Palestinian Talmud of Abba Hoshaya who once restored to a non-Jewish woman a piece of jewelry which she had lost in his place. The lady refused to accept it, saying: "This is not of much value to me, I have many other better and more valuable pieces". Abba Hoshaya, however, insisted that she take it back, for, says he, אורייתא גזרת דנחזור "the Torah commands us to return lost articles even to non-Jews." Compare also commentary *Pene Moshe ad loc.* and Menaḥem de Lonzano in his *Maarik* (ed. Jellinek Leipzig 1853), p. 124; and *Midrash Tehillim*, XII, ed. Buber, 104.

[57] *Sefer Ḥassidim*, 1080.

[58] Maimonides' view that the biblical law commands the Jew to charge interest on loans to non-Jews (*Malve ve-Love*, V, 1) is rejected by all authorities, see commentaries *ad loc.*; compare also Eliezer Zebi Zweifel in his *Sanegor*, Warsaw, 1894, p. 291ff.

[59] The reason why the rabbis forbade one to charge interest to non-Jews is given by a later Amora in the Talmud (*ibidem l. c.*) שמא ילמוד

ממעשיו It seems to me that the meaning of this phrase is that the Jew should not imitate the non-Jew in this unethical practice of charging interest. The sole reason why the Torah permitted the Jew to charge interest to the non-Jew was, as we have seen, because the non-Jew charged interest to the Jew. Against this the rabbis argued that the Jew must not imitate a non-Jewish unethical practice, hence he should not charge interest to the non-Jew even though the latter charges him interest. The commentators take the words שמא ילמוד ממעשיו to mean, lest the Jew learn from the non-Jew some other bad practices. But one fails to see how this danger is avoided by merely prohibiting the Jew from charging the non-Jew interest, while permitting him to lend the non-Jew money without interest and otherwise to associate in business with him. It must be admitted that the following words וכיון דתלמיד חכם הוא לא ילמוד ממעשיו which are added in the Talmud to the statement שמא ילמוד ממעשיו favor the interpretation of the commentators. On the other hand, it seems strange that while according to the talmudic statement וכיון דתלמיד חכם הוא לא ילמוד ממעשיו the learned, not being in danger of imitating bad practices, would be permitted to charge interest to non-Jews, R. Amram Gaon in a *Responsum* (*Shaare Zedek*, p. 40a) declares this prohibition of taking interest from the non-Jew to be especially strict in the case of the learned. Did Amram have a different reading in the Talmud?

⁶⁰ See his commentary to Deut. XXIII, 21; compare also David de Pomis (16th century) *Apologia Pro Medico Hebraeo*, extracts of which are given by Winter und Wuensche, *Juedische Literatur*, III, p. 698ff. De Pomis quotes a Christian theologian who observed that pious Jews abhor usury whether practiced upon Jew or non-Jew.

⁶¹ So it is quoted by Tossafot, (*Abodah Zarah*, 26b s. v. ולא מורידין (וֹלֹא מורידיו from the Palestinian Talmud and so it is also found in tractate *Soferim*, XV, 10; compare Mueller, p. 211. See also I. B. Lewinsohn, *Zerubabel* II, p. 97; Graetz, *Monatschrift*, XIX, p. 486; Zweifel, *Sanegor*, pp. 290-291; G. Deutsch, *Jew and Gentile*, (Boston, 1920) pp. 122-123.

⁶² Another such saying which has been misunderstood even by early Jewish authorities, is the one found in the *Tosefta B. M.* II, 32, and also quoted in the Talmud, *Abodah Zarah*, 26ab, which reads as follows: העובדי כוכבים והרועים בהמה דקה ומגדליה לא מעלין ולא מורידין The meaning of this *Baraitha* is either that the idol worshipers of those days, as well as the Jewish shepherds, both of whom did not enjoy a high reputation for honesty, were not to be appointed to public offices, but if once appointed to such an office were not to be removed from it (Graetz, *ibidem l. c.*) or, what is more likely, that they were to be refused the privilege of getting up in public to announce that they lost certain articles and to claim them from the finder, for they were suspected of making false claims (Rector A.

Schwarz in *Hazofeh Meerez Hagar*, I, 3 (Budapest 1911) p. 488ff.) The latter interpretation is supported by the context in the *Tosefta*.

[63] A similar exaggerated expression is the saying עובר כוכבים ששבת חייב מיתה (*Sanhedrin*, 58b). See Zweifel, *op. cit.*, pp. 285-86.

[64] See *Sifra, Aḥare Mot*, XIII, Weiss 86a; *Tosefta Sabbath*, VI-VII.

[65] R. Joseph Colon (2nd half of the 15th century) in his *Responsa*, No. 88, quoted by Joseph Caro in *Bet Joseph* and Moses Isserles in *Darke Moshe* to *Tur Yoreh Deah*, 178.

[66] R. Solomon Lurja (1510-73) in his work *Yam shel Shomoh* to *Baba Kamma* (Prague 1616) p. 39a.

RESPONSA

TALMUDIC-RABBINIC VIEW ON BIRTH CONTROL

In considering the question of the Talmudic-Rabbinic attitude towards Birth-control we must seek to clear up the confusion that prevails in the discussion of the subject and define the principles involved in the whole question.

Some rabbis are inclined to regard all forms of Birth-control, excepting self control or continence as הוצאת שכבת זרע לבטלה and therefore put them in a class with masturbation or self-abuse. Hence, they believe that, with the citing of agadic sayings from the Talmud and Midrashim against the evil practice of self-abuse, they have also proved the opposition of rabbinic law to the various forms of Birth-control. Such a method, however, is unscientific and not justified in the discussion of such a serious and important question.

In the first place, the method of adjudging questions of religious practice on the basis of agadic utterances is altogether unwarranted. The talmudic rule is אין מורין מן ההגדות that "we cannot decide the questions of practice by citing agadic sayings" (P. *Hagigah* I, 8 76d). The Agadah may set up an exalted ideal of the highest ethical living. It may teach the lofty precept קדש עצמך במותר לך to aspire to a holy life and to avoid even such actions or practices which, though permitted by the law, do not measure up with its high standard. But it does not rest with the Agadah to decide what is forbidden or permitted by the law. "The Agadist cannot declare anything forforbidden or permitted, unclean or clean," says the Talmud ובעל אגדה שאינו לא אוסר ולא מתיר לא מטמא ולא מטהר P. *Horayot* III, 7 48c). The answer to questions of practice, that is, as to what is permitted by Jewish law and what is not, can be given only on the basis of the teachings of the Halakah.

Secondly, it is absolutely wrong to consider cohabitation with one's wife under conditions which might not result in procreation, an act of הוצאת שכבת זרע לבטלה and to class it with sexual perversions such as self abuse.

Reprinted from *Central Conference of American Rabbis Year Book,* Vol. XXXVII, 1927.

In the following, therefore, we must consider only what the Halakah teaches about the various forms of birth-control and ignore what
the Agadah has to say in condemnation of the evil practices of self-
abuse and sexual perversions.

In order to avoid confusion and for the sake of a clearer understanding and a systematic presentation of the rabbinic teachings bearing
upon our subject, it is necessary to formulate the question properly.
It seems to me that the correct formulation of our question is as follows: Does the talmudic-rabbinic law permit cohabitation between
husband and wife in such a manner or under such conditions as
would make conception imposible; and if so, what are the conditions
under which such cohabitation is permitted?

As to the first and main part of the question, there is no doubt that
it must be answered in the affirmative. To begin with, the rabbinic
law not only permits but even commands the husband to fulfil his
conjugal duties to his wife, even after she has experienced the change
of life and has become incapable of having children. Likewise, the
husband is permitted to have sexual intercourse with his wife even
if she is congenitally incapable of conception, as, for instance, when
she is an עקרה sterile, or an איילונית that is a wombless woman
(Tossafot and Mordecai, quoted by Isserles in Shulhan Aruk
Eben Ha-Ezer XXIII, 2). The later rabbinic law goes even
further and permits even a man who has never had children and thus
has not fulfilled the duty of propagation of the race מצות פ'ור
to marry a woman incapable of bearing children, that is, a sterile
woman עקרה or an old woman זקנה (Isaac b. Sheshet quoted
by Isserles op. cit. I. 3). From all this it is evident that the act
of cohabitation, even when it cannot possibly result in conception
is in itself not only not immoral or forbidden, but in some cases even
mandatory. Hence we may conclude that the discharge of sperm
through sexual intercourse even though it does not effect impregnation
of the woman, is not considered an act of "wasteful discharge of
semen", הוצאת שכבת זרע לבטלה which is so strongly condemned by
the agadic sayings of the Talmud. For while, as regards procreation,
such a discharge is without results and purposeless, yet since it
results from legitimate gratification of a normal natural desire, it
has fulfilled a legitimate function and is not to be considered as
in vain.

Now it may be argued that only in such cases where the parties
through no fault of their own are incapable of procreation does the
law consider the mere gratification of their natural desire a legitimate
act and hence does not condemn it as הוצאת שכבת זרע לבטלה. We have,
therefore, to further inquire whether the gratification of their legitimate desire by sexual intercourse in a manner not resulting in
procreation would be permissible even to young and normally healthy
husband and wife who are capable of having children.

To my knowledge, the Halakah, aside from recommending decency
and consideration for the feelings of the wife in these matters, does
not put any restrictions upon the huband's gratification of his sexual
desire for his wife and certainly does not forbid him any manner of
sexual intercourse with her. This is evident from the following passage in the Talmud (Nedarim 20b) where R. Joḥanan b. Nappaha,
commenting upon a saying of R. Joḥanan b. Dahabai in disapproval
of certain practices indulged in by some husbands, says: "These are
but the words (i. e. the individual opinion) of Joḥanan b. Dahabai
the sages, however, have said that the decision of the law, i. e. the
הלכה is not according to Joḥanan b. Dahabai, but a husband
may indulge with his wife in whatever manner of sexual gratification
he desires."

אמר רבי יוחנן זו דברי יוחנן בן דהבאי אבל אמרו חכמים אין הלכה כיוחנן בן
דהבאי אלא כל מה שאדם רוצה לעשות באשתו עושה.

This Halakah of R. Johanan b. Nappaha, supported by the decisions
of Judah ha-Nasi and Abba Areka, reported in the Talmud (*ibidem*
l. c.) has been accepted as law by all medieval rabbinic authorities,
and they accordingly permit intercourse with one's wife in any
manner כדרכה ושלא כדרכה. (Maimonides Yad, Issure Biah XXI,
9; Tur Eben ha-Ezer 25 and Isserles in Shulhan Aruk, *Eben
ha-Ezer* 25, 2). Maimonides (l.c.) would limit the permission of sexual
indulgence שלא כדרכה only to such forms of שלא כדרכה which do
not result in הוצאת שכבת זרע לבטלה for he says: ובלבד שלא יוציא
שכבת זרע לבטלה But other medieval authorities permit intercourse
שלא כדרכה even when resulting in הוצאת שכבת זרע לבטלה. The only
restriction they would put on this permission is that a man should
not habituate himself always to do it only in such a manner.

דלא חשוב כמעשה ער ואונן אלא כשמתכוין להשחית זרע ורגיל לעשות כן תמיד
אבל באקראי בעלמא ומתאוה לבא על אשתו שלא כדרכה שרי.
(Tossafot, Yebamot 34b s. v. ולא כמעשה ער ואונן; Tur and Isserles l.c.)

From the fact that they permit שלא כדרכה even when it necessarily
results in הוצאת ש"ז לבטלה we need not, however, necessarily conclude
that these authorities would also permit such practices of שלא כדרכה
as are performed שלא במקום זרע or ממקום אחר (See Rashi to Yebamot 34b s. v. שלא כדרכה and Rashi to Genesis XXIV, 16, compared
with Genesis R. XL, 5), which are really sexual perversions and not
sexual intercourse. See R. Isaiah Horowitz in his *Sh'ne Luḥot ha-
Brith* שער האותיות (Josefow, 1878, pp. 132-133). It seems rather that
the Rabbis were of the opinion that when intercourse is had by what
they euphemistically term הפיכת השולחן whether היא למעלה והוא למטה
or פנים כנגד עורף the very position of the woman is such as to prevent
conception. Compare their saying אשה מזנה מתהפכת כדי שלא תתעבר
(Yebamot 35a); also Tur Eben ha-Ezer 76 end. Hence according
to their theory, though not sustained by modern medicine, there
are forms of sexual intercourse שלא כדרכה which cannot result
in conception. These alone, not sexual perversions, do they
permit. The statement of Raba (Sanhedrin 58b) taking for granted
that an Israelite is permitted (read דלישראל שרי see Tossafot and
מהרש"א ad loc.) to have intercourse with his wife שלא כדרכה is also to be
understood in this sense, though from the phrase ודבק ולא שלא כדרכה
used in the amended saying of Raba it would appear that the term
שלא כדרכה means ביאה ממקום אחר. From a Baraita in *Yebamot,* 34b
we learn that during the period of lactation the husband is allowed,
if not commanded, to practice coitus abruptus when having intercourse with his wife. The Baraita reads as follows:

כל עשרים וארבעה חדש דש מבפנים וזורה מבחוץ דברי רבי אליעזר אמרו לו
הללו אינו אלא כמעשה ער ואונן, כמעשה ער ואונן ולא כמעשה ער ואונן

"During the 24 months in which his wife nurses, or should nurse,
the child, the husband when having intercourse with her should, or
may practice coitus abruptus (to avoid her becoming pregnant again.
For in the latter eventuality she will not be able to continue nursing
the child and the child might die as a result of an early weaning
Rashi ad loc.) כדי שלא תתעבר ותגמול את בנה וימות The other teachers,
however, said to R. Eliezer that such intercourse would be almost like
the acts of Er and Onan." One may argue that this permission or

recommendation of practicing coitus abruptus represents only the opinion of R. Eliezer and we should decide against him, according to the principle יחיד ורבים הלכה כרבים. But such an argument does not hold good in our case. In the first place, when the individual opinion has a good reason in its support דמסתבר טעמיה, as, according to Rashi, R. Eliezer's opinion in our case has, the decision may follow the individual against the many (see Alfasi and Asheri to B. B. Chapter 1, end, and comp. Maleachi Cohn, Yad Maleachi 296). Secondly, we cannot here decide against R. Eliezer since the other teachers do not express a definite opinion contrary to his. For we notice that the other teachers do not say "It is forbidden to do so." They do not even say that it is Onanism. They merely say: "It is almost like the conduct of Er and Onan." This certainly is not a strong and definite opposition to R. Eliezer's opinion. It seems to me that even the other teachers did not forbid the practice under the circumstances. They merely refused to recommend it as R. Eliezer did, because they hesitated to recommend a practice which is so much like the acts of Er and Onan, even under circumstances which make it imperative that conception be prevented. And we have to understand R. Eliezer's opinion as making it obligatory for the husband to perform coitus abruptus during the period of lactation.

That this interpretation of the respective positions of R. Eliezer and the other teachers in our Baraita is correct will be confirmed by our consideration of another Baraita dealing with the question of using contraceptives. This other Baraita is found in Yebamot 12b, 100b, Ketubot 39a, Nedarim 35b and Niddah 45b. It reads as follows:

תני רב ביבי קמיה דרב נחמן שלש נשים משמשות במוך קטנה מעוברת ומניקה, קטנה שמא תתעבר ושמא תמות מעוברת שמא תעשה עוברה סנדל מניקה שמא תגמול בנה וימות. ואיזו היא קטנה מבת י"א שנים ויום אחד עד י"ב שנים ויום אחד פחות מכאן ויתר על כן משמשת כדרכה והולכת דברי רבי מאיר וחכמים אומרים אחת זו ואחת זו משמשת כדרכה והולכת ומן השמים ירחמו משום שנאמר שומר פתאים ה'

Before we proceed to interpret this Baraita, we must ascertain the correct meaning of the phrase משמשות במוך as there are different interpretations given to it. According to Rashi, (*Yebamot*, 12b) it means putting cotton or another absorbent into the vagina before the cohabitation, so that the semen discharged during cohabitation will fall upon the cotton and be absorbed by it and conception will not take place. According to R. Jacob Tam (Tossafot, ibidem s. v. שלש נשים) however, it means using cotton or the absorbent after the act of cohabitation in order to remove the semen and thus prevent conception. Whether the latter is according to modern medical science an effective contraceptive or not is not our concern; the rabbis believed it to be such.

It is evident that according to R. Tam the use of a douche or any other means of removing or destroying the sperm would be the same as משמשות במוך. Likewise, according to Rashi the use of other contraceptives, on the part of the woman, would be the same as משמשות במוך. Possibly, R. Tam would permit the use of chemical contraceptives even if employed before cohabitation. For his objection to the cotton put in before cohabitation is that then the semen is discharged upon the cotton, it does not touch the mucous membrane of the vagina. This he considers "no real sexual intercourse, but like scattering the semen upon wood and stone."

דאין דרך תשמיש בכך והרי הוא כמטיל זרע על העצים ועל האבנים כשמטיל על המוך

a practice which, according to the Midrash (Genesis R. XXVI, 6) was indulged in by the "generation of the flood" דור המבול. This objection, then, would not hold good when chemical contraceptives are used.

Again, according to Rashi (*Yebamot*, 100b) the phrase משמשות במוך means מותרות ליתן מוך באותו מקום שלא יתעברו, that is, that in these three conditions women are allowed to use this contraceptive; this would imply that other women who do not expose themselves or their children to danger by another pregnancy are forbidden to do so. According to R. Tam (Tossafot, *Ketubot*, 39a s. v. שלש נשים). Asheri and R. Nissim (on *Nedarim*, 35b) the phrase משמשות במוך means צריכות or as R. Nissim puts it חייבות לשמש במוך משום סכנה וכו', that is, that these three women because of the danger of possible harm which might result from pregnancy are obliged to use this precaution. If we interpret the phrase in this sense, it would imply that other women, not threatened by any danger from pregnancy are merely not obliged to use this precaution against conception but are not forbidden to do so. It would also follow from this interpretation that if the other teachers differ from R. Meier, they differ only in so far as they do not consider it obligatory upon these three women (or to be

more correct, upon the קטנה) to take this precaution, but as to
permitting these three women or any other woman to use a contraceptive, there is no difference of opinion between R. Meier and the
other teachers. R. Solomon Lurya (1510-1573) in his ים של שלמה
to Yebamot ch. I, No. 8 (Altona, 1739) p. 4 bc, has indeed so
interpreted our Baraita. He points out that from the Talmud,
Niddah, 3a, it is evident that Rashi's interpretation of משמשות במוך
as meaning "putting in the absorbent before cohabitation takes
place" is correct. As to R. Tam's objection, Lurya correctly states
that such a practice is not to be compared to מטיל על עצים. For after
all, it is a normal manner of having sexual intercourse, and the two
bodies derive pleasure from one another and experience gratification
of their desire. It is, therefore, not different from any other normal
sexual intercourse with a woman who is incapable of having children
ואין זה כמטיל על עצים דסוף סוף דרך תשמיש בכך וגוף נהנה מן הגוף ודמי
למשמש הקטנה.
Lurya further points out that since from *Nidda*, 3a, it is also evident
that all women are permitted to use this contraceptive, the meaning of the phrase משמשות במוך in our Baraita must therefore
be that these three women *must* use this precaution—which implies
that all other women may use it. From this, argues Lurya, we
must conclude that even if we should decide that the law הלכה
follows the חכמים who differ from R. Meier, it would only
mean that we would not make it obligatory for these three women to
use this precaution. But these three women like all other women are
permitted to use it if they so desire. This is in essence the opinion
of Lurya.

It seems to me that a correct analysis of the Baraita will show that
Lurya did not go far enough in his conclusions, and that there is no
difference of opinion between R. Meier and the other teachers on the
question whether a pregnant or a nursing woman must take this precaution. For this is what the Baraita says: "There are three women
who, when having intercourse with their husbands, must take the
precaution of using an absorbent to prevent conception, a minor, a
pregnant woman and a woman nursing her baby. In the case of the
minor, lest she become pregnant and die when giving birth to the
child (it was believed by some of the Rabbis that if a girl became

pregnant before having reached the age of puberty, she and her child would both die at the moment of childbirth. (comp. Saying of Rabbah b. Livai, *Yebamot*, 12b and Tossafot ad loc. s. v. שמא תתעבר also saying in P. Pesahim, VIII, 1 (35c)

עיברה וילדה עד שלא הביאה שתי שערות היא ובנה מתים.

In case of a pregnant woman, this precaution is necessary, lest, if another conception takes place the embryo becomes a foetus papyraceus (com. Julius Preuss, Biblisch-Talmudische Medizin, Berlin 1921 p. 486-7).

In the case of a nursing mother, this precaution is necessary, for if she should become pregnant, she will have to wean her child before the proper time (which was considered to extend for twenty-four months) and the child may die as a result of such an early weaning. So far the Baraita apparently represents a unanimous statement. It then proceeds to discuss the age up to which a woman is considered a minor in this respect. R. Meier says that the minor in this case is a girl between the age of eleven years and one day and twelve years and one day, and that during that period only must she take this precaution. Before or after this age she need not take any precaution, but may have natural intercourse משמשת כדרכה והולכת The other teachers, however, say that even during the period when she is a קטנה i. e., between the age of eleven and twelve she may have natural intercourse and is not obliged to take any precaution. For the heavenly powers will have mercy and protect her from all danger as it is said, "The Lord preserveth the simple" (Ps. 116, 6). The other teachers evidently did not consider the danger of a minor dying as a result of child-birth so probable. They must have believed that a girl even before the age of puberty could give birth to a living child and survive (comp. Preuss, *op. cit.*, p. 441). But as regards the nursing or the pregnant woman, even the other teachers do not say that she may dispense with this precaution, for we notice that they do not say כולן משמשות כדרכן והולכות.

The rules of law laid down in this Baraita according to our interpretation are, therefore, the following: When there is a danger of harm resulting to the unborn child or the child already born, all teachers agree that it is obligatory to take the precaution of using a contraceptive. According to R. Meier, however, this obligation holds good also in the case when conception might result in danger or harm to the mother. But even if we should understand the Baraita to indicate that the other teachers differed with R. Meier in all three cases, it would still only follow, as Lurya correctly points out, that in all three cases we decide the הלכה according to the חכמים and do not make it obligatory upon these three women to take the precaution of using contraceptives; the rule indicated by the Baraita would still teach us that, according to the opinion of all the teachers, it is not forbidden to use a contraceptive in cases where conception would bring harm either to the mother or the child born or unborn. And I cannot see any difference between the protection of a minor from a conception which might prove fatal to her and the protection of a grown up woman whose health is, according to the opinion of physicians, such that a pregnancy might be fatal to her. Neither can I see any difference between protecting a child from the danger of being deprived of the nourishment of its mother's milk, and protecting the already born children of the family from the harm which might come to them due to the competition of a larger number of sisters and brothers. For the care and the comfort which the parents can give to their children already born, will certainly be less if there be added to the family other children claiming attention, care and comfort.

The Talmudic law also permits a woman even to permanently sterilize herself האשה רשאי לשתות כוס של עיקרין (Tosefta, *Yebamot*, VIII, 4). And the wife of the famous R. Hiyya is reported to have taken such a medicine כסא דעקרתא which made her sterile. Yebamot 65b. Whether there be such a drug according to modern medicine or not, is not our concern. The Rabbis believed that there was such a drug which, if taken internally makes a person sterile (see *Sabbath*, 110ab and Preuss, *op. cit.* p. 439-440 and p. 479-80, and they permitted the woman to take it and become sterile. According to Lurya (*op. cit., Yebamot*, IV, 44) this permission is given to a woman who experiences great pain at child-birth, which she wishes to escape, as was the case of the wife of R. Hiyya. Even more so, says Lurya, is this permitted to a woman whose children are morally corrupt and of bad character, and who fears to bring into the world other moral delinquents

אלא למי שיש לה צער לידה כעין דביתהו דרבי חייא וכל שכן אם בניה אין הולכין
בדרך ישרה ומתייראה שלא תרבה בגידולין כאלו שהרשות בידה

To these I would also add the woman who, because of a hereditary
disease with which she or her husband is afflicted, fears to have children who might be born with these diseases and suffer and be a burden
to their family or to society.

From the passage in the Talmud (*Yebamot*, 65b) we learn, however, that there is an objection which the Jewish law might have to
a man's using contraceptive means, or having intercourse with his
wife in such a manner as to make conception impossible. This objection is based, not on the view that such an act is in itself immoral
or against the law, but merely on consideration for another religious
duty which could not be fulfilled if such a practice would be indulged
in all the time. The wife of R. Hiyya, so the Talmud tells us, inca-
pacitated herself only after she had learned that the duty of propagation of the race was not incumbent upon her, since, according to the
decision of the Rabbis, women were not included in the commandment, "Be fruitful and multiply" (Genesis I, 28), which was given
to men only. Since a man must fulfill the duty of propagation of
the race מצות פו"ר he cannot be allowed the practice of having intercourse with his wife only in such a manner as to make conception impossible. For in doing so he fails to fulfill the law commanding him to have children. It is accordingly a sin of omission
but not of commission; for the practice as such is not immoral or
against the law.

But—and this is peculiar to the Jewish point of view on this question—the man who practices absolute self-restraint or total abstinence
is also guilty of the same sin of omission, for he likewise fails to fulfill the duty of propagation of the race. No distinction can be made,
according to Jewish law, between the two ways of avoiding the duty
of begetting children, whether by total abstention from sexual intercourse or by being careful not to have intercourse in such a manner
as would result in conception. For, as has already been pointed out,
the act of having intercourse with one's wife in a manner not effecting
conception is in itself not forbidden by Jewish law. If, however, a
man has fulfilled the duty of propagation of the race, as when he
already has two children (i. e. two boys according to the school of
Shammai or a boy and a girl according to the school of Hillel) and is

no longer obliged by law to beget more children (*Yebamot*, 61b and Shulḥan Aruk, *Eben ha-Ezer*, I, 5) there can be no objection at all to the practice of birth control. For while the Rabbis of old, considering children a great blessing, would advise a man to continue to beget children even after he has already fulfilled the duty of propagation of the race, yet they grant that any man has a right to avoid having more children, when for one reason or another he does not consider it a blessing to have too many children and deems it advisable in his particular case not to have more than the two, that the law commands him to have.

But even in the case of one who has not yet fulfilled the duty of propagation of the race מצות פריה ורביה it might, under certain conditions, be permitted to practice birth control, if it is done not for selfish purposes but for the sake of some higher ideal or worthy moral purpose. For the rabbinic law permits a man to delay his marrying and having children, or even to remain all his life unmarried, like Ben Azzai, if he is engaged in study and fears that having a family to take care of would interfere with his work and hinder in the pursuit of his studies (*Kiddushin*, 29b, Maimonides, *Yad Ishut*, XV, 2-3; Shulḥan Aruk, *Eben ha-Ezer*, I, 3-4).

Since, as we have seen, the act of having intercourse with one's wife in a manner not resulting in conception is in itself not against the law, there can be no difference between the failure to fulfill the commandment of propagation of the race by abstaining altogether from marriage and the failure to fulfill this commandment by practicing birth control. The considerations that permit the one permit also the other. It would even seem that the other, i. e. the practice of birth control should be preferred to the one of total abstention. For, in granting permission to practice the latter, the Rabbis make the proviso that the man be so constituted, or so deeply engrossed in his work, as not to be troubled by his sexual desires, or be strong enough to withstand temptation (והוא שלא יהא יצרו מתגבר עליו) (Maimonides and Shulḥan Aruk l. c.) Now, if a man is so constituted that he is troubled by his desires and suffers from the lack of gratification of them and yet is engaged in some noble and moral pursuit like the study of the Torah, which pursuit hinders him from taking on the responsibilities of a family, he may marry and avoid having children. He may say with Ben Azzai, "I am very much attached to my work and cannot afford to have a family to take care of. The propagation of the race can and will be carried on by others." איפשר לעולם שיתקיים על ידי אחרים) *Yebamot*, 36b, Tosefta, *ibidem*, VIII, end). For the Rabbis also teach that "it is better to marry" even if not for the sake of having children, "than to burn" with passion and ungratified desires. And, as we have seen above, the rabbinic law permits marriage even when it must needs result in failure to fulfill the commandment "be fruitful and multiply", as when a young man marries an old or sterile woman. The rabbis did not teach total abstention. They did not agree with Paul that "it is good for a man not to touch a woman" (I Corinth. VIII, 1). While the institution of marriage may have for its main purpose the propagation of the race, this is not its sole and exclusive purpose. And the Rabbis urge and recommend marriage as such without regard to this purpose, or even under conditions when this purpose cannot be achieved. The companionship or mutual helpfulness in leading a pure, good and useful life, achieved by a true marriage is also a noble purpose worthy of this divine institution. In fact, according to the biblical account, this was the first consideration in the Divine mind when creating woman for man. He said: "It is not good that the man should be alone, I will make him a help meet for him" (Genesis II, 18). He did not say I will make him a wife that he have children by her. The commandment to have children God gave to Adam later on. When husband and wife live together and help each other to lead a good life, whether they have children or not, God is with them and their home is a place for the שכינה the Divine presence, says R. Akiba (Sotah 17a). Ben Azzai did not say like Paul: "I would that all men were even as I myself" (I Corinth. VII, 7). He did not set up celibacy in itself as an ideal, nor would he recommend it to others (comp. H. Graetz, *Gnosticismus und Judenthum*, Krotoshin, 1846, p. 73 ff). Ben Azzai considered marriage a Divine institution and recognized the obligation of propagating the race as a religious duty. But he believed that he was exempted from this duty in consideration of the fact that it might interfere with another religious duty like the study of the Torah in which he was engaged. Of course, the same right would, according to Ben Azzai, be given to others in a similar position, i. e., pursuing studies or engaged in any other moral religious activities which might be interfered with by the taking on of the obligation of having children. We have seen that the medieval rabbinic authorities have concurred in the opinion of Ben Azzai and allowed a man engaged in a religious pursuit like the study of the Torah to delay or even altogether neglect fulfilling the commandment of "Be fruitful and multiply." And we have also found that no distinction can be made between neglecting this duty by abstaining from marriage or neglecting it by practicing birth control.

The above represents the logical conclusion which one must draw from a correct understanding and a sound interpretation of the halakic statements in the Talmud touching this question, disregarding the ideas expressed in the agadic literature as to the advisability of having many children.

The later Jewish mystics emphasized these agadic sayings, as well as the agadic condemnations of the evil practices of הוצאת שכבת זרע לבטלה. They came to regard any discharge of semen which might have resulted in conception but did not, almost like הוצאת שכבת זרע לבטלה. Nay, even an unconscious seminal emission is regarded a sin against which one must take all possible precautions and for which one must repent and make atonement. But even the mystics permit intercourse with one's wife even when she is incapable of having children, see Zohar Emor 90b

ואי תימא דאפיק ליה באתו דלא מתעברא הכי נמי? לא. אלא כדאמרן.

Some rabbinic authorities of the 18th and 19th centuries, under the spell of the agadic sayings of the Talmud and more or less influenced by the mystic literature, are loath to permit birth control. But even these authorities do not altogether prohibit the practice when there is a valid reason for exercising it. The reasons given by some of them for opposing the practice are not justified in the light of the Halakic statements of the Talmud which we discussed above. Their arguments are not based upon correct interpretations of the talmudic passages bearing upon this question, and they utterly ignore or overlook the correct interpretations and the sound reasoning of R. Solomon Lurya quoted above. In the following I will present the opinions of some of the authorities of the 18th and 19th centuries on this question.

R. Salom Zalman of Posen, Rabbi in Warsaw (died 1839) in his

responsa חמדת שלמה (quoted in Piṯḥe Teshubah to Eben ha-Ezer
XXIII, 2) in answer to a question about a woman to whom,
according to the opinion of physicians, pregnancy might be dangerous, declares that she may use a contraceptive. He permits
even the putting into the vagina an absorbent before cohabitation,
declaring that since the intercourse takes place in the normal way,
the discharge of the semen in such a case cannot be considered
השחתת זרע.

R. Joseph Modiano, a Turkish Rabbi of the second half of the
18th century in his Responsa collection ראש משביר part II (Sa-
lonica 1840) No. 49, discusses the case of a woman who during
her pregnancy becomes extremely nervous and almost insane. He
quotes the great rabbinical authority R. Michael who declared that
the woman *should* use a contraceptive. R. Michael argued that since
the woman is exposed to the danger by pregnancy she is in a class
with the three women mentioned in the Baraita of R. Bibi and should
therefore, like them, use an absorbent, even putting it in before cohabitation שישמש בעלה במוך כדי שלא תתעבר and her husband cannot
object to it. Modiano himself does not concur in the opinion
of R. Michael; he argues that the use of the absorbent could only
be permitted if employed after cohabitation, and the husband who
may find the use of this contraceptive inconvenient or may doubt its
effectiveness should therefore be permitted to marry another woman.
But even Modiano would not forbid the use of this contraceptive if
the husband had no objection.

R. Akiba Eger in his Responsa, No. 71 and 72 (Warsaw 1834)
p. 51b-53a also permits the use of an absorbent but only if it is employed after cohabitation. The questioner, R. Eleażar Zilz, a rabbinical authority of Posen, however, argued that it should be permitted even when employed before cohabitation.

R. Moses Sofer in his Hatam Sofer, part Yore Deah No. 172
(Pressburg 1860) p. 67d-68a, likewise permits it only when used
after cohabitation. R. Abraham Danzig in his Hokmat Adam and
Binat Adam, שער בית הנשים No. 36 (Warsaw 1914) p. 156 permits
the use of an absorbent or a douche or any other method of
removing or destroying the semen after cohabitation. He adds,
however, that according to Rashi's interpretation, it would be

permitted to the woman in question to whom pregnancy was dangerous, to use this contraceptive even before cohabitation.

R. Jacob Etlinger (1798-1871) in his Responsa *Binyan Zion* (No. 137) (Altona 1868) p. 57b-58b and R. Joseph Saul Nathanson (1808-1875) in his Responsa שואל ומשיב מהדורא תנינא part IV (Lemberg 1874) No. 13 are inclined to forbid the use of any contraceptive even when used after cohabitation.

The authorities objecting to the use of an absorbent before cohabitation do so, of course, on the ground that, like R. Tam, they consider such a practice כמטיל על העצים ועל האבנים. On the same ground they would no doubt object to the use of a condum. But as already pointed out above, they could have no objection to the use of chemical contraceptives on the part of the woman.

In summing up the results of our discussion, I would say that while there may be some differences of opinion about one detail or another or about the exact meaning of one talmudic passage or another, we can formulate the following principles in regard to the question of birth control as based upon a correct understanding of the halakic teachings of the Talmud as accepted by the medieval rabbinic authorities, and especially upon the sound interpretation given by R. Solomon Lurya to some of these talmudic passages:

1). The Talmudic-Rabbinic law does not consider the use of contraceptives as such immoral or against the law. It does not forbid birth control but it forbids birth suppression.

2). The Talmudic-Rabbinic law requires that every Jew have at least two children in fulfillment of the biblical command to propagate the race which is incumbent upon every man.

3). There are, however, conditions under which a man may be exempt from this prime duty: (a) when a man is engaged in religious work like the study of the Torah, and fears that he may be hindered in his work by taking on the responsibilities of a family. (b) when a man because of love or other considerations marries a woman who is incapable of having children, as an old or sterile woman. (c) when a man is married to a woman whose health is in such a condition as to make it dangerous for her to bear children. For, considerations for the saving of human life פקוח נפש or even ספק פקוח נפש set aside the obligation to fulfill a religious duty. In this case, then, the woman is allowed to use any contraceptives or even to permanently sterilize herself in order to escape the dangers that would threaten her at childbirth.

4). In case a man has fulfilled the duty of propagation of the race, as when he has already two children, he is no longer obliged to beget children and the law does not forbid him to have intercourse with his wife even in a manner which would not result in conception. In such a case the woman certainly is allowed to use any kind of contraceptive or preventive.

Of course, in any case, the use of contraceptives or of any device to prevent conception is allowed only when both parties, i. e., husband and wife consent.

Some rabbinic authorities of the 18th and 19th centuries would object to one or another of the above rules, and especially put restrictions upon the use of contraceptives. But we need not expect absolute agreement on questions of rabbinic law. We must be content to have good and reliable authority for our decisions, even though other authorities may differ. We have the right to judge for ourselves which view is the sounder and which authorities are more correct. We have found that the arguments of those authorities of the 18th and 19th centuries who would oppose or restrict the use of contraceptives in cases where we would recommend it, are not convincing. With all our respect for these authorities we may ignore their opinions just as they in turn have ignored the opinions of other authorities, especially those of R. Solomon Lurya, on our question.

SHOULD ONE COVER THE HEAD WHEN PARTICIPATING IN DIVINE WORSHIP?

QUESTION:

Where can one find the rabbinic law prescribing that men should cover their head when participating in Divine worship or when entering a Synagog? If there is no law to this effect will you please tell me where and when did the custom of covering one's head now generally observed in Orthodox Synagogs originate among the Jews?

ANSWER:

There is no law in Bible or Talmud prescribing the covering of the head for men when entering a sanctuary, when participating in the religious service or when performing any religious ceremony. The saying in the Mishnah (Berakot IX, 5): *"Lo yakel adam et rosho keneged shaar ha-mizrah"* does not mean: "one should not bare his head in sight of the Holy of Holies," as understood by some scholars (comp. K. Kohler, The Origin and Function of Ceremonies in Judaism, in Yearbook of C. C. A. R. 1907, p. 7). For, one must distinguish between *Giluj ha-rosh,* which means "bareheadedness" and *Kaluth rosh,* which means "lightheadedness." The latter is considered a sin. The former is no sin at all and no prohibition against it can be found in either Mishnah or Talmud. It is true that among the garments prescribed for the priests (Exod. XXVIII, 4 and 40) a headgear is mentioned. This headgear was to be worn by the priests only when officiating at the altar or performing any other priestly function in the sanctuary. (This may have been intended to distinguish the priests in the Temple at Jerusalem from the priests of some heathen deity, who sit on seats in their temples ... and "nothing upon their heads." Epistle of Jeremy 31. Comp. note in Charles' *The Apocrypha and Pseudepigrapha,* I, p. 604, though some heathen priests, like the Roman, were also in the habit of sacrificing with covered head.) But it cannot be justifiably concluded from this that any person per-

Reprinted from *Central Conference of American Rabbis Year Book,* Vol. XXXVIII, 1928.

forming any religious ceremony must cover his head. The priests of old performed all their functions at the altar and in the Temple bare-footed. Yet the conclusion was never drawn from this fact that one must be barefooted while performing any religious ceremony. And, certainly, the custom of covering one's head when entering a synagog has no precedent in the practice of the priests in the Temple at Jerusalem. For, the priests were not forbidden to enter the Temple bareheaded (see Jacob Reischer in his Responsa "Shebut Jacob" III, No. 5 (Metz, 1789, 2b). Indeed, from B. Yoma 25a, it is evident that when not performing any priestly function, the priests in the Temple would go without a hat. I do not know on what ground I. Scheftelowitz makes the statement that the priests, while allowed to enter the Temple barebeaded, were not permitted to come within four yards of the altar with uncovered head (*Alt-Palästinensischer Bauernglaube*, (Hannover, 1925) p. 154). The Midrash Genesis, R. XVII and Numbers R. V, to which Scheftelowitz referred, does not contain any saying that would justify such a statement. (Comp. my review of Scheftelowitz's work in the Hebrew Union College Monthly, December, 1925, pp. 15-17.)

The practice of covering the head when entering a synagog, and when reciting prayers or performing any other religious ceremony, is not based upon any talmudic law and cannot be supported by any express statement in the Talmud. Many express statements and implied teachings of the Talmud rather point to the contrary. This practice is merely a custom, *Minhag*, that first appeared among the Jews in Babylon. In the course of time it spread to other countries and gradually became a generally observed custom among Orthodox Jews. Its origin probably goes back to a non-Jewish source. It furnishes another instance of how sometimes the Jews in one country, subject to the influence of their environment, would borrow a ceremony or custom from their non-Jewish neighbors and pass it on to Jews of other countries, and how in the course of time such a borrowed non-Jewish custom is interpreted by Jewish teachers as having some religious significance and regarded as a genuinely Jewish custom. In the following I present a brief account of the origin and the development of this supposedly Jewish custom of covering the head during religious devotion or when in a holy place.

Now, as regards its origin, no such custom can be found in ancient Israel. The Jews in Palestine, in so far as biblical and talmudical records show, would ordinarily not wear any headgear. The covering of the head was an expression of grief or a sign of mourning, as is evident from II Samuel, XV, 2. When a person was in mourning he would cover his head (B. M. K. 15a and 24a) but not while the people came to comfort him and recite the comforting prayers and benedictions (comp. saying from Ebel Rabbati as cited by R. Nissim to Alfasi and quoted by N. Brüll in his Jahrbücher I, p. 54). Sometimes a person would cover his head as a protection from cold or excessive heat (see Midrash, Lev. R. XIX, 4). But this was done with a shawl or some other protective covering, but not by wearing a headgear in our sense of the word. The shawl, occasionally used to cover one's head because of being a mourner or for the sake of protection from heat or cold, the *Sudar ha-Rosh,* was not considered a regular garment or as part of a man's outfit, and hence was not subject to the law of *Zizit* prescribed for garments only (saying from Sifre cited by R. Estori ha Parchi in his *Kaphtor wa-Pherach,* ch. 60 (ed. A. M. Luncz, Jerusalem, 1897) p. 781, though not found in our editions of the Sifre). This also points to the fact that Jewish men, ordinarily, would not wear a hat nor otherwise cover their head. One of the innovations forced upon the Jews by Antiochus Epiphanes, to which the pious Jews objected very much, considering it against Jewish law or practice, was that the young men were made to "wear a hat" (II Macc. IV, 12, according to the authorized version, though Charles has "wear the *petasus*", that is, a broad-brimmed felt hat, which being the mark of Hermes, may have been especially objectionable. Compare, however, A. T. Olmstead, *Wearing the Hat,* in the American Journal of Theology, January, 1920, p. 94ff.) From the saying of Rabbi Meier that every day, "when at sunrise the kings of the earth put on their crowns upon their heads and bow down to the sun, God gets angry" (Berakot 7a, Abodah Zorah 4b) it also appears that it was the non-Jewish custom of covering one's head when worshipping.

The Mishnah Nedarim III, 8, takes it for granted that men go bareheaded and only women and children cover their head. (The remark in the Gemara b. Nedarim 30b וקטנים לעולם מולו cannot be harmonized with the plain meaning of the Mishnah, unless

it refers only to infants or reflects a different Babylonian custom.)
According to a story found in Tractate Kallah it was, therefore, considered impudence on the part of young boys to walk on the street,
and especially to pass older people, without covering their head.
The conclusion drawn from this story in Kallah Rabbati II,
ש״מ נילוי הראש עזות חקיפא היא   is to be understood that it is
marked impudence on the part of a young boy to go bareheaded and
not, as R. Isaac Aboab (Menorat ha-Maor ch. 337 (Warsaw 1890) p.
325) seems to have understood it, that even on the part of adults it
would be impudent to walk with uncovered head. For, according to
the Mishnah, it was the usual thing for grown up men to go bareheaded.

And when Paul said: "Every man, praying or prophesying, having
his head covered, dishonoreth his head ... For a man, indeed ought
not to have his head veiled forasmuch as he is the image and glory
of God" (I Corinthians XI, 4-7), he merely stated the Palestinian
Jewish practice of his time and did not express any new or un-Jewish
doctrine. It is a mistake—and one that involves a reasoning in a circle—to interpret this passage in the Epistle as aiming to sever the
Christian worshipers from the synagog by distinguishing their appearance at worship from that of the Jewish worshipers, and then to
assume that it was Paul's insistence upon his followers worshipping
without a hat that, in turn, caused the Jews to attach great importance
to the covering of the head during religious service (W. Rosenau,
Jewish Ceremonial Institutions and Customs (Baltimore, 1912) p.
49; also M. Gaster as reported in the Jewish Chronicle of London,
March 17, 1893, p. 17). In the first place Gaster's alleged statement
that the founder of Christianity "in one of his Epistles" said: "My
followers, pray bareheaded to distinguish you from the Jews" is without any justification. No such saying of Jesus is found in the New
Testament or among the Agrapha of the New Testament. (Comp. The
Jewish Chronicle, London, April 17, 1893, question by "A Sub-
scriber" to which, as far as I could see, no answer was given by
Gaster.) And if Gaster had in mind the saying of Paul in I Corinthians he gave it the wrong interpretation. Paul could not have meant
by his saying to put himself and his followers in opposition to Jewish
custom or traditional practice, since what he recommends actually

was the Jewish practice of his days. (Against Jonathan Altar in his *Antwort auf das Sendschreiben eines Afrikanischen Rabbi,* Prag, 1826, 30ab).

Secondly, had the later Jewish custom of covering the head during religious worship been the result of the Jewish reaction to the Christian practice intended as a protest against Paulinian doctrine, it is but reasonable to expect that traces of it would be found in Palestinian Jewish sources. For, during the talmudic period, it was in Palestine, more than in any other country, that the Jews came into close contact with the Christians and there, if anywhere, surely the teachers would have good reason to introduce such customs as were calculated to prevent Jews from following Christian practice. But, as a matter of fact, we do not find in Palestinian Jewish sources of talmudic times, the least indication of any decree or enactment by the rabbis requiring the covering of the head during religious service or while in a synagog. On the contrary, we find many indications and a few express statements to the effect, that in Palestine men would usually go bareheaded and remain bareheaded even when entering the synagog and reading from the Torah or reciting their prayers. Thus, R. Joshua b. Hananiah, a younger contemporary of Paul, states that the reason why a man, as a rule, goes bareheaded and a woman covers her head is because the woman is ashamed of her sin in having listened to the serpent (Gen. R. XVII, 13; also Abot d. R. Nathan, Version B, ch. 14, Schechter, p. 13; comp. V. Aptowitzer, *Monastchrift fuer Geschichte und Wissenchaft des Judentums,* 1913, p. 148ff.) The implication is that man need not be ashamed of having listened to his wife. Evidently R. Joshua b. Hananiah does not know of any custom of men covering their heads during religious service. From the Palestinian Talmud, Berakot II, 3 (4c) it appears that R. Johanan would cover his head during the winter as a protection against the cold, but would go bareheaded during the summer. Compare the commentaries and especially the discussion of this passage by R. Menahem de Lunsano (in the Wilna edition of the Jerushalmi, Wilna 1922, 14a-15a).

From another story in the Palestinian Talmud (M. K. III, (82c), also Gen. R. 100, 7) it is also evident that in Palestine it was the usual thing to go bareheaded. For, we are told that the two sons of Rabbi (Jehudah ha-Nasi) differed in their observing the mourning for their father. On the Sabbath day during the mourning period, one of them would cover his head, like on week days. The other, however, would not observe this custom of mourning on the Sabbath day, and hence on the Sabbath during the mourning period, he would go out bareheaded. He believed that no mourning rites should be observed on the day of the Sabbath (comp. B. M. K. 24a). This clearly tells us, that for people who are not in mourning or on a day when no mourning was to be observed, it was customary to go bareheaded. This passage in the P. Talmud has been misunderstood by I. Scheftelowitz (op. cit., 1. c.) and by A. Marmorstein in *Haolam* December 24, 1926, No. 53, pp. 1010-1011, and in *Monatschrift fuer Geschichte und Wissenschaft des Judentums*, 1926, p. 211. They understood it to mean that even on the week days of the mourning period one of the sons of Rabbi would disregard the custom for mourners, and go around bareheaded. Scheftelowitz, therefore, draws the conclusion that "in some places in Palestine it was customary for *every mourner* to go bareheaded." But the two sons of Rabbi lived in the same place! And Marmorstein concludes, that "the one son of Rabbi, for reasons of his own, refused to observe the mourning rites for his father" (*Haolam*, 1. c., p 1011), or "that in the time of Judah ha-Nasi it was not yet the general custom for mourners to cover their heads" (*Monatschrift*, 1. c.) From a correct understanding of the passage, however, neither one of these conclusions can be justified.

In Lev. R. XXVII, 6 (also Pesikta d. R. K. IX (Buber, 77a) and Tanhuma Emor 10 (Buber 13), p. 47a) it is implied that the Jew need not trouble himself to remove his hat, if he has one on, or to stand up, if he happens to be sitting, when he is about to recite the Shema, but may do it even while sitting and even with his head covered. From this it is evident that not only could there be no objection to reciting the Shema bareheaded but that it would ordinarily be more reverential to do so. (See R. Solomon Lurya in his Responsa No. 72, and comp. Gronemann in Rahmer's *Literaturblatt*, 1880, No. 42; also M. Duschak, *ibid.*, No. 44, p. 176; M. Auerbach, *ibid.*, p. 192, and Simon Wolfsohn, *ibid.*, 1881, p. 36). The Targum to the Prophets, a work Palestinian in origin if not in form (comp. W. Bacher, *Jewish Encyclopedia* XII, p. 61) interpreting Judges V, 9 as speaking in praise of the scholars and teachers in Israel who in times of trouble and persecution did not cease to study the Torah, expressly says, that "it is fitting that these scholars and teachers sit in the synagogs with uncovered heads, teaching the people the words of the Torah and reciting praises and prayers of thanksgiving to God."

וכדו יאי להון דיתבין בבתי כנישתא בריש גלי ומאלפין ית עמא פתגמי אורייתא ומברכין ומודין קדם יי.

And in another Palestinian work, the tractate Soferim XIV, 15 (ed. Joel Müller (Leipzig 1878) p. XXVI) it is expressly stated that one with uncovered head may act as the reader, leading the congregation in the recital of the Shema מי שראשו מגולה פורס על שמע (comp. Müller's remark on p. 198-199 and I. Elbogen, *Der Jüdische Gottesdienst,* pp. 497 and 515). It is true that the tractate Soferim in the same passage also mentions another opinion that would not allow one who is bareheaded to utter the name of God in prayer. But, as will be shown presently, this latter opinion reflects the Babylonian custom. For, in Palestine throughout the entire talmudic period and even later, people would not hesitate entering a synagog, reading from the Torah, and participating in the religious service with uncovered head.

It was different in Babylon, though even in Babylonian Jewish sources of talmudic times, one could not find any express regulation for covering the head during religious service. Nay, from the Babylonian Talmud it might even be proved that one is allowed to recite prayers with uncovered head. For, in B. Berakot 60b, the Talmud prescribes certain benedictions to be recited every morning before one covers his head. (Comp. also Sh. Ar. O. H. 46, 1 and especially R. Elijah Gaon of Wilna in his commntary ביאורי הגרייא to Sh. Ar O. H. 8, 6). But there did develop in Babylon during talmudic times, especially among very pious people, the custom of covering the head when reciting prayers or performing any religious ceremony, as well as the practice of avoiding going bareheaded. Thus R. Huna the son of R. Joshua, a Babylonian Amora of the fifth generation, second half of the fourth century, (not Rab Huna, the disciple and successor of Abba Areka, as the head of the academy at Sura, who died about 297 C. E., see below), prides himself on the fact that he never walks four yards with uncovered head (Sabbath 118b, also Kiddushin 31a). This, however, could not have been the general practice for all scholars and for those who read the prayers, as Scheftelowitz (op. cit., l. c.)

assumes. For in that case Huna could not have prided himself on observing this practice. Scheftelowitz's other statement (*ibid.*, l. c.) that from the second century on, it became the general "custom of always keeping the head covered," is likewise without any justification in the sources. The covering of the head was especially considered a sign of respect which one must show to his elders or to scholars. Thus we are told (b. Kiddushin 33a) that R. Jeremiah of Difte considered it impudent on the part of a man passing him without showing him the respect of covering the head. It is evident from the context there that R. Jeremiah did not mind the man's going without a hat, for even in Babylon it was not a generally observed custom for men to cover their heads (see Rabbinnovicz in Rahmer's *Literaturblatt* XXII, 1893, No. 15, p. 58). But R. Jeremiah expected the man to show him the respect due to a scholar by not passing him without covering the head. Rabina, who happened to be with R. Jeremiah, however, sought to mitigate the man's offence by suggesting that that man might have come from Mata Mehasya where the people were rather on familiar terms with the rabbis and not so punctilious in the usual manner of showing respect to scholars.

The covering of the head seems also to have been considered as tending to help one acquire the fear of God. Thus, the mother of R. Nahman b. Isaac whom the astrologer had told that her son Nahman was destined to become a thief, would never allow him to go around bareheaded, evidently fearing that such conduct on his part might tend to hasten to bring about the evil destiny predicted for him by the astrologers. She would also say to her son: "Cover your head so that the fear of heaven may be upon you," כסי רישיך כי היכי דתיהוי עלך אימתא דשמיא   B. Sabbath 156b). According to J. H. Schorr (*Heḥalutz* VII, p. 34) the practice of covering the head, and especially the idea that it is disrespectful to go without a hat, was borrowed by the Babylonian Jews from the Persians. One is also justified in surmising that there were some elements of primitive superstition connected with this practice (comp. Hastings, *Encyclopedia of Religion and Ethics*, VI, p. 539) But be this as it may, this much is certain, that among the Babylonian Jews already in talmudic times the covering of the head was considered a sign of respect. It was observed especially when in the presence of prominent men. It was also regarded as conducive to inculcate in one the fear of God. Pious people would be careful not to walk around with uncovered head. A prominent scholar's outfit included also a headgear (B. Kiddushin, 8a, case of R. Kahana), though even prominent scholars would not wear a headgear before they were married (*ibid.*, 29b, case of R. Hamnuna). According to R. Abraham ibn Yarḥi in Ha-Manhig, Tefillah 43, (Berlin 1855) p. 15, it would have been regarded presumptuous or haughty pride   דמחזי כיוהרא   on the part of an unmarried scholar to cover his head. But for the people in general, there was no fixed rule. Some of them would cover their heads and some would go bareheaded

אנשים זמנין דמיכסו רישייהו וזמנין דמגלו רישייהו

(b. Nedarim 30b). As to how they appeared in the synagog we have no record. Scheftelowitz's statement that the scholars in general and those who read the prayers would always keep their head covered (op. cit., l. c.) has no justification in the talmudic sources. Some pious people, however, would, no doubt, cover their head when praying. For, we are told in the Talmud (b. Berakot 51a) that R. Ashi (not Asi as in the printed editions, see Rabbinnovicz, *Dikduke Soferim*, ad loc.) would cover his head when reciting the benedictions after the meal. We may justly assume that he would also cover his head when reciting other benedictions and prayers.

In the very early post-talmudic times, however, we find that the Babylonian Jews considered it already forbidden to utter the name of God in prayer with uncovered head. (The opinion of the יש אומרים   "Some say" in tractate Soferim, which, as already suggested above, represent Babylonian authorities). And in the *Hilufe Minhagim* (published by Joel Müller in *Haschachar*, VII), it is stated that one of the differences in custom and ritual between the Palestinian and Babylonian Jews was that among the former the priests would recite their benedictions bareheaded while among the latter the priests were not permitted to recite their benedictions with uncovered head. בני בבל אוסרין שיברכו הכהנים לישראל וראשם פרוע. בארץ ישראל מברכין כהנין כהנים לישראל בראשם פרוע   This is the correct reading. (Comp. Müller's discussion there, No. 44). This, by the way, also implies that even in Babylon it was not absolutely forbidden to enter the synagog and participate in the religious service with uncovered head. Had this been the case, the special mention of a law prohibiting the priests from pronouncing their blessings bareheaded would have been gratuitous.

There was, accordingly, a difference in custom as regards wearing hats between Palestine and Babylon. In the former the people would not cover their heads while praying or when in the synagog and in general would go bareheaded. In the latter, however, it was the custom of pious people to cover their head. This custom, however, had not been brought to Babylon from Palestine by Abba Areka, as Marmorstein (*Haolam*, 1926, p. 1010, and *Revue des Etudes Juives*, 1928, pp. 66-69) assumes. The custom could not have been imported from Palestine where it did not exist. And we have no indication in the Talmud that Abba Areka ever observed it. The Geonim do mention among the ten practices of extreme piety עשרה מילי דחסידותא observed by Rab, the practice not to walk four yards with uncovered head. (See Responsa of the Geonim, *Shaare Teshubah* No. 178 (Leipzig 1858) p. 18, and *Sefer Ha-Orah* of Rashi ed. Buber (Lemberg 1905) p. 4). They also add that his disciple R. Huna, followed this practice. But the Talmud reports this practice only of R. Huna the son of R. Joshua who lived one century later than R. Huna the disciple of Rab, and nowhere says that Rab himself observed this custom

Marmorstein's arguments for his theory that the Palestinians would cover their head and the Babylonians would go bareheaded (*ibid.*, l. c., also Haolam, 1926, No. 8, p. 159ff) are not at all convincing. The contradiction which he finds between B. M. K. 24a and B. Berakot 60b, can be explained without recourse to his theory. (Comp. also A. S. Herschberg, *Haolam* (November 1926, No. 47) pp. 889-890.)

Like the two centers in Asia, Palestine and Babylon, the European countries in the Middle Ages, at least up to the thirteenth century, were also divided as regards the propriety of covering the head during prayer or not covering it. Spain followed Babylon, while France and Germany followed Palestine. The Spanish rabbinical authorities require the covering of the head during prayer and in general consider it praiseworthy to avoid going bareheaded. Thus, Maimonides declares that one should not recite his prayers with uncovered head (*Yad*, Tephillah, IV, 5) and he also says, that it is the proper thing for a scholar not to go bareheaded (*ibid.*, Deot, V, 6). The *Zohar* in

Vaethhanan (Lublin, 1872) p. 520, likewise says, that one must cover his head ובעי לחפיא רישיה when praying. R. Abraham ibn Yarhi in *Ha-Manhig*, Tephillah, 43, (Berlin, 1855) p. 15, states that it is a custom to pray with covered head and he recommends this custom as well as the general practice of covering the head, but he expressly characterizes them as the custom and practice of the Jews in Spain. (This plainly contradicts the statement of David ben Jehudah Hasid as quoted by A. Marmorstein in *Monatschrift fuer Geschichte und Wissenschaft des Judentums*, 1927, p. 41) R. Jeroham b. Meshullam in his Toledot Adam we-Hawaah I, Natib 16 (Kopys 1808) p. 118d requires the covering of the head when reciting benedictions. Judah Asheri in his Responsa *Zikkaron Jehudah*, No. 2 (Berlin 1846) 4a recommends the coverinng of the head when studying the Torah, but would not insist upon it in hot weather when one feels uncomfortable to have his head covered. And Joseph Karo in *Shulḥan Aruk, Orah Hayyim* 91, 3 merely mentions that some authorities forbid the uttering of the name of God in prayer with uncovered head, and also that some authorities would even prevent people from entering the synagog with uncovered head, but he himself does not decide the question. He recommends, however, as a pious practice מדת חסידות not to go around bareheaded (*ibid.*, 2, 6 according to R. Abraham Abali Gumbiner in his commentary *Magen Abraham* to 91, 3; comp. also Tur O. H. 2 and the discussion of Isserles in *Darke Moshe* and especially of R. Joel Sirkes in *Bayyit Ḥadash* ad loc.)

In France and Germany, however, following the Palestinian custom, there was no objection to praying or reading from the Torah with uncovered head. Thus R. Isaac b. Moses Or Zarua of Vienna (1200-1270) expressly reports that it was the custom of the French rabbis to pray with uncovered head, מנהג רבותינו שבצרפת שמברכין בראש מגולה (*Or Zarua*, II, 43, (Zitomir, 1862) p. 20), though he does not favor it. Likewise R. Meier of Rothenburg (1215-1293) is quoted by his disciple R. Shimsohn b. Zadok in Tashbaz 547 (Warsaw, 1875) p. 93 as having said that it was not forbidden to go around bareheaded. He is said to have explained the conduct of R. Huna the son of R. Joshua reported in *Kiddushin*, 31a and *Sabbath*, 118b as having been an exceptional case of extreme piety which the average man need not follow. Compare also Kolbo, *Tephillah*, XI (Lemberg 1860) 8a.

Beginning, however, with the thirteenth century the Babylonian-Spanish custom began to penetrate into France and Germany. We accordingly find Ashkenasic authorities of the thirteenth century and of the following centuries favoring the Spanish custom and recommending, or requiring, that one should cover his head when praying or reading from the Torah (R. Isaac of Vienna, in *Or Zarua* l. c. and R. Moses Isserles in *Darke Moshe* to *Tur Oraḥ Ḥayyim* 282, 3, arguing against the French custom, and in Shulhan Aruk, Orah Ḥayyim 282,3, forbidding one to read the Torah bareheaded, and many others) But even as late as the sixteenth century it was in German-Polish countries not generally considered as forbidden to read the Torah or to pray bareheaded.. R. Solomon Lurya, one of the greatest rabbinical authorities of his time (1510-1573) in his Responsa No. 72, referred to above, expressly says אין אני יודע איסור לברך בלא כיסוי הראש "I do not know of any prohibition against praying with uncovered head. (Comp. also Joseph Solomon Delmedigo in his מצרף לחכמה Odessa 1864, p. 76). In the seventeenth century, R. David Ha-Levi of Lemberg (1586-1667) in his commentary *Ture Zohab*, to Shulḥan Aruk, *Orah Hayyim* 8, 3 advanced the argument that praying with uncovered head be forbidden on the ground that since it is a custom generally practiced by non-Jews, it be regarded as חוקת הגוי. This argument, however, is fallacious. For, according to the definition given by R. Moses Isserles in Sh. Ar. Yore Deah 178, 1 (comp. also Tossofot to Abodah Zarah 11a s. v. ואי חוקה only such non-Jewish practices as are observed by the non-Jew because of some foolish superstition לשם שטות or because they express or symbolize some of his peculiar religious beliefs, are to be regarded as חוקת הגוי which the Jew is forbidden to imitate. But practices which the non-Jew observes for the sake of comfort and convenience or because they are expressions of politeness and good manners, not involving any particular doctrine, cannot be classed as Ḥukat ha-Goyyim and the Jew need have no scruples in practicing them as the non-Jew does. (Comp. A Chorin in Iggereth Elassaph, Prag, 1826, pp. 23-24). And, indeed, many great rabbinical authorities of the seventeenth and eighteenth centuries utterly disregard this argument on the ground of the law against חוקת הגוי and declared that there is no prohibition against praying with uncovered head,. Thus, R. Hezekiah Silva (1659-1698) in his comentary Peri Hadash to Sh. Ar. Orah Hayyim 93, 1 says: "The opinion of those who permit the utterance of the name of God in prayer with uncovered head seems to be reasonable and valid", מסתברא כמאן דמתיר להוציא אזכרה בראש מגולה

And R. Jacob Reischer (died 1733) in his Responsa Shebut Jacob III, referred to above, says: ואיסור גלוי הראש אין לו עיקר ומקור

ברור בש"ס And the famous Gaon of Wilna in his commentary ביאורי הגר"א to Sh. Ar. Orah Ḥayyim 8, 6 expressly says: "According to Jewish law it is permitted to enter a synagog and to pray without covering one's head," דמדינא אפילו להתפלל ולכנס

לבית הכנסת הכל מותר And after some discussion in which he cites many proofs for his statement, he closes with the following words: "There is no prohibition whatever against praying with uncovered head, but as a matter of propriety it would seem to be good manners to cover one's head when standing in the presence of great men and also during the religious service,"

כללא דמילתא אין איסור כלל בראש מגולה לעולם רק לפני הגדולים וכן בעת התפלה או נכון הדבר מצד המוסר.

In the nineteenth century as a reaction to the first attempts of modern Reform which suggested the removal of the hat by the worshipers in the synagog (see *Iggereth Elassaph* by A. Chorin (Prag 1826) pp. 17-24 and 29b-31b) the strict Orthodox rabbinical authorities became more emphatic in their insistence upon the requirement of covering the head when entering a synagog, and when praying or performing any religious ceremony. (Comp. Ḥayyim Ḥiskiyah Medini in his *Sde Ḥemed*, vol. II, מערכת בית הכנסת (Warsaw 1896) pp. 159-160 where most of these authorities are quoted). But none of these authorities succeeded in proving that there is in Jewish law or tradition an express prohibition against praying with uncovered head. (Recently it has been argued that the custom of covering the head during prayer is against the Halakah, see Kahan in *Revue des Etudes Juives*, vol. LXXXIV, 1927, pp. 176-178). Neither have the reasons for the custom of covering the head in the synagog and the arguments for retaining it, advanced by modern Orthodox authorities any validity. Thus, to mention but a few of them, Gaster, as reported in the Jewish Chronicle referred to above, says that one of the reasons why the Jews covered their head when praying was because the Roman slaves used to go bareheaded. The Jews did not wish to appear as slaves, hence they cŏvered their heads when praying. But according to Raba (b. Sabbath 10a) it is the proper attitude when reciting the prayers to appear like a slave. כעבדא קמיה מריה. An anonymous writer in *Orient-Literaturblatt* VII, p. 388 arguing in favor of retaining the custom of covering the head in the synagog, even though that ordinarily it is a sign of respect to remove the hat, gives two reasons for it. The first one is that we need not be so formal with God as to show him the ordinary outward signs of respect, for only man looketh on the outward appearance, but the Lord looketh on the heart: "Dem alten Gotte des Judentums sollen keine Komplimente gemacht werden, er soll überhaupt nicht auf äussere Erscheinung sehen sondern in den Herzen lesen." But according to this argument God would not mind if we came to him without a hat but with a pure heart. His second reason is, that the covering of the head while in the synagog shows that the worshipers are like one family and feel themselves at home in the synagog without any need of observing the social convention of removing the hat while there. But, by such an argument one might excuse any lack of decorum in the synagog. Compare further G. Deutsch, *Jewish Encyclopedia* II, pp. 530ff., s. v. "Bareheadedness" and "The Covering of the Head," *The Jewish Chronicle* of London, October 10, 1919, p. 15.

In summing up the discussion I would say that from the point of view of Jewish law or ritual there can be no objection to either covering or uncovering the head in the synagog or when praying and when reading the Torah. The custom of praying bareheaded or with covered head is not at all a question of law. It is merely a matter of social propriety and decorum. As such it cannot, and need not, be the same in all countries and certainly not remain the same for all times. For it depends on the ideas of the people as to what is the proper attire for worshipers in the Temples or what is the proper thing to wear or not to wear at solemn occasions and at public worship. These ideas are, of course, in turn subject to change in different times and in different places. Hence, in countries where the covering of the head is a sign of showing respect and reverence, it certainly would be improper to appear before God in the house of prayer with uncovered head. And even in countries where it is generally regarded more respectful to remove the hat, if there be congregations who still feel like their grandfathers and consider it disrespectful to pray with uncovered head, they are within their right if they retain the custom of their fathers. We can have no quarrel with them and should rather respect their custom. In visiting them in their synagogs or when participating in some religious service at their homes, we should do as they do. For their motive and their intentions are good, and they observe these practices out of a feeling of respect and a sense of propriety, misguided as they may appear on this point to the occidental and modern mind. On the other hand no one should find any fault with those people who, living in countries where it is considered to be disrespectful to keep the hat on while visiting in other people's homes or in the presence of elders and superiors, deem it proper to show their respect for the synagog by removing the hat on entering it. These people also observe their practice with the best intentions and with a respectful spirit. They are not prompted by the desire to imitate non-Jewish practice. Their motive rather is to show their respect for the synagog and to express their spirit of reverence by praying with uncovered head. And although in the last century this question of "hat on or hat off" was the subject of heated disputes between the Conservative and Liberal groups of Jewry, we should know better now, and be more tolerant and more liberal towards one another. We should realize that this matter is but a detail of custom and should not be made the issue between Orthodox and Reform. It is a detail that is not worth fighting about. It should not separate Jew from Jew and not be made the cause of breaking of Jewish groups or dividing Jewish congregations.

RESPONSUM ON QUESTION, "SHALL WOMEN BE ORDAINED RABBIS?"

The very raising of this question is due, no doubt, to the great changes in the general position of women, brought about during the last half century or so. Women have been admitted to other professions, formerly practiced by men only, and have proven themselves successful both as regards personal achievement as well as in raising the standards or furthering the interests of the professions. Hence the question suggested itself why not admit women also to the rabbinical profession?

The question resolves itself into the following two parts: first what is the attitude of traditional Judaism on this point, and second, whether Reform Judaism should follow tradition in this regard. At the outset it should be stated that from the point of view of traditional Judaism there is the following important distinction to be made between the rabbinate and the other professions in regard to the admission of women. In the case of the other professions there is nothing inherent in their teachings or principles which might limit their practice to men exclusively. In the case of the rabbinate on the other hand, there are, as will soon be shown, definite teachings and principles in traditional Judaism, of which the rabbinate is the exponent, which demand that its official representatives and functionaries be men only. To admit women to the rabbinate is, therefore, not merely a question of liberalism, it would be acting contrary to the very spirit of traditional Judaism which the rabbinate seeks to uphold and preserve.

It should be stated further, that these traditional principles debarring women from the rabbinate were not formulated in an illiberal spirit by the rabbis of old out of a lack of appreciation of

Reprinted from *Central Conference of American Rabbis Year Book,* Vol. XXXII, 1922.

women's talents and endowments.   Indeed the rabbis of old entertained a high opinion of womanhood and frequently expressed
their admiration for woman's ability and appreciated her great
usefulness in religious work.   Thus, e. g. they say: "God has
endowed woman with a finer appreciation and a better understanding than man." (Niddah 45b).   "Sarah was superior to
Abraham in prophecy" (Tanḥuma Exodus beginning) "It was
due to the pious women of that generation that the Israelites were
redeemed from Egypt" (Sotah 11b) and "The women were the
first ones to receive and accept the Torah" (Tanḥuma Buber, Me-
zora 18, p. 27a) ; and "They refused to participate in the making
of the golden calf."   These and many other sayings could be
cited from rabbinic literature in praise of women, her equality to
man and in some respects, superiority to him.   So that we may
safely conclude that their excluding of women from the rabbinate
does not at all imply deprecation on their part of woman's worth.

But with all their appreciation of woman's fine talents and noble
qualities, the rabbis of old have also recognized that man and
woman have each been assigned by the Torah certain spheres of
activity, involving special duties.   The main sphere of woman's
activity and her duties centered in the home.   Since she has her
own duties to perform and since especially in her position as wife
and mother she would often be prevented from carrying on many
of the regular activities imposed upon man, the Law frees her
from many religious obligations incumbent upon man, and especially exempts her from such positive duties the performance of
which must take place at certain fixed times, like reciting the Shma,.
or at prescribed seasons, like Succah.
(M. Kiddushin I, 7).

וכל מצות עשה שהזמן גרמה אנשים חייבין ונשים פטורות

This fact, that she was exempt from certain obligations and
religious duties, necessarily excluded her from the privilege of
acting as the religious leader or representative of the congregation,
שליח צבור She could not represent the congregation in the performing of certain religious functions, since, according to the
rabbinic principle, one who is not personally obliged to perform a
certain duty, cannot perform that duty on behalf of others and
certainly cannot represent the congregation in the performance of

such duties.   כל שאינו מחויב בדבר אינו מוציא את הרבים ידי חובתן
(R. H. III, 8, Berokot 20b).

On the same principle she was expressly disqualified from writing Torah scrolls. Since she could not perform for the congregation the duty of reading from the Torah, the text prepared by
her was also not qualified for use in connection with the performance of that duty (Gittin 45b Mas. Soferim I, 14). Women
were also considered exempt from the obligation to study the
Torah (Erubin 27a; Kiddushin 29b-30a). Some rabbis even
went so far as to object to women studying the Torah (M. Sotah
III, 4). This opinion, of course, did not prevail. Women were
taught the Bible and given a religious education and there were
some women learned in the law even in talmudic times. But to use
the phrase of the Talmud (M. K. 18a)   אשה בי מדרשא לא שכיחא
women were not to be found in the בית המדרש in the academies
and colleges where the rabbis assembled and where the students
prepared themselves to be rabbis. Evidently, for the reason that
they could not aspire to be rabbis, the law excluding them from
this religious office.

This law that women cannot be rabbis was always taken for
granted in the Talmud. It was considered to be so generally
known and unanimously agreed upon that it was not even deemed
necessary to make it a special subject of discussion. The very
idea of a woman becoming a rabbi never even entered the mind of
the rabbis of old. It is for this reason that we find only few direct
and definite statements to the effect that women cannot be rabbis.
Only occasionally when the discussion of other questions involved
the mentioning of it, reference, direct or indirect, is made to the
established law that women cannot act as judges or be rabbis.
Thus in a Baraita (pal. Talm. Shebuot. IV, i 35b and Sanhedrin
IV, 10, 21c) it is stated: הרי למדנו שהאשה אינה דנה "We have
learned that a woman cannot act as judge, i. e., cannot render decisions of law." The same principle is also indirectly expressed in
the Mishnah (comp. Niddah VI, 4 and Shebuot IV, i). In the
Talmud (Gittin 5b) it is also indirectly stated that a woman
cannot be a member of a Beth Din, i. e., a rabbi, or judge. For
there it is taken for granted that she could not be one of three who

form a tribunal or בית דין to pass upon the correctness of a bill of divorce or of any other document. (See Rashi ad. loc.)

In the Midrash Num. R. X, 5, it is also quoted as a well known and established principle that women may not have the authority to render decisions in religious or ritual matters, שהנשים אינם בנות הוראה

These talmudic principles have been accepted by all medieval Jewish authorities. Maimonides, Yad, Sanhedrin II, 7, declares that the members of every tribunal or בית דין in Israel, which means every rabbi, *Dayyan* or *More Horaah* in Israel, must possess the same qualities which characterized the men whom Moses selected to be his associates, and whom he appointed judges and leaders in Israel. These qualities, Maimonides continues, are expressly stated in the Torah, as it is said: "Get you from each one of your tribes *men,* wise and understanding and full of knowledge, and I will make them heads over you." (Deut. I, 13). Maimonides here has in mind the idea, entertained by the rabbis of all generations, that the rabbis of each generation continue the activity and are the recipients of the spirit of those first religious leaders of the Jewish people. For, as is well known, *Moshe Rabenu* and the seventy elders who formed his council were considered the prototypes and the models of the rabbis of all subsequent generations (comp. Mishnah R. H. II, 9). Likewise, R. Aaron Halevi of Barzelona (about 1300 C. E.) in his Sefer Ha Ḥinuk (Nos. 74, 75, 77, 79, 81, 83) as well as Jacob Asheri in Tur Ḥoshen Mishpat VII and Joseph Karo in Shulhan Aruk, Ḥoshen Mishpat VII, 3, all expressly state the principle that a woman cannot officiate as judge or rabbi. It hardly need be stated that when some of the sources use in this connection the term judge דיין they, of course, mean rabbi for which Dayyan is but another name. In rabbinic terminology the functions of a rabbi are spoken of as being לדין ולהורות to judge and decide religious and ritual questions. And even in our modern rabbinical diploma we use the formula יורה יורה ידין ידין giving the candidate whom we ordain the authority to judge and decide religious questions and to give authoritative rulings in all religious matters.

To be sure, the rabbis do permit the women to be religious teachers, like Miriam, who according to the rabbis, taught the

women while Moses and Aaron taught the men (Sifre Zutta
quoted in Yalkut, Shimeoni Behaaloteka 74i end) and Deborah
whom the rabbis believed to have been merely teaching the law
(Seder Elijahu R. IX-X Friedmann, p. 50, compare also Tossafot B. K. 15a s. v. אשר תשים and parallels). Some authorities would put certain restrictions upon women even in regard to
her position as teacher (see Kiddushin 82a and Maimonides, Jad.
Talmud Torah II, 4) but in general the opinion of the rabbis was
that women may be teachers of religion (see Ḥinuk 152 and comp.
Azulai in Birke Joseph to Ḥoshen Mishpat VII, 12) ; and as a
matter of fact, there have always been learned women in Israel.
These women-scholars were respected for their learning in the
same manner as learned men were respected.   (See Sefer
Ḥasidim, 978 and comp. also Sde Ḥemed I, letter Kaf No. 99)
and some of these women scholars would occasionally even give
lectures in rabbinics, but they have never been admitted to the
rabbinate since all the rabbinic authorities agree, at least implicitly,
that women cannot hold the office of a rabbi or of a שליח צבור
and cannot perform any of the official functions requiring the
authority of a rabbi.

This is the attitude of traditional Judaism towards the question
of women rabbis, a view strictly adhered to by all Jewry all over
the world throughout all generations even unto this day.

Now we come to the second part of our question, that is, shall
we adhere to this tradition or shall we separate ourselves from
Catholic Israel and introduce a radical innovation which would
necessarily create a distinction between the title rabbi, as held by
a reform-rabbi and the title rabbi in general.   I believe that hitherto no distinction could rightly be drawn between the ordination of
our modern rabbis and the ordination of all the rabbis of preceding
generations. We are still carrying on the activity of the rabbis
of old who traced their authority through a chain of tradition to
Moses and the elders associated with him, even though in many
points we interpret our Judaism in a manner quite different from
theirs. We are justified in considering ourselves the latest link
in that long chain of authoritative teachers who carried on their
activity of teaching, preserving and developing Judaism, and for

our time we have the same standing as they had (Comp. R. H. 25a). The ordination which we give to our disciples carries with it, for our time and generation, the same authority which marked the ordination given by Judah Hannasi to Abba Areka or the ordination given by any teacher in Israel to his disciples throughout all the history of Judaism.

We should, therefore, not jeopardize the hitherto indisputable authoritative character of our ordination. We should not make our ordination entirely different in character from the traditional ordination, and thereby give the larger group of Jewry, following traditional Judaism, good reason to question our authority and to doubt whether we are rabbis in the sense in which this honored title was always understood.

Nor is there, to my mind, any actual need for making such a radical departure from this established Jewish law and time honored practice. The supposed lack of a sufficient number of rabbis will not be made up by this radical innovation. There are other and better means of meeting this emergency and that is, by the rabbis following the advice of the Men of the Great Synagog, to raise many disciples and thus encourage more men to enter the ministry. And the standard of the rabbinate in America, while no doubt it could be improved in many directions, is certainly not so low as to need a new and refining influence such as women presumably would bring to any profession they enter. Neither could women, with all due respect to their talents and abilities, raise the standard of the rabbinate. Nay, all things being equal, women could not even rise to the high standard reached by men in this particular calling. If there is any calling which requires a whole-hearted devotion to the exclusion of all other things and the determination to make it one's whole life work, it is the rabbinate. It is not to be considered merely as a profession by which one earns a livelihood. Nor is it to be entered upon as a temporary occupation. One must choose it for his lifework and be prepared to give to it all his energies and to devote to it all the years of his life, constantly learning and improving and thus growing in it. It has been rightly said that the woman who enters a profession, must make her choice between following her chosen profession or the calling of mother and home-maker. She cannot do both well at the same time. This certainly would hold true in the case of the rabbinical profession. The woman who naturally and rightly looks forward to the opportunity of meeting the right kind of man, of marrying him and of having children and a home of her own, cannot give to the rabbinate that whole-hearted devotion which comes from the determination to make it one's lifework. For in all likelihood she could not continue it as a married woman. For, one holding the rabbinical office must teach by precept and example, and must give an example of Jewish family and home life where all the traditional Jewish virtues are cultivated. The rabbi can do so all the better when he is married and has a home and a family of his own. The wife whom God has made as a helpmate to him can be, and in most cases is, of great assistance to him in making his home a Jewish home, a model for the congregation to follow.

In this important activity of the rabbi, exercising a wholesome influence upon the congregation, the woman rabbi would be deficient. The woman in the rabbinical office could not expect the man to whom she be married to be merely a helpmate to her, assisting her in her rabbinical activities. And even if she could find such a man, willing to take a subordinate position in the family, the influence upon the families in the congregation of such an arrangement in the home and in the family life of the rabbi would not be very wholesome. Not to mention the fact that if she is to be a mother she could not go on with her regular activities in the congregation.

And there is, to my mind, no injustice done to woman by excluding her from this office. There are many avenues open to her if she choose to do religious or educational work. I can see no reason why we should make this radical departure from traditional practice except the specious argument that we are modern men and, as such, we recognize the full equality of women to men, hence we should be thoroughly consistent. But I would not class the rabbis with those people whose main characteristic is consistency.

THE JEWISH ATTITUDE
TOWARD AUTOPSY

Question:

What is the attitude of Jewish law towards the practice of autopsy? Are there any objections to it on the part of the Jewish religious consciousness? If there are such objections will you please inform me whether they are based on valid grounds and whether, in your opinion, these objections hold good even in our day?

Answer:

To my knowledge no law or regulation, expressly forbidding the practice of autopsy, can be found in the Bible or the Talmud or the Shulhan Aruk. It may safely be stated that in case the autopsy would not unduly delay the funeral one could not find the least support for any objection to it in these authoritative sources of Jewish law. In case the autopsy would unduly delay the burial one might object to it on the ground that the ancient Jewish law recommended burial on the same day in which the death occurred. For the law in Deuteronomy XXI, 23 "But thou shalt surely bury him the same day," though originally prescribed for the criminal who has been put to death as punishment for his sin, was understood by the rabbis of the Talmud to apply to every dead person even to one who died a natural and peaceful death. Hence they recommend that, unless delay is necessary for the sake of showing honor to the dead person or in order to have time for making the proper arrangements for the funeral, burial should take place on the same day in which the death occurred. One might, therefore, cite this talmudic regulation—which, however, is nowadays generally disregarded even by the orthodox—as a reason for objecting to a'utopsy if it would unduly and unnecessarily delay the funeral. But to the practice of autopsy as such one cannot find any express objection in the Talmud. On the contrary, one could cite the Talmud in support of the practice since it is evident from talmudic reports that some of the rabbis of the Talmud, no doubt prompted by their interest in the science of medicine, actually performed an autopsy.

According to the talmudic theory of anatomy, the human body contains 248 parts or joints רמ"ח אברים and 365 sinews or veins שס"ה גידין (b. Makkot 23b). Whether this theory of the rabbis is scientifically correct or not is not our concern now. But it is evident that they could not

Reprinted from *Central Conference of American Rabbis Year Book,* Vol. XXXV, 1925.

have obtained the knowledge of anatomical detail upon which they based
their theory except by dissecting a human corpse and counting its joints
and sinews. Had they acquired this knowledge indirectly from non-Jewish
physicians they would have quoted their authority or expressly mentioned
that this was a theory of the non-Jewish scientists חכמי אומות העולם
as they do in other cases when they mention theories of the wise men of
the Gentiles (Comp. b. Sanhedrin 91b, R. H. 12a, Pesahim 94b). The
fact that this theory is stated by the rabbis in an unqualified form as an
indisputable fact certainly justifies the assumption that they learned this
fact from their own direct observations by dissecting a human body. This
assumption is confirmed by the following express report found in the
Talmud (b. Bekorot 45a). Here we read that the disciples of R. Ishmael
who had learned from their teachers that the human body contains 248
joints, had the opportunity to test this anatomical theory of their teachers.
They obtained the body of a woman who had been sentenced to death and
executed by the Roman authorities. They boiled the body and dissected
it and counted the number of the joints and to their great surprise they
found that it contains 252 joints instead of only 248. This fact seemed
to refute the theory which they had learned from their teachers. They
came to their master and told him that they have found by their own observation in dissecting a corpse that the theory about the 248 joints was
not correct. The master answers them by saying שמא באשה בדקתם
"Perhaps you have examined the body of a woman?" And he informed
them that the theory about the 248 joints applied only to the body of a
male but that the female of the species had four more joints. It is evident
from this report that the practice of autopsy was not considered by the
rabbis as forbidden or objectionable. The master does not express any
surprise when he hears that his disciples dissected a human body. He
does not reproach them for having done such a thing. He does not even
ask where they obtained the body or whether it was a Jewish or a non-
Jewish corpse. It evidently made no difference to him who the body was.
This consideration would also answer the possible argument that it was
only because the woman had been sentenced to death and executed as a
criminal that they did not mind performing the autopsy on her body. In
the first place it is doubtful if the rabbis considered the woman a criminal
even though the Roman government treated her as such. The rabbis may
have disagreed with the Roman law on the question whether the woman
in the case deserved death or not. Secondly, even if the woman had been
sentenced to death and executed by a Jewish court and according to the
Jewish law, the rabbis could not have treated her differently from any
other dead person. After she had paid the penalty for her crime her
death brought her atonement and her body was not to be mistreated. Had
there been a law against dissecting a dead body they could not have ignored such a law in this case on the ground that the body was executed
to death and did not die a natural death. But above all, it is evident from

our report that when the disciples first reported the case to their master they did not give any details, they did not tell him whether it was the body of a Jew or a non-Jew, man or woman, saint or criminal, and the master did not care to ask for any details. Only when it was necessary for him to maintain the theory about the 248 joints, did it occur to him to ask: "Was it perhaps the body of a woman that you dissected and examined?" It is also significant that no discussion or remarks by later teachers follow this report in the Talmud. This *argumentum e silencio* has some weight considering that usually when some action or practice of older teachers is reported in the Talmud the later teachers if they know of some law forbidding such a practice, take up the discussion of the whole question. Evidently in this case, the later teachers did not know of any law forbidding the practice.

The objection to the practice of autopsy which is prevalent among Jewish people is based merely on the assumption that such a practice is a disgrace to the human body ניוול and an insult to the dead person בזיון המת And, of course, we are not permitted to treat disrespectfully a dead person. This supposition, however, that a post mortem examination constitutes a disgrace to the human body has no real basis in Jewish literature. It is true, in the Talmud (Hullin 11b) it is assumed that to dissect and examine a dead body might be considered a disgrace ניוול to that body, which, of course, should be avoided. This, however, holds good only in the case when it is done unnecessarily and for no good purpose. For in the same passage in the Talmud it is taken for granted that if such a post mortem examination might possibly result in saving another man's life—e. g., in the case of a suspected murder when a post mortem examination of the killed person might prove the innocence of the suspected murderer—we should by all means dissect and examine the dead body, so that we may possibly avoid the loss of another life משום איבוד נשמה דהאי נינוליה

And on general psychological grounds we have no reason to assume that the dead person would feel insulted if subjected to a post mortem examination. We may rather assume the contrary. Just as a living person, while undergoing an operation, has no objection to physicians and students seeing him cut open and watching the surgeon performing the operation, so also the dead person, since it gives him no pain, would have no objection to the physicians cutting him up in order to learn the cause of his death or the nature of his disease. To apply the Talmudic phrase דניחא ליה לאיניש לקיומי מצוה בגופיה (Pesahim 4b) in a somewhat different sense than the one in which it was originally used in the Talmud, we may say it would rather be pleasing to the dead person to know that he is benefiting humanity in that from his body the physicians might learn to combat disease and to alleviate the sufferings of other people. The consideration that by a post mortem examination the physicians may learn the nature of a certain disease and thus be enabled to help other people suffering from the same disease has indeed led two great rabbinical authorities of the 17th and 19th century to permit autopsy under certain conditions. R. Ezechiel Landau (1713-1793) in his Noda bi-Yehudah Tinyana, part of Yore Deah No. 210, and, following him, R. Moses Sofer (1763-1839) in his Hatam Sofer part of Yore Deah No. 336 permit autopsy but only when there is in the same locality another person suffering from the same disease from which the person to be subjected to autopsy died. Their reasons for permitting the autopsy are very cogent. Since by the autopsy the physicians may learn to understand better the nature of the disease and thus be enabled to save the life of the other person afflicted with it, it is a case of פיקוח נפש . And according to the talmudic-rabbinic law, all the laws of the Torah, excepting those against idolatry, incest and murder, may and should be violated if necessary for the saving of a human life (b. Ketubot 19a). According to this talmudic-rabbinic law, then, even if there could be found an express law in the Torah prohibiting the dissecting of a human body it would have to be ignored in favor of autopsy which might lead to the saving of a human life. Thus far we can fully agree with these two great rabbinical authorities. But with all due respect to them we cannot see any reason for limiting, as they do, the permission of autopsy only to cases when there is right then and there another person suffering from the same disease who might immediately be benefited by the findings of the physicians. The talmudic law that consideration for the saving of a human life sets aside any law of the Torah except the three mentioned above applies also to doubtful cases, that is, when we are not sure that by the act involving a violation of the law we shall save a human being, but there is merely a chance of saving a human life, we should nevertheless proceed with the act and ignore the law (b. Yoma 88a). And certainly there is more than a mere chance or probability that the enrichment of the medical science and the wider knowledge and experience gained by physicians from their findings through autopsy will result in the saving of human life here and now or somewhere else and at some other time. For in our days any discovery made in one hospital and the knowledge acquired by one physician in one part of the world is easily communicated through books or medical journals to physicians living in other parts of the world. We can, therefore not argue against autopsy even in such an instance when we do not know of any person suffering from the same disease. For if there is no such case here it may be elsewhere and if there is none right now it may turn up tomorrow or next year.

I believe that in the above I have proved that there can be no objection to autopsy on the ground of any biblical or talmudic-rabbinic law. I would go still further and state that in our days there are good reasons why Jewish people should modify their customary attitude towards autopsy. This attitude on the part of the Jews has created bad feelings among Christian students of medicine. In some universities in Europe Jewish medical students find it very difficult and almost impossible to get admission to the medical laboratories for this very reason because Jews ordinarily refuse to deliver Jewish corpses for purposes of anatomical dissection (comp. Yearbook of C. C. A. R. vol. XXXIII, 1923, p. 452). The exclusion of Jewish students from the anatomical laboratories ultimately means that Jewish students will be deprived of the opportunity of studying medicine. For we must consider the possibility of such an attitude towards Jewish medical students on the part of Christian students or university authorities, spreading to all other universities outside of Poland, Austria-Hungary and Roumania, if we Jews persist in our unjustified objections to autopsy. These considerations have prompted orthodox Jewish communities in Europe to change their attitude towards autopsy and to agree to deliver Jewish corpses for purposes of anatomical dissection. According to a report from Bucharest, Roumania, printed in the Jewish Daily Bulletin, March 10, 1925, p. 3, the Jewish community in Jassy has agreed and has actually already begun to deliver Jewish corpses for dissection to the university of that city. No doubt this decision of the Jassy community had the approval of the rabbinate of that city. Another dispatch of the Jewish Telegraph Agency brings the following report from Kishineff (printed in the Jewish Daily Bulletin April 7, 1925, p. 1) : "An unparalleled scene took place in the hall of the local rabbinate when an aged Jewish physician made a declaration of his intentions with regard to his body after death. Dr. Rabinovitch, sixty years of age, before Rabbi Zirelson and a "Minyan" (ten men, the quorum necessary for solemn declarations) declared that after his death his body should be delivered to the Medical College of Jassy University for dissection in order to remove the cause of the anti-Semitic riots among the Roumanian students, who claim that the Jews refuse to submit Jewish corpses." And according to press reports the Jewish Burial Society in Szegedin, Hungary, resolved to deliver Jewish corpses for purposes of anatomical dissection to the medical laboratory of the university of that city (see American Jewish Yearbook XXVII (1925) p. 33). If all these reports are true, and we have no reason to doubt them, they certainly prove that the authorities of the Jewish community in Jassy and the members of the Hebra Kadisha in Szegedin, as well as Rabbi Zirelson of Kishineff and the ten men associated with him who received the declaration of Dr. Rabinovitch, were all of the opinion that the Jewish religious consciousness can have no valid objection to autopsy. To this opinion I fully subscribe, as I cannot find any law in Bible, Talmud or Shulhan Aruk, which would justify such an objection.

BURIAL PRACTICES

I.

"Our congregation has just purchased adjoining territory to its burial grounds. The plot runs north and south. It runs from street to street and our plans are to make an entrance by the north side and the exit by the south side. This would mean that the graves and lots when laid out would either be facing north or south and not the east as is customary. The question, therefore, which I desire to ask is this: Is there anything in traditional Judaism concerning this matter? Is there any prohibition concerning the burying in graves that run north and south or vice versa"?

Answer: There is, to my knowledge, no prohibition of this kind in rabbinic Judaism. Neither the Talmud nor the Shulḥan Aruk have any definite ruling about the direction in which the graves should run. On the contrary, from the Mishnah, *Baba Bathra,* VI, 8, and the discussion of the Gemara (*ibidem,* 101b) it is evident that they would have graves in every direction, east-west, west-east, north-south and south-north. Lest it be argued that this was only in Palestine, we have now the evidence from the Jewish catacombs in Rome, Italy, that some of the graves were arranged so that the head was in the direction of northwest and the feet towards the southeast, and others again in the opposite direction, head southeast and feet northwest. (See Nikolaus Müller, *Die Jüdische Katakombe am Monteverde zu Rom,* Leipzig, 1912, p. 48-49). And R. Moses Sofer in his *responsa, Hatam Sofer, Yoreh Deah* No. 332, expresses his surprise at certain people who would fix the direction in which graves should run. In Pressburg where he was rabbi, the cemetery was so laid out that the graves ran west-east, that is, the head was to the west and the feet towards the east, while in the city from which the question was addressed to him, the graves ran north-south, that is, the head was placed towards the north and the feet towards the south. It would seem that certain people, believing that at the time of the resurrection the dead will get up and march to Palestine, would be careful to place the body in the grave with the feet toward Palestine, so that when the time comes the dead would be able to get up and walk right ahead without having to turn around. But, argues R. Moses Sofer, there are many roads toward Palestine, since from European countries, one can go first south to a Mediterranean harbor and then by ship east, or one can go east by land to Constantinople first and thence to Palestine, therefore, he concludes that there is absolutely no difference in what direction the graves run.

Reprinted from *Central Conference of American Rabbis Year Book,* Vol. XXXIII, 1923.

II.

Will you please tell me what is the origin and the significance of the custom to put small sticks of wood into the hands of the dead body when placing it in the grave

Answer: This custom is not universally observed, and is not mentioned in the codes. R. Moses Sofer in his Responsa (*Ḥatam Sofer, Yoreh Deah*, No. 327) mentions the custom and states that when he was in Prossnitz, he heard from the members of the *Ḥebra Kadisha* there that the purpose of the custom was to indicate the belief in the resurrection of the dead. The dead are provided with these sticks on which to lean and support themselves when getting up at the time of the resurrection. To this explanation of the *Ḥebra Kadisha* men of Prossnitz, R. Moses Sofer remarks that it is rather weak and unsound, just as the thin wooden sticks are weak and not strong enough to lean upon them. With all due respect to R. Moses Sofer, however, I must say that he forgot or overlooked a passage in the Palestinian Talmud (*Kilayim* IX, 4, 32b) where it is related that R. Jeremiah requested among other things, that a staff be put into his hand when placed into the gave, so that when the Messiah will come, he, R. Jeremiah, should be ready to get up and march.